# GUIDEBOOK FOR DIRECTORS OF NONPROFIT CORPORATIONS

## THIRD EDITION

NONPROFIT ORGANIZATIONS COMMITTEE

WILLARD L. BOYD III
JEANNIE CARMEDELLE FREY
EDITORS

AMERICAN BAR ASSOCIATION
Business Law Section

Cover design by Tamara Kowalski/ABA Publishing.

Page layout by Quadrum Solutions.

Printed in the United States of America.

17 16 15 14 13  7 6 5 4 3

Library of Congress Cataloging-in-Publication Data

Boyd, Willard L., III, and Jeannie Carmedelle Frey, editors
Guidebook for directors of nonprofit corporations / Edited by Willard L. Boyd III and Jeannie Carmedelle Frey.—3rd ed.

    p. cm.

Includes bibliographical references and index.

ISBN 978-1-60442-093-7 (alk. paper)

1. Directors of corporations—Legal status, laws, etc.—United States. 2. Nonprofit organizations—Law and legislation—United States. I. Title.

KF1388.7.Z9B69 2012

346.73'064—dc23

2012029811

# Summary of Chapters

# Table of Contents

## Chapter 2:

## Chapter 4:
## Taxation

# Preface

This third edition of the *Guidebook for Directors of Nonprofit Corporations* has been prepared by the Committee on Nonprofit Organizations of the Business Law Section of the American Bar Association. The purpose of the *Guidebook* is to assist directors of a nonprofit corporation in performing their duties. Primarily designed for the lay reader, the *Guidebook* provides a description of general legal principles as they apply to nonprofit corporations. On a more practical level, the *Guidebook* offers what is intended to be useful suggestions and procedures for both the individual directors and the corporation they serve.

The *Guidebook* is designed to serve as a useful reference book for directors and prospective directors of the thousands of nonprofit corporations in the United States—from the smallest corporation that operates principally at a local or even neighborhood level, to the largest nonprofit corporation having operations that extend not only across this country but internationally as well. Nonprofit corporations have always played a large role in American life; they play a bigger role today than most people realize. In the future, it is likely that even more people will look to nonprofit corporations to help address issues and solve problems.

In general, the *Guidebook* addresses general legal principles and broad areas of concern and is not intended to be a source of specific legal advice or solutions to particular problems. Rather, its goal is to provide nonprofit corporation directors with an overall understanding of their role. It is designed to help directors identify the information they need in certain areas, and to suggest methods for obtaining this information within the framework of the corporation's particular circumstances.

This third edition of the *Guidebook* attempts to reflect the issues that affect directors of nonprofit corporations today. In many respects, the issues facing nonprofits now are unchanged from what they were when the previous editions came out: What does a director do? What is the scope of his or her duties? Although these questions may be timeless, the answers necessarily reflect today's realities and legal developments. We also attempted to identify developing trends and legal issues that are likely to affect nonprofit corporations and their directors in the future.

It has been said that those who select directors of nonprofit boards should look for the following qualities: "wealth, wisdom, and work—never settle for less than two."[1] Through this *Guidebook*, the Nonprofit Organizations Committee hopes to add to your wisdom, and make your work as a nonprofit director more effective; as for wealth, we can't do much for you. But if all who care for the nonprofits that they direct are wise and dedicated, there will be wealth, in many forms, for all.

The principal authors and editors of this edition are Willard L. Boyd III, and Jeannie Carmedelle Frey. George W. Overton of Chicago and Ms. Frey were the principal authors and editors of the second edition. Mr. Overton was the principal author of the first edition, together with William Humenuk of Philadelphia, and other members of the Committee on Nonprofit Organizations (then known as the Committee on Nonprofit Corporations) of the ABA Business Law Section.

The following members of the Committee on Nonprofit Organizations assisted with editing and shaping the overall content:

Lisa A. Runquist of Northridge, California
Richard Sevcik of Chicago
Patrick Sternal of Northridge, California

In addition, the following ABA members served as contributing editors for specific chapters and subject matter:

- Elizabeth M. Mills of Chicago and Stephanie Switzer of Cleveland (Taxation, Chapter 4)
- Scott A. Edelstein of Washington, D.C. (For-Profit Subsidiaries and Joint Ventures, Chapter 5)
- Frank B. Harty of Des Moines, Iowa (Employees, Chapter 7)
- Harold L. Kaplan of Chicago (Bankruptcy Section, Chapter 10)

Special thanks and appreciation also are owed to Steven J. Roy of Des Moines, Iowa, Denise M. Mendt, also of Des Moines, Jennifer Smith of Iowa City, Iowa, and Jan Murray of Cleveland for subject matter assistance, and to the following lawyers and other individuals who provided valuable research and editorial assistance:  Hilary Hippen-Leek, Jessica McKeigan, Brian Rockwell, and Sarah Hmoud Davis.

WILLARD L. BOYD III
Des Moines, Iowa

JEANNIE CARMEDELLE FREY
Chicago, Illinois

---

1.     A common variant of this qualification standard is "time, treasure, and talent." The originators of the sayings are unknown.

# Introduction

## Who Should Read This Guidebook?

This *Guidebook* was prepared to aid directors of a nonprofit corporation in performing their duties.[1] It is written for anyone presently serving as such a director, as well as anyone contemplating such service.

There are a wide variety of nonprofit corporations: Art museums, health care providers, social clubs, trade associations, foundations, and homeowners' associations, just to name a few, and this *Guidebook* is written for the directors of all of them. You may ask how this *Guidebook* can address the needs of directors of all nonprofit corporations, given the vast range of nonprofit activities. Despite their variety of purposes, nonprofit corporations have many things in common. For instance, most nonprofit corporations are organized and maintained pursuant to a single state statute, and are managed by a single governing board. Although the size of the resources managed by nonprofit boards varies widely, their fundamental responsibilities are the same.

The rights and duties of directors of nonprofit corporations are in many respects similar to those imposed on directors of for-profit or business corporations. In a large number of states, the statute governing nonprofit corporations has been modeled at least to some degree on the statute governing business corporations. Further, the legal analysis of many corporate governance issues in the nonprofit context often draws on the lessons learned from the law applied to business corporations. A new or prospective director of a nonprofit corporation who is familiar with the working of business corporation boards is therefore likely to feel comfortable that he or she understands the basic requirements of this new role. Still, nonprofit directors need to be aware that, because of the unique nature of nonprofit organizations, in some circumstances both state and federal law may impose additional or different duties on directors of these organizations—especially directors of tax-exempt corporations and corporations deemed to be public charities or public benefit corporations.

Nonprofits play an important and sometimes irreplaceable role, not only in this country, but throughout the world. The conduct of all nonprofit boards is important not only to their organizations, but also to the constituencies they serve. To help effectively direct these organizations, directors need two things: an informed understanding of their role and effective procedures for making decisions and taking action.

Directors of smaller nonprofit organizations may feel that some of the suggestions in this *Guidebook* only apply to larger entities with bigger staffs and greater resources. Although there are practical limitations imposed on directors of many nonprofits, consistency and regularity in board procedures typically found in established, well-managed corporations (whether for-profit or nonprofit) are not accidental. This *Guidebook* aims to help directors of all nonprofit corporations, big and small, to use their resources to greatest effect.

# A Few Definitions

***Nonprofit Corporation.*** A nonprofit corporation is an artificial creation of a government—usually a state. Corporations do not exist simply by mutual agreement of members or directors but come into being only by a specific act of a state or federal government and are kept in existence only by compliance with the regular requirements of that government.

***Articles of Incorporation.*** As part of the creation of the corporation, the articles of incorporation are filed with the government. These articles are sometimes referred to as a charter, certificate of incorporation, or constitution. The *Guidebook* uses the term "articles of incorporation."

***Bylaws.*** The detailed rules of the corporation's governance of the corporation, as adopted by the directors, are usually referred to as the bylaws but sometimes are labeled with other names, such as standing rules or constitution. The *Guidebook* uses the term "bylaws."

***Board of Directors.*** Every nonprofit corporation statute provides for a board of directors; however, in a given corporation, the name of this body varies with the history, tradition—and whim—of the organization involved. It may be called a board of trustees, a board of overseers, a governing committee, or any one of a dozen other names.[2] This *Guidebook* will use the terms the "board of directors" or "board," and refers to the board's members also as "directors." Throughout this *Guidebook*, the term "director" is used to denote a member of the governing body of a nonprofit corporation. Any other type of director will be qualified in the text.

*Officers.* There is similar variety in the titles of officers. The individual who is responsible for overseeing the day-to-day operations of the corporation may be referred to as the president, CEO, executive director, executive officer, or other title. In this *Guidebook*, the term "chief executive" is used to describe the principal executive officer of the corporation, and "chair" to describe the individual who presides over the board of directors.

*Members.* In the nonprofit world, the term "member" may refer to an individual or entity having the power to elect one or more of the corporation's directors and having other voting rights that are similar to, or even greater than, those of a stockholder of a business corporation. On the other hand, a nonprofit corporation may use the term "members" for supporters who have no voting rights, with the term member being mostly an acknowledgement of such support, used by a charitable corporation to express appreciation (and sometimes offer special benefits or discounts) to its donors. Although numerous nonprofit corporations have different categories of members, with differing rights and powers, many nonprofit corporations have no members at all. In some organizations, the term "delegate" identifies individuals, such as persons participating in conventions or other representative assemblies, who may have some of the attributes of members but whose rights may be limited to the context of a specific assembly or gathering.[3] In this *Guidebook*, the term "member" is used only to refer to a person or entity with rights to vote for directors.

*Focus of this Guidebook.* This *Guidebook* deals only with nonprofit entities that are organized as corporations. Other nonprofit entities, such as unincorporated associations, charitable trusts, or limited liability companies are outside the scope of this book.[4]

# Legal Requirements versus Good Corporate Practice

Throughout this *Guidebook*, we seek to answer two principal questions:

- What does the law require?
- What is good corporate practice, as shaped by the needs of the particular corporation involved and the practical limitations of the director's service?

Neither of these questions has a simple answer. Much of the law concerning a director's responsibility is derived from practices in business corporations where the accountability of a director may differ from that arising in a nonprofit

xxii    *Guidebook for Directors of Nonprofit Corporations*, **Third Edition**

context. What constitutes good corporate practice also will vary with the nature and resources of the corporation, its purposes, and the nature of its exposures. The practical expectations of nonprofit directors are shaped in part by the needs and resources of each corporation involved. Nonetheless, there are significant areas of common ground that apply to all nonprofit corporation directors.

# The Law's Commands

In writing for directors we must first, as lawyers, alert our readers to the commands and prohibitions imposed by the law. All legal systems necessarily deal with minimum requirements of behavior: "You must do at least X" or "No matter what the circumstances, you must not do Y." This *Guidebook* indicates legal requirements by the use of imperative verbs such as *must, must not, shall, shall not, is required to,* and the like.

Our statements of the law's commands are sometimes a summary of a specific statute or regulation—such as the Internal Revenue Code and the related regulations—and sometimes a reference to the body of judge-made law concerning corporations. The Model Nonprofit Corporation Act, Third Edition (Model Act) is used in this *Guidebook* as the prototype or presumptive guide to issues of statutory corporate law.[5] Still, directors should be aware that state statutes and legal precedent applicable to specific nonprofit corporations may differ from the Model Act in various respects.

# Good Corporate Practice

Equally important is the *Guidebook's* advice—based on experiences of lawyers for nonprofit corporations—outlining what a director should, is expected to, may, or should not do.

The *Guidebook's* statements as to what a director *should* do reflect: (a) policies underlying legal requirements; and (b) general standards of corporate management evolved from the experience of both business and nonprofit corporations.

With respect to good corporate practice, this *Guidebook* describes in part what a director is generally expected to do today and in part what a director may be expected to do in the future. Good corporate practice also describes the behavior dedicated directors will want to see from their fellow directors, and hence from themselves.

# Limitations of Time vs. the Corporation's Needs

The most important practical limitation on a director's service is time. Each individual director should determine how much time he or she can devote to the corporation's affairs. The board of directors as a whole should organize its affairs on a shared assumption as to the time all directors can give. Given that most directors are chosen on the basis of their experiences and activities, director time constraints are an ever-present issue. The board needs to determine how much time directors should spend to appropriately carry out their duties, and make sure that each director is willing and able to do so.

In many of the areas examined in this *Guidebook*, there are no ready-made answers to the conflict of needs versus resources; it will be up to the directors to evaluate how to mediate between these conflicts, and to reassess these decisions periodically in the light of current circumstances. Directors need to be aware of changes in the legal and business climate that affect their corporation, and that may change the determination of what is "enough" time to fulfill their individual duties to the corporation and their fellow board members.

# The Organization of This Guidebook

This *Guidebook* is organized as follows:

Chapters 1 through 3 discuss matters of concern to all directors of all corporations: how a board works, the directors' rights and duties, and the functions of committees, advisory bodies, and officers.

Chapter 4, on taxation, surveys tax-exemption issues, an area of concern for most nonprofit corporations and their directors.

Chapter 5 discusses the tax-exemption issues that arise when tax-exempt nonprofit organizations create for-profit subsidiaries or contemplate joint ventures with for-profit entities.

Chapter 6 discusses a host of potential legal issues that may be relevant to a nonprofit organization's Internet activities.

Chapters 7 and 8 discuss legal issues relating to use of a nonprofit corporation's human resources, and suggest standards and procedures for the effective use of volunteers and employees.

Chapter 9 notes some of the general legal issues that arise in fundamental change events, such as  mergers, sales, and bankruptcy.

Chapter 10 discusses issues relating to the investment of institutional funds and expenditures from endowment funds.

Chapter 11 covers issues relating to insurance and other liability protection for nonprofit corporation directors.

Chapter 12 offers suggestions on the steps that a nonprofit's directors can take to understand the legal environment in which the organization operates, and on how to select and use legal counsel.

Chapter 13 discusses best practices for orientation of new board members, and ways to revitalize existing board members and the board as a whole.

At the end of each chapter, the reader will find questions that we suggest each individual director review concerning the issues relevant to the subject matter of the chapter.  Following the questions in each chapter is a checklist that board members may find helpful to review in light of their organization's specific circumstances.

# Endnotes

1.   This *Guidebook* is the work of the Committee on Nonprofit Organizations of the Business Law Section of the American Bar Association (ABA).

2.   The Model Nonprofit Corporation Act, Third Edition (Model Act) and most state laws specifically reject the trust law standard for the conduct of nonprofit directors. *See* Model Act § 8.30(e). Thus, the use of the term "trustee" does not connote duties different from or additional to those of a director.  In some states and in certain circumstances, however, nonprofit directors may be considered trustees of charitable assets and thereby subject to duties beyond those generally applicable to nonprofit directors.  See *Chapter 2, "Duties and Rights of Nonprofit Corporation Directors."*

3.   *See, e.g.,* Colorado Revised Nonprofit Corporation Act, Colo. Rev. Stat. § 7-121-401(1); Indiana Nonprofit Corporation Act, Ind. Code §§ 23-17-2-8 and 23-17-9-1.

4.   For a discussion regarding other types of nonprofit entities, *see* Lisa A. Runquist, *The ABCs of Nonprofits* (American Bar Association 2005).

5.   The Model Act was approved by the Committee on Nonprofit Organizations of the Business Law Section of the ABA in 2008.  It was published by the Business Law Section of the ABA in 2009.

# Chapter 1:
## The Nonprofit Corporation and Its Directors: What They Do, How They Do It, And For Whom

# Chapter 1

# The Nonprofit Corporation and Its Directors: What They Do, How They Do It, and for Whom

*There are many types of nonprofits with some created for a charitable or public purpose, some created for a religious purpose and some created for the benefit of the nonprofit corporation's membership. Regardless of the type, it is important that the nonprofit corporation have governance documents—typically in the form of articles of incorporation and bylaws—that accurately describe the purposes and governance structure of the corporation. In addition, a nonprofit corporation—regardless of its purpose—is generally required to have a board of directors that has the ultimate legal authority and accountability for the management of the affairs of the corporation. The composition and election of boards vary among nonprofits. Still, a common theme for all nonprofits is that the members of the board act as a collective body and not individually when acting on behalf of the corporation.*

## The Zoology of the Nonprofit World

### Basic Concepts

Nonprofit corporations are corporations organized under the laws of a state and have as their objective something other than enriching shareholders. The laws of each state vary, of course, so this section describes a few basic nonprofit corporate law concepts in very general terms. As noted below, nonprofits can be generally characterized as being one of three major categories: public benefit, religious, or mutual benefit.

### *"Public benefit" corporations*

Most highly visible nonprofit corporations (e.g., educational institutions, art museums) are sometimes referred to as *"public benefit" corporations.* These corporations exist to benefit the public rather than members by engaging in a purpose that historically has been viewed as primarily "charitable" in nature. Public benefit corporations may or may not have members. Members may have important rights or no rights depending on how the corporation's articles of incorporation or bylaws define those rights. For example, members may be entitled to vote only on a proposed merger or sale of the corporation's assets or they also may be entitled to elect some or all of the directors. Still, members of a public benefit corporation have no franchise or ownership interest in the nonprofit. Public benefit corporations are typically eligible to be exempt from federal taxation under Internal Revenue Code (Code) section 501(c)(3), which is described in more detail later, as well as other sections of the Code, such as 501(c)(4). See Chapter 4, *Taxation.*

### *A "religious" corporation*

A *"religious" corporation* is similar to a public benefit corporation in many respects but is established for religious purposes. Some state nonprofit corporation acts distinguish between public benefit corporations and religious corporations. Organizations that meet the Internal Revenue Service (IRS) definition of churches, conventions or associations of churches, and integrated auxiliaries of churches are automatically considered to be exempt under Section 501(c)(3), whether or not they file with the IRS to establish their exempt purposes. Still, religious organizations that are not churches or the church-related entities listed above remain subject to the same filing requirements to establish their exempt status as other nonprofits.[1]

### *A "mutual benefit" corporation*

A *"mutual benefit" corporation*, in contrast to a public benefit or religious corporation, is operated to benefit its members. Its members will generally be a well-defined group, such as members of a trade association, homeowners' association, or country club. The rights of the members of a mutual benefit corporation are defined in its organizing documents. A mutual benefit corporation does not qualify for federal tax exemption under 501(c)(3) although it may qualify for exemption under another Code section, such as 501(c)(6).

State nonprofit corporation statutes may or may not use the classifications described above. For example, the Model Nonprofit Corporation Act, Third

Edition (Model Act) recognizes certain differences between charitable corporations and other types of nonprofit corporations but does not use the "public benefit," "mutual benefit," and "religious" classifications.[2]

### *"Articles of incorporation" and "bylaws"*

As noted in the Introduction, the organizing documents of a corporation are often referred to as the *"articles of incorporation"* and *"bylaws."* The articles of incorporation is a public document filed with the secretary of state or another state governmental office. The document generally provides basic information, such as the type of corporation, its purpose, and any special restrictions related to its status. It may include provisions such as identifying the organizers, initial board of directors, and other required or optional provisions. The bylaws set out in detail how the corporation is governed: requirements for members, if any, member voting rights, and procedures for member action (i.e., notice of meetings, quorum, voting); number, qualification, and responsibilities of directors; committees of the board; number, qualifications, and responsibilities of officers; and may address other topics such as conflict of interest. In addition, the articles or the bylaws might address other special provisions, such as indemnification and limitation of liability.

## The Director's Role

### *A director acts as a part of a board*

Anyone serving as a director of a nonprofit corporation must be aware of what a director is—and isn't. As a body, a board of directors has considerable powers. In most nonprofit corporations the board plays a substantial part in the beginning or end of any corporate activity, and the board appoints or removes corporate agents, executives, and officers.

In contrast, an individual director, acting alone, has no power; rather, each director exerts his or her power as one participating element in the board of directors.[3] Nonetheless, the individual director is still legally accountable for corporate actions in certain circumstances and has legally protected rights and duties to participate in the board's decisions and all information related to them.[4]

### *A director directs, but does not perform, the corporation's activities*

The corporate structure contemplates that corporate actions, as determined by the board, will be carried out by officers, employees, and agents—persons chosen, directly or indirectly, by the board of directors. Often a person serving as a director also may wear another hat, such as that of an officer or agent, but corporate theory assumes that neither the board itself nor any individual director, acting solely as a director, carries out day-to-day activities.

### The directors act on behalf of one or more constituencies

In a business corporation, the director's constituents are, by and large, the stockholders. The stockholders elect the directors. The directors understand that their primary function is to advance the stockholders' wealth, and it is the stockholders, in most instances, who may call the director to account.

In the nonprofit world, identifying a director's constituencies is often not so simple. The persons or entities electing or appointing nonprofit directors, the interests they serve, and those who may call the director to account can be, and often are, separate parties.

## Director Selection

Directors of nonprofit corporations can be selected in three ways.

### Election by members or others

Membership corporations, including, for practical purposes, all mutual benefit corporations, elect directors somewhat as stockholders elect business corporation directors. Often the members are presented with a slate of candidates for election or reelection at an annual meeting; each member has one vote, and the candidate or candidates having the most votes win. The same basic structure is used where the members are institutions or even one single person or entity. For instance, a hospital may create a subsidiary nonprofit corporation for a particular purpose, with the hospital corporation as the sole voting member electing the subsidiary's directors.

In some cases, the corporation's articles of incorporation or bylaws may provide that a person or group who is not a member of the corporation may appoint one or more of the corporation's directors. For instance, some states permit bondholders or other creditors to vote for directors under certain circumstances.[5]

### Self-perpetuating boards

Many public benefit and religious corporations have self-perpetuating boards of directors in which the existing board elects—or reelects—the persons who serve as directors.

### Election by status

A director may serve ex officio by virtue of holding another position, such as chief executive of the corporation, or officer of an affiliate organization or constituency group. As noted below, ex officio directors have the same voting rights as other directors unless the bylaws specify that the ex officio directors have no voting rights.

# Special Categories of Directors

Frequently a nonprofit board will describe some person as an *honorary, life, emeritus,* or *ex officio* director. These designations often cause confusion.

### *Honorary directors*

An honorary or emeritus director is, almost by definition, not a true director. If a nonprofit corporation's member or board wishes to recognize someone—usually a longtime member of the board—as deserving of special respect, but to be relieved of regular duties as a board member, they are free to do so. Still, referring to such a person by the term "director" raises three legal issues.

**Status should be provided for in the bylaws.** It is helpful to have both the method of designating and the status of honorary directors described in the bylaws. Otherwise, the distinction between "regular" and honorary directors can be confusing for the board as well as for staff and other persons who deal with the board. Especially where the honorary director has recently served as a regular director (such as a board chair who has been bumped up to honorary status), these bylaw clarifications are helpful for all concerned. Among other things, it is important to address voting rights, terms, and removal of honorary directors in the bylaws.

**No voting rights.** Although a board may at any time invite any person, including honorary or emeritus directors, to attend any board meeting, such person's presence may not be counted for a necessary quorum, and such person may not vote, even if she or he is allowed to participate in discussion at the meeting (unless the articles or bylaws provide otherwise). The invitation to attend the meeting confers no voting rights.

**Attorney-client privilege issues.** The board, in consulting legal counsel concerning matters that the corporation may wish to consider in confidence, must realize that *the presence at a meeting of nondirectors (including persons referred to as honorary directors), or their receipt of confidential documents, may jeopardize the attorney-client privilege*—the corporation's right to communicate with counsel while keeping that communication secret even in court.[6]

### *Life directors*

Life directors usually occupy much the same position as honorary directors and use of such category merits the same cautions as set forth above. Still, if a corporation intends to create one or more full voting directorships with a lifetime term, the board must first examine the applicable nonprofit corporation statute—some will not permit it. The bylaws then must clearly define the status of such a director and address the rights that are associated with such position.

### *Ex officio directors*

Ex officio is the term commonly used to describe a person whose status as a director is tied to the holding of some other office or position (inside or outside the corporation). For example, a hospital may designate whoever is chief of the medical staff as an ex officio director, to serve as long as, and only as long as, she or he is chief of staff. A museum, as a condition of its using park district land, may be required to include the park superintendent as an ex officio director. Ex officio directors may be voting or nonvoting, as specified in the articles or bylaws. If the bylaws and articles of incorporation are silent on voting rights, it is likely that an ex officio director will be deemed to have voting rights. If an ex officio director has voting rights, he or she is considered a regular director, with the same rights and duties as other directors.

Sometimes, however, the term ex officio is used to describe someone who needs to be recognized (or appeased) but who is *not* regarded as a fully participating director. For example, the individual may not only be nonvoting, but his or her presence at every meeting may neither be expected nor counted for purposes of determining a quorum. All the cautions mentioned with regard to honorary directors (particularly with regard to the attorney-client privilege) apply in these situations, and the ambiguity of the term ex officio dictates that its use should be limited to the situation outlined in the preceding paragraph. It is particularly important, in these cases, that the bylaws define the rights and duties of any ex officio directors, including whether or not they have any voting rights.

# The Corporation's Purpose and How It Affects a Director

## Defining the Corporation's Purpose and the Persons or Interests It Serves

Any person serving or asked to serve as a director must ask: For what purpose is the corporation maintained? What is the constituency that it is serving? It has been said that all organizations exist to maximize something for somebody; the nonprofit corporation is no exception.[7] Defining the something and the somebody is a duty of every nonprofit board and every director. Once it has been determined what the corporation is maximizing and for whom, all persons serving or asked to serve as directors should determine if these aims are compatible with their reasons for serving on the board.

# Statements of the Corporation's Purpose and Its Constituencies Should Be Consistent with the Corporation's Activities

## *Statements of corporate purposes*

In all nonprofit corporations, the corporate purposes should be stated, at least in general terms, in the articles of incorporation and, if desired, the bylaws. The corporate purposes also may be reflected by a mission statement adopted by the board. Unfortunately, the foregoing places for inquiry may give inconsistent answers, or no answer at all. To the extent the corporate purpose is described in more than one document, it is important that these descriptions be consistent. Moreover, although the articles of incorporation will legally control in the event of conflicts, the purposes stated therein may be as broad as legally allowable and the bylaws may be equally vague.

## *Use of mission statements*

Especially if a nonprofit corporation has no governance instrument that clearly details its present purposes, a director should urge the creation of a mission statement. Even where a nonprofit corporation is conducting a specific program or activity, with a clear consensus among its directors, it may be beneficial to describe that activity and its purpose in a brief mission statement. The articles of incorporation and/or bylaws may define the broad general purposes of the corporation; however, the mission statement should be more specific. As a practical matter, confusion over mission impairs the efficiency of the board in the discharge of its duties. On the other hand, adoption or renewal (such as at an annual board retreat) of a corporate mission statement can rekindle the energies and help focus the attentions of the board members, both individually and collectively.

Mission statements come in varying styles and shapes. An effective mission statement succinctly reflects the board's agreement regarding the corporation's purposes and constituencies. It is very important that the mission statement is consistent with any purposes statement set forth in the articles of incorporation or bylaws. Three examples of how a mission statement may help focus the activities of a nonprofit corporation are described below:

(1)   The board of a condominium association usually operates within a fairly tight structure dictated by its declaration and statutory law, but clear choices may have to be made as to the constituency served (all owners? only owner-occupants?) or the corporate purpose (bare structural maintenance? enhanced value through annual improvements?). A mission statement enables the board to reach these decisions with minimum—or greatly lessened—interpersonal controversy.

> (2)    A local community organization—no matter how small—may have to make choices concerning the constituency served (all residents? only merchants? only youth?) or purposes (all welfare? specific social services?).
>
> (3)    The parent corporation of a regional healthcare system may use a mission statement to help guide its planning and strategic decisions, as well as to communicate its commitments to its employees, medical staff, and the community in which it provides services.

The board should reexamine its mission statement on a regular basis. Any vigorous nonprofit corporation will find that demands and opportunities will continually shape and alter what the corporation actually does; the environment in which it acts will change as well. Regular consideration of a mission statement also helps ensure that newer directors both understand the corporation's mission and know that they have been part of the articulation of the mission. Further, a periodic examination will reveal whether the current mission statement is consistent with the purposes statement and other provisions of the articles and bylaws, and if not, what changes in these documents may be required. Tax-exempt nonprofit corporations also should evaluate whether any variations between the corporation's current activities and the statements in its articles and bylaws necessitates a filing with the IRS to confirm the organization's tax-exempt status.

# Understanding the Corporation's Constituencies and Their Representatives

## Director Accountability to Defined Classes of Persons or Entities

All nonprofit directors are legally responsible to certain parties. In other words, some classes of persons or entities have the right to question the director's conduct, and even, in extreme cases, to bring him or her into court. By implication, there are others who do not have that right.[8]

# Directors Accountability of Mutual Benefit Corporations is Similar to That of Business Corporation Directors

It has been emphasized that the nonprofit corporation serves to maximize something for somebody, and the director must be able to identify the something and the somebody. In mutual benefit corporations, as a general rule, the somebody involved will be the party or parties who control the tenure of the directors—for example, in a trade association the members usually elect the directors—and those same persons will be the parties who may, in appropriate circumstances, call the board of directors to account.

Thus, the directors of most mutual benefit corporations hold a relationship to their members similar to that held by the directors of business corporations to stockholders. Nevertheless, in some circumstances (such as when a mutual benefit corporation holds some assets in trust or considers merging with or selling its assets to a business corporation), the directors of a mutual benefit corporation may be called to account by the state attorney general, or other community representatives, on the basis that those assets are charitable assets that may not be disposed of without state approval.[9]

# Director Accountability of Public Benefit and Religious Corporations

### Direct beneficiaries generally have no legal oversight power over nonprofit corporation directors

From the beginning of public charities, there was a class of beneficiaries of the charitable corporation (for example, the poor of a parish) who were not the parties appointing the director or trustee to office. Further, those beneficiaries were generally deemed incapable of enforcing the director's obligations or were persons who, it was felt, should not have that power. In some cases, moreover, the direct beneficiaries of a nonprofit organization are not people—for example, nonprofits devoted to animal welfare or preserving natural resources. The absence of a mechanism for direct action and oversight by beneficiaries of nonprofit organizations leaves an accountability vacuum. In the United States, this vacuum is often filled by the state, generally represented by the state attorney general.

### Attorney general oversight

In many states, a state attorney general is generally deemed to speak for the beneficiaries of any entity, such as a public benefit corporation, which has assets that are considered to be held in a charitable trust. In effect, the attorney general becomes the voice of the constituency for whom a charitable corporation was

organized.[10]  In comparison, except in unusual circumstances, the attorney
general does not assert a right to scrutinize activities of noncharitable
corporations, such as mutual benefit corporations.

Traditionally, the attorney general's authority has been understood as giving
him or her the power to enforce the public's interest in the maintenance of
property and funds for the original charitable purpose: to prevent a divergence
of these funds for improper purposes and intervene if the persons holding
this property attempted to change the purpose, even if the new purpose was a
proper charitable activity. As a result, a public benefit corporation planning a
major change in the use of its assets may be required to consult the attorney
general or join him or her in a so-called *cy pres* proceeding in a court. Statutory
provisions have broadened the power of the attorney general in most states
to include a general supervision over the solicitation of monies for charitable
purposes.[11]

States vary in the degree to which the attorney general is specifically
empowered to investigate transactions of nonprofit corporations, such as public
charities, which are deemed to hold some or all of their assets in a charitable
trust.[12] Many states have adopted laws affirmatively requiring some or all
nonprofit corporations to give the state attorney general prior notice and the
opportunity to review transactions involving disposition of substantially all
of the corporation's charitable assets, particularly in the case of a merger or
sale of assets to a for-profit institution.[13]

In recent years, nonprofit organizations, especially nonprofit health care
entities, have experienced increased state attorney general scrutiny of their
activities.[14] This has resulted in high-profile enforcement actions and legislation
enhancing the enforcement authority of the attorney general around the
country.[15]

## Despite Their Importance, Donors Are Not Considered Part of Nonprofit's Legal Constituency

A director of a public benefit corporation, such as a conventional charity, will
note an omission from the list of the persons to whom directors of a nonprofit
corporation may be accountable: donors are not listed as a party with whom the
director has a legal relationship. In general, the omission is correct, although
obviously the corporation will be sensitive to the concerns of its principal
donors. Although there are exceptions, as a general rule, assets acquired by
a charitable corporation are no longer subject to the donors' control, unless
the donors have specified restrictions in the gift instrument that the assets be
used or invested in a specific manner.[16]

The corporation's board of directors may use the donated assets in whatever
way the board believes appropriate, consistent with the corporation's purpose.
If donors or others believe these uses are not appropriate, they may petition

the state attorney general to review the matter.[17] In some circumstances, donors may bring an action against the nonprofit corporation for enforcement of restrictions on a gift.[18] A donor also may have a contract action available based on the written instrument that sets forth the term of the gift.[19]

## Accountability to Members Responsible for Appointing Directors

Although the attorney general's powers may extend to all public benefit corporations within a given state, many such corporations also have a membership to whom the director may be accountable, to the extent this membership has the power to remove or fail to reelect the director, to sue directors on the corporation's behalf, or to bring a derivative action.[20] If a director is elected by one or more members, the director may have—or feel—a duty to the member or members electing the director to make sure that their viewpoint is represented on the board. Still, such duty to articulate a member's individual perspective does not change the director's obligation to make decisions and take other actions in accordance with the *corporation's* best interest—irrespective of any individual member interests. The only exception to this rule occurs when the corporation's articles and bylaws specify that certain member interests should be taken into account, such as a requirement that no action be taken that would result in the corporation losing its tax-exempt status.

## Constitutional Considerations Limiting Public Accountability of Religious Corporations

The directors of religious corporations are generally subject to the foregoing considerations. Still, because United States constitutional law restricts the role of government in dealing with religious corporations to a minimum enforcement of basic fiscal integrity, oversight is more limited, lest the government intrude on freedom of religion.

*See the Suggested Questions and Checklist following the Endnotes below to review the issues discussed in this chapter.*

# Endnotes

1.   *See* Lisa A. Runquist and Jeannie Carmedelle Frey, Eds., *Guide to Representing Religious Organizations* 55 (American Bar Association 2009).

2.   The drafters of the Model Act eliminated the classification system because of the lack of uniform acceptance by states adopting the revised Model Nonprofit Corporation Act. *See* Lizabeth A. Moody, Foreward to Model Act, at xxii (American Bar Association 2009).

3.   A good analogy is that of a representative in Congress, who may, on the floor or through committee, exert immense influence on the actions of government, but is given no function, under the Constitution, when acting alone. But (again paralleling a member of Congress) the individual director has legally protected rights to participate in corporate decisions and has legally recognized rights and duties to be informed concerning corporate transactions.

A one-person board of directors is permitted under some state statutes; where such a board exists, the single director's act is an exercise of the board's powers. The Model Act § 8.03 (and other state statutes) requires a minimum of three directors.

4.   *See* Comment to Model Act § 8.01 (describing rights and duties of directors). *See also Chapter 2, "Duties and Rights of Nonprofit Corporation Directors"* in this *Guidebook.*

5.   *See, e.g.,* DEL. CODE ANN., tit. 8 § 221; N.Y. NOT-FOR-PROFIT CORP. LAW § 703.

6.   *See generally* John William Gergacz, *Attorney-Corporate Client Privilege* (2010) at § 5.10 (discussing factors to be considered in determining whether attorney-client confidentiality applies); *see also id.* at § 2.05 (using Kirby v. Kirby, 1987 WL 14862 (Del. Ch. July 29, 1987) to explain why in nonprofit corporations the privilege is considered to attach to directors as part of the corporate entity).

7.   Attribution unknown.

8.   *See, e.g.,* Cook v. The Lloyd Noland Foundation, Inc. & Tenet Healthcare, Inc., 825 So. 2d 83 (Ala. 2001) (holding that under the state Alabama Nonprofit Corporation Act, the only persons authorized to bring a legal proceeding to challenge an act, conveyance, or transfer of property by a nonprofit corporation were members or directors of the corporation, representatives of the corporation, and the state attorney general, and that the local district attorney and other community representatives therefore lacked standing to challenge the corporation's actions).

9.   *See* James K. Orlikoff and Mary K. Totten, *Governing Conversion Foundations: A Practical Guide for Trustees,* TRUSTEE 51, no. 4 (April 1998), at T1-T4; Gary Claxton, Judith Feder, David Shactman, and

Stuart Altman, *Public Policy Issues in Nonprofit Conversions: An Overview*, HEALTH AFFAIRS 16, no. 2 (March/April 1997), at 9-28.

10.   *See, e.g.,* CONN. GEN. STAT. § 3-125; MASS. ANN. LAWS ch. 12 § 8.

11.   *See, e.g.,* MO. REV. STAT. § 407.450, et seq.; N.Y. EXECUTIVE LAW § 171-a, et seq.

12.   *See, e.g.,* OHIO REV. CODE ANN. § 109.24 (giving the state attorney general the power to "investigate transactions and relationships of trustees of a charitable trust for the purpose of determining whether the property held for charitable, religious, or educational purposes has been and is being properly administered in accordance with fiduciary principles. . ." and providing that the attorney general "shall institute and prosecute a proper action to enforce the performance of any charitable trust, and to restrain the abuse of it whenever he considers such action advisable. . ."). *See also* RESTATEMENT (THIRD) OF TRUSTS No. 5, 2009 § 94 (Tentative Draft) ("A suit for the enforcement of a charitable trust may be maintained only by the Attorney General or other appropriate public officer, or by a co-trustee or successor trustee, by a settlor, or by another person who has a special interest in the enforcement of the trust").

13.   *See* TENN. CODE ANN. § 48-62-102(g); *see also* OHIO REV. CODE ANN. § 109.34 (referring solely to nonprofit healthcare entities); National Conference of Commissioners on Uniform State Laws, Model Protection of Charitable Assets Act.

14.   *See, e.g.,* People ex rel. Spitzer v. Grasso, 893 N.E.2d 105 (N.Y. 2008); Michael W. Peregrine and Ralph E. DeJong, *State AGs' Powers Over Nonprofits After Spitzer v. Grasso*, National Law Journal (June 18, 2007).

15.   *See, e.g.,* California Nonprofit Integrity Act of 2004, CAL. GOV'T CODE § 12585. The National Conference of Commissioners on Uniform State Laws has developed the "Protection of Charitable Assets Act," which articulates the state attorney general's protection authority over charitable assets.

16.   *See* Newman v. Forward Lands, Inc., 430 F. Supp. 1320, 1324 (E.D. Pa. 1977) ("[t]hat only the Attorney General, a co-trustee, or someone with a special interest may sue to enforce a charitable trust."), citing RESTATEMENT (SECOND) OF TRUSTS § 391. The PRINCIPLES OF THE LAW OF NONPROFIT ORGANIZATIONS (Tentative Draft No. 3, 2011) in §§ 670 and 680 address standing issues relating to gift-enforcement suits. Section 670 provides that a private suit for specific enforcement of the charitable purpose of a charitable trust or restrictive gift may be maintained only by: (1) the sole or primary settler of the trust or donor of the gift; (2) a person granted authority in the trust or gift instrument to enforce the performance of the charitable purpose of the trust or gift; or (3) a person with a special interest. Section 680 provides that a person has a special interest with standing to sue to

enforce or modify the charitable purpose of a charitable trust or a restrictive gift or to bring a derivative suit only upon demonstrating the following: (1) the attorney general approved of the complained-of behavior by settlement or other agreement or is unavailable due to an official conflict of interest; (2) the complained-of behavior is egregious or the circumstances are exigent, and the remedy sought is particularized to address the injury to the trust or gift or to the charity; and (3) the plaintiff bears a special relationship both to the matter at issue and to the trust or gift or to the charity.

17.   *See* Linda Grant, *Acts of Charity: Furious Donors Blame a Lax Board after a Fund's Scandal Toppled the Lavish-Living Hand of the United Way,* Los Angeles Times Magazine, Sept. 13, 1992, at 39; *see also* Aramony v. United Way, 28 F. Supp. 2d 147 (S.D.N.Y. 1998), *reversed on other grounds,* 254 F.3d 403 (2d Cir. 2001).

18.   For example, in Iowa, a donor of a gift in excess of $100,000 may be able to bring an action against the nonprofit corporation to enforce the restrictions placed on the gift. *See* Iowa Code § 540A.106.

19.   *See, e.g.,* Principles of the Law of Nonprofit Organizations § 670, Cmt. d, *supra* note 16.

20.   *See, e.g.,* Cal. Corp. Code §§ 5710; 7710; N.Y. Not-for-Profit Corp. Law § 623; *see also* Model Act, Chapter 13; Del. Code Ann. Tit. 8 § 141(k).

# Suggested Questions for Directors Regarding the Nonprofit Corporation and Its Directors

(1)   What group of members elected me? If I wasn't elected by a voting membership, how was I elected?

(2)   If I was elected by a voting membership, how is that membership defined? Where can I find: The bylaws? The articles of incorporation? Are the records of voting membership kept in good order? By whom?

(3)   When does my term of office expire? Can I be reelected? Does my term run until a specific date, or until my successor is chosen?

(4)   Can I be removed from my position as director? By whom? On what basis?

(5)   Was I selected by some group of members or some entity so that my term differs from that of the other directors?

(6)   Is the nonprofit corporation in good standing under the laws of state in which it was incorporated (this usually can be confirmed

by an online search of the website for the Secretary of State's office in that state).

(7)     What is our corporation supposed to do and for whom? Is our purpose expressed in the articles of incorporation, bylaws, and/or a separate mission statement?

(8)     Does the corporation have a mission statement? If not, why not? If so, when was the mission statement last reviewed? Is it consistent with the "purposes" of the corporation as described in the articles of incorporation or bylaws?

(9)     What parties or officials can question what we do as directors of the corporation?

# Checklist: The Nonprofit Corporation and Its Directors

*Note:*    For simplicity, these checklists describe a corporation having a chair, who presides over the board of directors; a chief executive, who may be a staff person; an executive committee; a governance/nominating committee; and an audit committee. (We recognize, however, that in many smaller and other nonprofits, these committee functions may be performed by either the executive committee or the board as a whole.) We also assume a legal counsel—someone, paid or unpaid, having primary responsibility for the corporation's legal affairs. Many corporations, especially larger nonprofits, may have other committees established for specific purposes, such as establishing executive compensation; monitoring compliance with legal requirements; and overseeing investments and other financial matters.

| Subject | Review By | How Often | Comment |
|---|---|---|---|
| 1. Review the articles of incorporation | a) Full board or governance/ nominating committee, with legal counsel<br>b) By new directors | a) Periodic review, probably every three years<br>b) Upon joining board | Review should include: conformity to corporate purpose/mission; compliance with tax and corporate laws; any explicit provisions relating to directors and officers, including indemnification and availability of limitations on liability. |
| 2. Review the bylaws | In general:<br>a) Chair, legal counsel, governance/ nominating or other committee<br>b) By new directors | In general:<br>a) Periodic review, probably every three years<br>b) Upon joining board | Review should include conformity to articles of incorporation, corporate purpose/mission; problems possibly arising from changes in program; compliance with tax and corporate laws; any explicit provisions relating to directors and officers, including indemnification, insurance, and availability of limitations on liability. |

| Subject | Review By | How Often | Comment |
|---|---|---|---|
| a. Does the number of directors stated in the bylaws conform to the number actually serving (or the size the board will reach if new directors are elected)? If the corporation has a rotating board with a percentage elected each year, is the percentage being elected correct? | Chair or chief executive; governance/ nominating committee | Annually in all cases; always before notice goes out for meeting to elect directors | Consistency of actual board composition with bylaw requirements is a frequent problem, particularly in smaller public benefit corporations. |
| b. Do the bylaws have a statement of corporate mission or purpose consistent with the articles of incorporation, or other mission statement? | Chair or chief executive; governance/ nominating or other committee | Annually and every time either of these documents is changed | Bylaws may have no statement of mission or purpose and there does not have to be one; but if there is one, it should be consistent with other documents, especially the articles of incorporation. |
| c. Are there, or should there be honorary directors? | Chair and chief executive | Probably every three or four years | Voting rights (or lack thereof) should be clearly defined and understood. |

| Subject | Review By | How Often | Comment |
|---------|-----------|-----------|---------|
| d. If the corporation has members with voting rights, is there an accurate list of the members consistent with whatever definition of eligibility is contained in the bylaws? | Chief executive, governance/ nominating or other committee | At least annually, and before notice goes out for any meeting where elections are to be held | There is probably no area with greater record-keeping problems than this. Nonprofits, particularly public benefit and religious corporations, will often designate as "members" persons who are simply donors or friends, keeping no accurate membership records. The rights (or lack thereof) of these persons to vote should be clearly defined and any problems reviewed with legal counsel. |
| 3. Review of a corporate mission statement | Chief executive reporting to board | Probably every three or four years | If there is no mission statement, a board should consider creating one. |

| Subject | Review By | How Often | Comment |
|---|---|---|---|
| a. Is there a single mission statement; is it consistent with the purposes of the corporation as set forth in the articles of incorporation and/or bylaws; in what document is it embodied? | Chief executive reporting to board | Probably every three or four years | There should be a single overall mission statement; separate statements for individual programs may be in order, but they should be consistent. |
| b. Are the corporation's public statements (e.g., brochures, press releases, etc.) as issued during the last year consistent with the mission statement? | Chief executive | Annually, and as each brochure or press release is issued | Nonprofits dealing with public controversies will often find problems here. |
| c. Has the board reviewed the mission statement and understood the constituency served by the corporation? | Chair, bringing issue to board | Probably every three or four years | Board should always understand the fundamental focus of the nonprofit corporation's work, such as the specific constituency served or services provided. |

# Chapter 2:
## Duties and Rights of Nonprofit Corporation Directors

# Chapter 2:
# Duties and Rights of Nonprofit Corporation Directors

*In carrying out their functions for the corporation, directors are subject to two primary obligations: a duty of care and a duty of loyalty.*

*The duty of care and the duty of loyalty are the common terms for the standards that guide all actions a director takes. These standards are derived from a century of litigation principally involving business corporations, but are equally applicable to nonprofit corporations.[1]*

*In recent years there has been an increased focus on the fiduciary duties of nonprofit corporation directors as a result of closer scrutiny being placed on nonprofits by both the government and the public. The United States Senate Finance Committee has, as part of its review of the activities of tax-exempt religious organizations, educational institutions, healthcare organizations, and other types of nonprofits, considered various proposals that would impact the governance of nonprofit organizations. The major 2008 revision and subsequent changes to the IRS Form 990 require a significant level of disclosure about exempt operations and governance issues.*

*State attorneys general have conducted high-profile investigations of nonprofit organizations (and their boards), which have resulted in various enforcement actions as well as legislation around the country.[2] Over time, the Sarbanes-Oxley Act, which focused on publicly traded companies, has affected views of best practices and recommended standards for governance of nonprofit organizations. Such developments have not resulted in any fundamental change in the standards to which nonprofit directors are held, but rather made clear the importance of a director fulfilling the duty of care and duty of loyalty.*

# The Duty of Care

The duty of care calls upon directors to act in a reasonable and informed manner when participating in the board's decisions and its oversight of the corporation's management.

The duty of care requires that first, directors be informed; and second, that they discharge their duties in good faith, with the care that a person in a like position would reasonably believe appropriate under similar circumstances.[3]

Each of the tasks outlined below requires the director's efficient allocation of time. The appropriate amount of time required to satisfy a director's duty of care must be decided by the director in his or her reasonable judgment, under the circumstances. Nonetheless, substantial compliance with the elements of care discussed below is commonly expected of the nonprofit director and may be required by law.

# Elements of the Duty of Care

The duty of care requires that a director be informed and exercise independent judgment. Satisfying the duty of care may be accomplished in part by the following activities:

### Attending meetings and proxy voting limitations

Regular attendance at meetings of the board of directors is a basic requirement of director service. Generally, directors may not vote by proxy.

**Importance of regular attendance.** All directors must remember that they act as a group, and therefore regular board meeting attendance is essential. Continuous or repeated absence may expose the director to the risk of not satisfying the duty of care. Moreover, sporadic board attendance by a director may be grounds for the director's removal. Most states permit directors to "attend" a meeting by telephone or use other mechanisms that allow all directors to hear or communicate with each other simultaneously. Therefore, even directors with busy travel schedules should be able to comply with the regular attendance standard.

**Attendance at committee meetings.** As discussed in *Chapter 3, Committees and Advisory Bodies*, boards typically delegate many important functions to committees. A director appointed to serve on a committee of the board is expected to regularly attend such committee meetings, and to be active in the committee's deliberations and other activities. A director must satisfy the duty of care in discharging his duties as a committee member.

**Limits on attendance or voting by proxy.** Generally, directors cannot designate another person as the director's proxy, to attend or vote at board or committee meetings in the director's place.[4] All directors should understand the reasons for this rule. First of all, whatever reasons a director's constituency may have had for choosing her or him, that choice was the selection of a specific person to perform a duty, not the grant of a transferable privilege. Second, all the other directors, as well as the nonprofit organization itself, are entitled to demand the director's own wisdom and judgment, not that of such surrogate as the director may choose. Third, such deference and accommodation the directors themselves may give to each other in the course of their work usually cannot, as a practical matter, be transferred to purely personal appointees.

If a board of directors encounters significant problems concerning the frequency of a director's attendance, it should consider adopting or recommending bylaws or policies permitting or requiring the removal of directors who regularly miss meetings or attend only portions of meetings.[5] As an alternative, the board could consider creating honorary directorships or advisory councils for these individuals.

## *Exercising independent judgment*

The duty of care requires that each director, no matter how selected, share *equally* in the responsibility of the board to act in the best interests of the corporation. Each director should exercise her or his independent and informed judgment on all corporate decisions. While such judgment may be informed by the director's individual expertise, experience and affiliations, and even knowledge of the viewpoints of any entity that contributed to his appointment, the director's decision must only be based on what is in the corporation's best interest. No director should vote solely on the basis of what another director thinks, even if that director has special expertise; each director must use his independent judgment to evaluate any position taken by another director, the corporation's staff, or an outside expert.

**Each director must judge what is in the corporation's best interest, irrespective of other entities with which the director is affiliated or sympathetic, or to which the director owes his board appointment.** The law conceives of a board of directors as an entity: each member  shares the same rights and the same duties and is accountable to the same constituency. Even if a director is specifically nominated or appointed by a particular group, or is chosen in part because of an association with a certain subset of the organization's members or beneficiaries, each director shares the same fiduciary duty to act in the best interest of the entire organization.

There are situations in which a board of directors may be explicitly structured to provide for representation of certain interests. For example, a trade association may have a board of directors composed of individuals who are selected by separate regions or states. A university alumni association may have a board on which each of the schools of the university is represented by one or more directors who are alumni of that particular school. Directors may be confused about how to address situations in which the interests of their constituency and the interests of the corporation are actually or potentially in conflict. In bringing to the attention of the board the particular sensitivities and concerns of their constituency, directors may aid the whole board in fulfilling its duty of care, and add wisdom to the whole board's deliberations. Nonetheless, the director's duty of loyalty lies with the interests of the corporation, not to any constituent group. (See the discussion in the section *"The Duty of Loyalty"* below.)

**Directors may give weight to the views of directors or others having special expertise, but must make an independent decision on any questions presented for board or committee determination.** The reason for having more than one director is to ensure that differing viewpoints have the opportunity to be heard, and that directors with different talents, expertise, experiences, and perspectives share their views and together decide on what course of action is in the corporation's best interests. To this end, it is important that each director use any expertise he or she may have when serving in the role of a board member. In other words, it is important that directors not "check" their talents at the door of the boardroom.

At the same time, although it is natural, and often appropriate, for a director to seriously consider the viewpoints of another director who has special expertise or knowledge on a matter being discussed, it is part of each director's duty of care to evaluate all views and information presented to the board or board committee, and to make an independent judgment regarding the proper course of action.

**The need for independent members of the board.** Since the passage of the Sarbanes-Oxley Act and as a result of greater scrutiny of tax-exempt organization operations by Congress and many state attorney generals, the concept of independent directors for a nonprofit has received increased attention. Some states place limitations on the number of directors who can be "interested" directors.[6]

In the context of nonprofits, an independent director generally means a director who is not employed by the corporation and does not receive compensation from the corporation other than as a director. There is a concern that directors who are not independent might give too much deference to management, or that conflicts of interest may not be appropriately recognized and avoided, resulting in actions that are not in the best interest of the organization.[7] Commentators have noted that independent and nonmanagement board members are an organizational resource that should be used to assure the exercise of independent judgment in key committees and general board decision making.[8]

The IRS requires nonprofits that file Form 990 to make certain disclosures about board member independence. In Form 990, the IRS defines "independence" differently than other legal sources and even from its own pronouncements in other contexts. For purposes of Form 990, a director who receives compensation from the organization as an officer or other employee or as an independent contractor exceeding $10,000, or a director involved in any disclosable interested persons transaction is considered to lack independence. Still, unless the state law limits the number of interested directors, the IRS has no power to limit the number.

In comparison, for determining whether a tax-exempt health care corporation would be considered to have a "community board," the IRS has indicated that practicing physicians "affiliated" with a hospital—such as medical staff members—are not considered independent, based on their "close and continuing connection" to the hospital, without regard to whether the nonprofit hospital compensates the physicians in any amount.[9] See also *Chapter 4, Taxation,* for more information on Form 990 requirements as it relates to the governance.

### Having adequate information

To function effectively, a director needs to be adequately informed.

**Assuring the adequacy and clarity of information.** To satisfy the duty of care effectively, directors need to have an adequate source of information flow. This information is generally supplied by the corporation's management and other staff. To the extent that it is not adequate, a board or an individual director will have to determine what additional information is needed. The directors should carefully read the information supplied. If the information is highly technical, lengthy, or otherwise difficult to comprehend, the board may find it helpful to request an executive summary or other version of the information, which is in a more understandable form. The directors also may want to insist that these materials be furnished far enough in advance that they have sufficient time to review and analyze the information.

In addition, a board member should ask questions at the board meeting as necessary to clarify the information or help assure the director that he or she has fully understood it. If a director has a special expertise with respect to a certain kind of information, he or she may assist the other board members by asking clarifying questions, or in pointing out specific items to the rest of the board. (However, such director should try to avoid stating opinions in such a way that other directors are tempted or pressured to "rely" on the director's opinion without engaging in independent analysis). (See the discussion in the section *"Directors may give weight to the views of directors. . ."* above.)

**Sources of board information.** In some small nonprofit entities, such as neighborhood improvement bodies or condominium associations, the board itself may be its own primary source of information. With larger organizations, however, the board will inevitably use and rely on information prepared by the corporation's officers and agents. This means that the corporation's staff will inevitably have a significant effect on the board's decisions since the staff will select much of the information the directors receive. Even when a director has total and justified confidence in the suppliers of information, he or she should be at least aware that for every piece of information received, other information may have been determined to be not necessary for the board's consideration.

Especially in heavily regulated areas or other areas that are significant to the organization's existence and purpose, the director should evaluate whether he or she needs additional information to fulfill the director's duty and to best serve the organization. If for any reason any member of the board thinks that the information provided to the directors is inadequate in any respect, he or she should not hesitate to request further information from the staff or other sources. Since boards tend to become accustomed to the status quo, new board members can often serve a valuable function by calling the board's attention to the question of whether the board should be receiving different or additional information in certain areas. It is also important that any director disclose information to other directors that is not already known to the other directors when this information is material to the discharge of the board's decision-making and oversight functions.[10]

# Reliance

In the ordinary course of business, a director may act in reliance on information and reports received from regular sources that the director reasonably regards as trustworthy.

A director may rely on the reports, communications, and information received from a committee or from any officer, employee, or agent, if the director reasonably believes the source to be reliable and competent. The Model Act, as well as many state nonprofit codes, expressly recognizes the concept of reliance on others. A director is entitled to rely on information, opinions, reports, or statements, including financial statements and other financial data, if prepared or presented by the persons or bodies referenced below:

## *Officers and employees*

A director may rely on information provided by officers or employees of the corporation whom the director reasonably believes to be reliable and competent in the matters presented. If the information is provided in written form, it is expected that the director would have independently reviewed or evaluated the information, or received a sufficiently detailed summary from a reliable source, before relying on it.[11]

## *Experts retained by the corporation*

A director may rely on legal counsel, public accountants, or other persons retained by the corporation as to matters the director reasonably believes are within the person's professional or expert competence.

### Board committees

A director may rely on information provided by a committee of the board of which the director is not a member as to matters within the committee's jurisdiction, if the director reasonably believes the committee merits confidence.

### Religious authorities presenting information to religious corporations

A director of a religious corporation may rely on information provided by religious authorities and ministers, priests, rabbis, imams, or other persons whose position or duties in the religious organization the director reasonably believes justify reliance and confidence and whom the director believes to be reliable and competent in the matters presented.[12]

### Inappropriate director reliance

These general rules of reliance *never* apply if the director has personal knowledge that would make reliance on the information provided by any of the above persons unwarranted.[13] In such circumstances, relying on such information would not constitute "reasonableness" or good faith on the part of the director. Moreover, a director having knowledge that brings into question the reliability of any information presented to the board may have a duty to share this knowledge with the other board members.

## Delegation

The board of directors, as such, does not operate the day-to-day business of the corporation. In delegating that function to others, it must adopt appropriate policies and procedures that ensure effective oversight of the actions of the corporation's management and other corporate agents.

### General rule: the directors oversee, but do not directly engage in the corporation's day-to-day operations

The board of directors is not expected to operate the corporation on a day-to-day basis. Even under statutes providing that the business and affairs of a corporation shall be "managed" by the board of directors, it is recognized that actual operation is a function of management, that is, the officers and agents of the corporation.[14] In conventional corporate theory, the responsibility of the board is limited to overseeing corporate operations. This principle does not relieve the board of its monitoring responsibilities; however, it does mean that directors are not personally responsible for actions or omissions of officers, employees, or agents of the corporation as long as these persons have been prudently selected and the directors have relied reasonably upon such officers, employees, or agents.

### *Adoption of appropriate monitoring and control procedures*

It is the board's responsibility to oversee implementation of a compliance program that helps assure the corporation's compliance with legal requirements applicable to the nonprofit corporation. Compliance programs are extremely important for mitigating risks of legal and operational problems for the nonprofit corporation. These programs also are important in the event there is ever a problem that arises for the corporation. Under the Federal Sentencing Guidelines, a corporation can receive significant fine reductions if it has an effective compliance program in place.

As part of their oversight responsibilities, directors and prospective directors of nonprofit corporations should be aware of the kind of legal claims and operational risks to which their corporation may be vulnerable, based on, among other things, trends in government enforcement actions or private litigation involving similar organizations. Directors should regularly evaluate whether the corporation has appropriate policies and procedures in place to ensure that the corporation complies with applicable laws.[15] (For a more detailed discussion of how a board can become aware of the legal environment of its corporation, see *Chapter 12, The Legal Environment of the Nonprofit Corporation.*)

### *Evidencing specific delegations of authority to officers*

While in the for-profit world, a corporation's board often makes clear written delegations of authority to the chief executive and other officers, this is often not the case in the nonprofit world. The board may wish to adopt bylaw provisions, or a general resolution or policy, setting forth the scope of management authority delegated to the chief executive (who may then be free to subdelegate portions of this authority). Formalizing the scope of delegated authority may be particularly useful in small nonprofit corporations, where lines of responsibility may be easily blurred. For example, a bylaw provision addressing the responsibility of an executive officer may specify that the officer has authority to execute contracts on behalf of the corporation within the scope of the corporation's ordinary conduct of business, and otherwise as specified by board resolution.

### *Directors with multiple "hats"*

When a member of the board occupies both the role of a director and that of an officer, employee, or other agent, corporate law treats that person, while acting in his or her capacity as an agent, just as the law would treat such a person who is not serving on the board. It is therefore essential that this person (and the other directors) always be aware of which "hat" the director is wearing at any particular time.

## *Delegations of director authority to members or other persons*

The Model Act, as well as many state laws, permit a nonprofit corporation's articles of incorporation to specify exceptions to the general management authority of the board.[16] In such cases, the articles or bylaws may name other parties, such as the corporation's members, a representative assembly, or a board-appointed committee, or other designated body, who are specifically responsible for certain corporate governance decisions that would ordinarily fall to the board of directors. Depending on the jurisdiction and the nature of the delegation, the directors of such corporations may be partially or wholly relieved of their fiduciary responsibilities in such specified areas (while the alternate decision-maker may become correspondingly subject to fiduciary obligations to the extent of its specified authority). It is incumbent upon any director to make sure that he or she clearly understands the extent to which such article or bylaw provisions serve to release the director of the fiduciary duties that would ordinarily apply.

## *Delegation to an executive committee*

Many nonprofit corporations make extensive use of an executive committee to make board-level management decisions. Such delegation of board authority may be both appropriate and practical, especially if the size of the board is very large or if it meets only a few times a year. Even fairly active boards may appropriately make use of an executive committee. The scope of such delegations of board authority to an executive committee, however, should be clearly set forth in the corporation's bylaws or in board resolutions, and state nonprofit corporation statutes often place some limitations on what can be assigned to a committee, including an executive committee.

In addition, directors who do not sit on the executive committee should understand the extent to which the board has (and has not) delegated its fiduciary duties to the executive committee. These directors should understand that they still retain a duty of oversight over the executive committee. The executive committee is accountable to the board, and the board members should receive sufficient information regarding executive committee decisions to be able to evaluate whether delegations of authority to the committee are appropriate. (See further discussion in the section *"Descriptions of Common Standing Committees"* in *Chapter 3, Committees and Advisory Bodies.*) One important way of making sure the entire board is aware of the executive committee's action is to distribute minutes of executive committee meetings to the entire board.

# Discharging the Duty of Care:
# Some Practical Suggestions

In all but the smallest and simplest corporations, the corporation's needs for the board's attention will often exceed the time the board has to furnish this resource. Hence, well-run nonprofit corporations will adopt certain procedures, including those set forth below, to enable the board and its individual members to use their time efficiently.

## Regular Schedule of Meetings

The board of directors should meet on a regular basis. The schedule of board meetings should be fixed at the beginning of each year, so that board members can place the meetings on their calendars well in advance, and thus assure attendance. While the appropriate frequency (monthly, quarterly, etc.) of scheduled board meetings will depend on the size of the corporation, the geographic nature of its constituency, budgetary considerations, the decisions to be made, and other considerations unique to each corporation, the need for a regular schedule of meetings applies to all nonprofit corporations. Without a regular schedule, the board is more vulnerable to claims that it has not adequately fulfilled its duties of oversight of the corporation. Because decisions regarding the corporation's management occur on a regular basis, some person or body other than the board is likely making management decisions in the board's absence. By allowing this situation to occur, the board members may have effectively, and inappropriately, transferred board power to persons other than the board.

## Executive Sessions

Many boards will meet in executive session where the chief executive and other staff members will be absent. These sessions can be helpful to the board in discussing sensitive issues outside the presence of the staff. As a result, a board can benefit from having executive sessions as part of its regular meetings. Regular executive sessions serve the dual purposes of encouraging candid discussions of issues among board members and avoiding management anxiety if it appears that the executive sessions are only called when major concerns have been raised.

## Meeting Agenda and Committee Reports

Although the items discussed will vary, most boards find it helpful to have a standard form of meeting agenda, to ensure the board routinely addresses issues important to the corporation. The agenda should include reports from the executive committee (if any), and from all other active committees, regarding significant actions taken and issues addressed since the last board meeting and the financial condition of the corporation.

## Action by Written Consent

The Model Act and many state statutes permit directors to act without a meeting by unanimous written consent.[17] A small number of states permit action by directors with less than unanimous consent.[18] For purposes of such authorization, many states and the Model Act permit "written" consents to be in electronic form if certain electronic transmission and signature requirements are met.

A procedure involving action by written consent may frequently be appropriate in  transacting routine business, or for approving specific actions that have already been fully discussed at prior board meetings. Directors should, however, be cautious about the ratification or authorization of major activities or decisions without a meeting or other opportunity for the board as a whole to raise questions and fully evaluate the ramifications of the action. The use of consents should not be a substitute for regular meetings.

## Board Voting Via E-mail

Many nonprofit boards will communicate via e-mail and seek to take action by an e-mail vote. A small number of state nonprofit corporation statutes expressly provide for the ability to take action by e-mail.[19] Most states, however, do not have statutory provisions that expressly address board action by email, even if members vote through electronic means.  As a result, any board "voting" via e-mail likely will need to comply with the state's requirements for action by written consent (discussed above). This means, among other things, that it may be necessary to have unanimous consent in order for an action to become effective.  Similar to written consents, voting by e-mail should not be a substitute for regular meetings.

# Regular Schedule of Information

As much information as practical should be provided to the directors on a regular schedule.

### Schedule of reports to be provided to the board

Information should be provided to the board of directors in a regular and timely manner, so that the board will have a realistic opportunity to review and consider it. The board's information needs will be more easily and efficiently satisfied if the directors establish a regularly scheduled system of reports and data for those corporate activities that are sufficiently repetitive to be predictable to all parties. This information will include financial reports, program reports, and the like. Just as with infrequent board meetings, when information is provided only sporadically, directors will find it much more difficult to satisfy their duty of care on the corporation's behalf. Furthermore, in almost all such situations, *some* board member is receiving information, and thus inequalities within the board's knowledge base may be created. Regularity of information distribution is important to the entire board's ability to be informed regarding significant corporate matters.

### Distribution of information in advance of board meetings

Directors should require distribution of as much material as possible in advance of a board meeting (preferably at least a week before the meeting). As noted above, certain types of reports—particularly financial reports— should be furnished on a regular schedule, whether monthly, quarterly, or semiannually.

### Practical limitations on staff time to prepare required reports and other information

The board's need for regular reports and other information must necessarily be balanced by its recognition of any limitations on staff time to prepare the information. The preparation of meaningful data for a board meeting consumes significant amounts of time, and particularly in small organizations, may take away from time needed for operational activities. The board should be mindful of this in defining the information it requires. The board—as a whole or through its chair or other representative—should discuss with its staff the most efficient way to provide the board with necessary information while not impeding the staff's operational responsibilities.

*Asking questions, getting answers, and taking action whenever there is a concern identified by a director*

It is incumbent upon each director to ask questions and raise concerns whenever there is a "red flag" or other concern or question identified by the director with regard to any information provided to the directors or any aspect of the nonprofit corporation's operations. A director should not be shy about raising such questions or concerns and the board, as a whole, should make sure whatever questions or concerns are raised receive adequate and acceptable responses.

In addition, it is important that the board of directors, upon becoming aware of any possible unethical or illegal acts of the corporation, its officers, or employees, investigate the matter and take appropriate corrective action.

# Rules of Procedure and Minutes

The board should adopt rules of procedure appropriate to its size, the constituencies represented on the board, and the diversity of its membership. Minutes of the board and committee meetings also should be prepared regularly.

Any working board will work out its own standard procedures for board meetings and the degree of formality, or lack thereof, used in submitting motions, amendments to resolutions, recording votes, etc. Matters of importance should always be acted on by formal resolution. Sometimes, formal procedural rules, such as Robert's Rules of Order, will be noted by a director for the proper procedure on a matter. Robert's Rules of Order are not applicable until the organization adopts them for use. Formal procedural rules can be very helpful to organizations that often have issues debated. On the other hand, because such rules are complicated, they can cause confusion for those who are not thoroughly familiar with them. Since such rules are generally intended for use by large membership organizations or delegated assemblies rather than small boards, many nonprofits opt to follow simpler rules of procedure, often based on general meeting conventions with which the directors are familiar.

The corporation's minutes should be prepared on a regular basis by a director or other individual with the ability to accurately record and produce in a timely manner the minutes of each meeting. At a minimum, minutes of board meetings should note the names of all directors and other persons who attended each meeting, and the outcome of each vote taken (specifically noting the names of the directors who voted for, against, or abstained). Further, when the board or committee is acting on a matter involving a conflict of interest for, or compensation or other benefit to, a director or executive officer, the minutes should recite the documentation and information relied on by the board or committee in making its decision. The minutes also should reflect the vote by the board (or committee) that indicates the director did not vote and whether or not the director was present at or participated in the discussion.

For tax-exempt corporations, the minutes and related documentation can be used to establish a rebuttable presumption of reasonableness for transactions covered by the IRS's "excess benefit" rule (including compensation decisions). (See the discussion of the excess benefits rules in the section *"Intermediate Sanctions: Excise Tax on Public Charities' Excess Benefit Transactions"* in *Chapter 4, Taxation*.) As noted above, the IRS has made clear through Form 990 that it prefers that governing bodies and subcommittees take steps to ensure that minutes of their meetings, and actions taken by written actions or outside of meetings, are contemporaneously documented.

Board committees also should prepare minutes, particularly when acting by authority delegated by the full board.

Questions can arise with regard to the handling of minutes for that portion of a board meeting that is conducted in "executive session." It is important that some form of record of the executive session be maintained. If no action is taken during the executive session, there do not need to be separate executive session minutes and the "regular" meeting minutes can simply note when the board went into and came out of executive session and that no action was taken during such session. If specific action is taken, or it is desirable to note some general or specific items discussed, such specific issues discussed can be described in the regular meeting minutes or, alternatively, in a separate set of minutes for the executive session. To the extent the minutes contain sensitive information, they should be maintained in a secure location within the organization or by another party, such as the attorney for the organization, and distributed only to board members.

It is important for each board member to review minutes carefully to ensure their accuracy. If there is ever a challenge to board action, the minutes will be an extremely important document in addressing such a challenge. As a result, draft minutes should be sent out soon after the meeting while the meeting is still fresh in directors' minds. It is also good practice for minutes to be approved no later than the next board meeting.

## The Business Judgment Rule

Even where a corporate action has proven to be unwise or unsuccessful, a director will generally be protected from liability arising from it if he or she acted in good faith and in a manner reasonably believed to be in the corporation's best interest, and with independent and informed judgment.[20]

### *Availability of the business judgment rule to prevent second-guessing of board decisions*

A director exercising good faith judgment will usually be protected from liability to the corporation or to its membership under the Business Judgment Rule. The Business Judgment Rule provides that a court, in an action brought by the corporation or its internal constituency, will not reexamine the actions of a director in authorizing or permitting a corporate action if the director's action was undertaken in good faith, in a manner reasonably believed to be in the best interests of the corporation, based on the director's independent and informed judgment, and the director is disinterested. The doctrine basically is a statement by the courts that it is inappropriate for them to second-guess corporate management decisions. This legal concept is well established in the case law applying to business corporations. It also has been recognized as applicable to the directors of nonprofit corporations.[21] The Model Act and some state nonprofit statutes have incorporated the Business Judgment Rule concept.[22] Still, in states where the Business Judgment Rule concept has not been incorporated in the nonprofit statutes, courts may be less willing to afford directors protection of the Business Judgment Rule when individuals are harmed, or other "bad facts" are present.[23]

Following good governance practices can help establish the Business Judgment Rule protection. In this regard, the Delaware Supreme Court has indicated that although aspirational ideals of corporate good governance practices do not define the standards of liability, following good governance practices can help directors avoid liability.[24]

### *Exceptions to availability of the rule*

The Business Judgment Rule defense is generally not available in situations in which basic breaches of duty by the director (such as criminal activity, fraud, bad faith, willful and wanton misconduct) are present.[25] In addition, for public charities, business decisions that would result in significant reduction or cessation of operations (such as the decision of a nonprofit health system to close down a money-losing hospital) may be challenged by the state attorney general on grounds that such action would violate the directors' duties to maintain the functions of a charitable trust.[26]

## Form 990 Governance Focus Areas

The IRS Form 990 asks certain questions regarding the governance of the tax-exempt organization, including whether certain policies relating to key governance or operational issues have been adopted. The IRS also has provided guidance regarding the content of certain governance-related policies and procedures for nonprofit organizations, such as in the areas of conflicts of interest, executive compensation, joint ventures, and fundraising. Although there is no specific law or provision of the Code mandating the adoption of many of these policies and procedures, the IRS focus and Form 990 questions have resulted in many nonprofit corporations adopting new or updating policies and procedures covering the topics identified in Form 990. Directors should know whether the nonprofit corporation has not only adopted but also in fact implemented policies and procedures relating to the following areas:

**Conflict of Interest.** Form 990 questions in this area focus on financial conflicts and ask if the nonprofit's conflicts policy applies to key employees as well as officers and directors. Issues regarding conflicts of interest are discussed in more detail later in this chapter, at *"Conflicts of Interest: General Principles."*

**Joint Ventures.** A policy on this topic may not be necessary or appropriate if the organization does not engage in joint ventures. If a joint venture policy is to be adopted, consideration should be given to the type of joint ventures that are expected and the specific issues that might arise for such ventures. If such a policy is needed, it should address means to assure that any joint venture is structured and operated consistently with the organization's tax-exempt status. Issues for directors to consider in connection with a nonprofit's participation in a joint venture with individuals or for-profit companies are discussed in more detail in *Chapter 5, For-Profit Subsidiaries and Joint Ventures: Tax Exemption and Other Issues.*

**Document Retention and Destruction.** An effective document retention and destruction policy is an important way to assure that documents considered to be legal records or other documents that pertain to or provide detail regarding the organization's operations are retained for any period required by law, or as useful for the nonprofit's functioning. Typically, document retention policies will include a retention schedule, organized by kind of document and specifying how long documents in specific categories should be retained; depending on the type of document a retention period may be fairly short (e.g., one year) or long (e.g., ten years after a contract termination, or indefinitely for organizational documents and amendments).

An equally important function of such a policy is to establish guidelines for appropriate destructions of documents, when their retention is no longer needed or legally required. Directors should expect that a document retention policy provides guidelines regarding storage of documents in electronic form, including back-up procedures, and permissible destruction periods and protocols. All document retention policies also should specify when and how routine document destruction standards for both paper and e-documents must be suspended, such as on the instruction of legal counsel in the light of actual or anticipated lawsuits or governmental investigations.

**Whistleblower Protection.** A whistleblower policy should specify a simple process (such as an anonymous telephonic or electronic "hotline") for confidentially reporting any potential wrongdoing. Such process gives the organization the opportunity to investigate and, if necessary, correct any problems. An essential part of any whistleblower policy is a prohibition on retaliation against any whistleblower based on the reporting of possible wrongdoing or noncompliance with law, whether the report was made internally or externally, such as to a government agency.

**Chapter, Affiliates, and Branches.** Form 990 asks if nonprofit organizations with extended operations through chapters, affiliates, and branches that are controlled by a parent organization have written policies and procedures governing the activities of those affiliated organizations, to assure that the activities are consistent with the nonprofit organization's exempt purposes.

**Fundraising.** A fundraising policy typically describes applicable federal and state requirements, such as registration requirements and donor acknowledgements, relating to the organization's fundraising activities.

**Investments.** An investment policy will describe the corporation's short-term, mid-term, and long-term financial needs, its tolerance for risk, asset allocation, and application of the Uniform Prudent Management of Institutional Funds Act. Investment policies and related issues for nonprofits are discussed in *Chapter 10, Investments and Expenditure of Endowment Funds.*

**Executive Compensation.** Form 990 asks about the process for determining executive compensation. It is recommended that a process be described in a policy that incorporates the steps required for the application of the safe harbor under the IRS's intermediate sanctions (also known as the "excess benefits") rules. Standards for setting and approving executive compensation are discussed in more detail in *Chapter 4, Taxation.*

**Documenting Governance Decisions.** Form 990 includes questions regarding the nonprofit organization's process for documenting governance decisions. Specifically, it asks if the organization contemporaneously documents the meetings held or written actions taken during the year by the nonprofit's governing board, and each committee that has authority to act on behalf of the governing board. The Form 990 instructions state that "contemporaneous" means the later of (1) the next meeting of the governing body or committee or (2) sixty days after the date of the meeting or written action.

**Governance Documents Availability.** Form 990 asks whether, and if so, how, an organization makes certain documents available to the public. The organization should consider what documents it determines are appropriate for public disclosure and adopt a policy it deems appropriate. Form 990 asks whether the Form 1023, Form 990, and Form 990-T, all of which are required to be made available to the public, are in fact made available—by request, on the organization's website, and/or other organization's website (e.g., GuideStar). Nonprofit practice varies regarding whether these documents are posted on the organization's website; this question should be periodically reviewed by the board or a board committee, such as the time the Form 990 is distributed each year. In addition, board members should be aware that some states require other documents, such as audited financial statements, to be made available to the public.[27]

Form 990 also asks whether and how any of the following documents are made available to the public, although none of these documents are required to be made publicly available: the organization's governing documents (e.g., Articles of Incorporation and Bylaws); conflict of interest policy; and financial statements.

**Form 990 Review.** Form 990 requires information on the board's receipt of the Form 990 in advance of its filing. It also asks about the process for reviewing the Form 990, but does not require the full board to review. The board may delegate responsibilities for an in-depth review to a committee; however, it is important that the Form 990 be distributed to all board members for review prior to filing with the IRS. In addition, directors should be aware that the Form 990 is not only an important regulatory document, but due to its public availability, it is also important for public relations purposes.[28]

Although most of the policies and procedures referenced above are not specifically required by the Code or other laws, most nonprofits will want to assure that they can answer "yes" to any questions regarding the existence of specific policies and procedures as posed in the Form 990, both to avoid unwanted attention from the IRS and to not appear out of step on good governance practices to the public (including potential donors and grant-makers). It is essential that directors be aware that adopting these policies and procedures is not sufficient; it is also very important that the corporation follow them. Accordingly, it is appropriate for the board or a board committee to ask management to report periodically on the effectiveness of such policies. This can be done annually in connection with review of the Form 990, or at other appropriate times for each applicable policy.

The list of governance policies and procedures above is not exhaustive. A nonprofit corporation likely will need other policies to assure its compliance with legal requirements.

# Internet Discussions by Board Members

Some nonprofit boards use e-mail, Internet chat rooms, discussion boards, or other designated Internet-based sites for board members to discuss issues. This may be a very helpful tool for board members to communicate between meetings. Board members should recognize that there can be issues relating to the use of these tools, including security breaches. In addition, to the extent that the subject matter relates to actual or potential litigation matters, the substance of the discussion may be discoverable and the corporation may have duties imposed on it with regard to not destroying such communication. Directors using social media should take care to avoid inadvertently communicating confidential organizational information through this media.

## Satisfying Other Legal Requirements

In discharging the duty of care, a nonprofit director should be mindful of the variety of legal requirements to which the corporation may be subject. For example, organizations that use volunteers should be aware of the variety of legal issues that can arise in connection with volunteers. See *Chapter 8, Employees.* (As noted in *Chapter 11, The Legal Environment of the Nonprofit Corporation,* an awareness of the corporation's particular legal environment and risk areas gives the board the opportunity to ensure that there are appropriate policies and procedures in place to avoid or address legal problems.)

# The Duty of Loyalty

The duty of loyalty requires directors to exercise their powers in good faith and in the best interests of the corporation, rather than in their own interests or the interests of another entity or person.

By assuming office, the director acknowledges that with regard to any corporate activity, the best interests of the corporation must prevail over the director's individual interests or the particular interests of the constituency selecting him or her. The basic legal principle to be observed here is a negative one: *The director shall not use a corporate position for individual personal advantage.* The duty of loyalty primarily relates to:

- conflicts of interest;
- corporate opportunity; and
- confidentiality.

## Conflicts of Interest: General Principles

Directors of nonprofit corporations may have interests that conflict with those of the corporation. The duty of loyalty requires that a director be conscious of the potential for such conflicts and act with candor and care in dealing with such situations.

Conflicts of interest involving a director are not inherently illegal nor are they to be regarded as a reflection on the integrity of the board or of the director. It is the manner in which the director and the board deal with a conflict that determines the propriety of the transaction.  In other words, a conflict is not necessarily bad, it just needs to be managed through a process that provides complete disclosure, is transparent, and helps prevent the organization from being harmed.

### *Conflicts of interest are not unusual*

Since nonprofit corporations generally look to populate their boards with civic, business, and community leaders, it is to be expected that from time to time a director of a nonprofit corporation will encounter situations in which a proposed corporate action will in some way relate to or affect the director's other activities and affiliations. In a situation where a conflict transaction is present, the board should document that it followed an appropriate procedure, consistent with its policies, to assure that the decision made was in the best interest of the nonprofit and not based on any influence from the conflict holder.

### *When is a conflict of interest present?*

A conflict of interest is present whenever a director has a material personal interest in a proposed contract or transaction to which the corporation may be a party. This interest can occur either directly or indirectly. The director may be personally involved with the transaction, have an employment or investment relationship with an entity with which the corporation is dealing, or have a family member who is either personally involved with the transaction or has a relationship with an entity that is involved in the transaction. A conflict of interest may result from a director performing professional services for the organization. For example, a banker, insurance agent, attorney, or real estate broker may benefit from employment by the organization.

*The board should understand that a conflict can still exist even when a director receives no direct monetary or other tangible benefit from a transaction with the corporation.* As discussed below, some personal interests of directors may result in the directors experiencing a conflict between their own interests and those of the corporation. In the nonprofit world, there also are common possible conflicts of interest arising from a director's simultaneous service on the boards of other (for-profit or nonprofit) corporations; it is therefore important that a director disclose such affiliations in general, as well as any specific circumstances in which a conflict between his role as a director for one corporation creates a conflict with respect to his director position with another corporation.

### *Determining whether a personal interest is a conflict of interest*

It is improper for a director to use his or her position to advance a personal interest. At the same time, the very reasons why a particular director is selected may relate to that director's concern for, and knowledge of, the particular business of the corporation. The following examples of personal interests illustrate that these interests may or may not be considered a conflict of interest, based on the circumstances:

- A director of an art museum may have—and probably should have—definite opinions as to the priority, in new purchases, of contemporary American painting versus Old Masters. The director's opinion and preferences present no conflict.
- If the art museum director was generally a collector of contemporary painting and the museum was faced with a particular possible acquisition in that field of art (which acquisition might then increase the recognition or value of pieces in the director's own collection), the director's personal interests might require disclosure.
- A director of a trade association might have been selected because of her familiarity with the impact of Pacific Rim competition on the products of the association's members. Her urging, based on her experience, that the association advocate a particular tariff bill would present no problem even if the director's own company would benefit along with others.
- Still, if that trade association director's own company was one of the relatively small group of manufacturers affected by Pacific imports, but most of the association's members were unaffected, a decision to use association assets and influence to advocate legislation benefiting the director's company on behalf of that minority might present a material conflict.
- A director who sits on a foundation board as well as a community service agency board would need to disclose her association with the service agency and recuse herself from a discussion by the foundation board of a grant to the community service agency.

### Dealing with conflicts: disclosure and approval requirements under nonprofit corporation laws and IRS rules

The law recognizes that conflicts of interest will occur. It deals with conflicts not by treating them as inherently immoral or illegal, but rather by prescribing the methods whereby affected directors should disclose conflicts and how a board of directors should proceed in the face of such situations. Under the Model Act, as well as many state nonprofit corporation laws, a director's conflict will not result in a deemed breach of the director's duty of loyalty, or render void the transaction under which the conflict arose, if the corporation can show that certain requirements were met, such as:

(1)    The transaction was approved by a disinterested majority of the board or in some cases a board committee (or by another disinterested party as specified by the statute), after full disclosure by the affected director of the material facts regarding the transaction and the director's interest therein; and/or

(2)    The transaction was fair to the corporation at the time entered into or when authorized, approved, or ratified by the board of directors.[29]

IRS Form 990 includes specific questions regarding conflict of interest management and related governance policies. It also requires disclosure of interested party transactions as well as director and officer relationships with the corporation and with each other. Form 990 requirements, which are further described in *Chapter 4, Taxation,* effectively require officers and directors to make fairly extensive disclosures to a nonprofit corporation of personal and professional relationships to enable the corporation to comply with new disclosure requirements on independence and interested party transactions. Form 990 requires disclosure of any family relationships or business relationships among the officers, directors, trustees, and key employees (which term includes the organization's officers and other employees who meet certain income and responsibility tests).

In addition, as discussed in the section *"Intermediate Sanctions: Excess Tax on Public Charities' Excess Benefit Transactions"* in *Chapter 4, Taxation,* the IRS has specified certain procedures for approving transactions with a corporation's "insiders" that must be followed to establish a rebuttable presumption of reasonableness under the IRS's excess benefits/intermediate sanctions rules. Failure to follow these procedures can result in liability for an insider who was found to be the beneficiary of an excess benefit transaction, as well as for organization leaders who approved the transaction.

**When is it appropriate to approve a transaction in which a director is interested?** Provided there has been appropriate disclosure and evaluation of transactions involving a conflict of interest, there are many situations in which such a transaction not only *can* but also, in the best interests of the corporation, probably *should* be approved. For instance, a board may legitimately choose to deal with a company affiliated with a director or other insider because of greater familiarity with the supplier's reliability or the supplier's favorable pricing. In some cases, a company's affiliation with a director may result in the corporation receiving better service or prices than can be obtained from other commercial sources. Nonetheless, the corporate records must still show that the affiliation was appropriately disclosed, and that the board made its decision to do business with the director's affiliated company based on the fairness of the transaction and the best interests of the corporation.

In addition, the board should be aware that all interested party transactions have to be disclosed in the Form 990, Schedule L. Finally, regardless of how beneficial the transaction is to the organization, it is important to recognize that third parties, including the press, may view the transaction as improper given the existence of a conflict. Therefore, thorough documentation of fair value and a robust process for disclosure and management of conflicts have become an important aspect of board decision-making.

**Conflicts of interest policies and disclosure statements.** In light of state and other laws that relate to how a board should handle the identification and evaluation of conflicts of interest involving directors and other insiders, it is good corporate practice for nonprofit corporations to adopt and adhere to a written conflict of interest policy. For instance, as noted in *Chapter 4, Taxation,* the IRS strongly encourages a nonprofit to have a conflict of interest policy. The IRS form also requests that directors and other persons having potential influence over the corporation fill out annual statements disclosing all of their significant affiliations, as well as contacts with entities doing business with the corporation. In other contexts, the presence of and adherence to a conflict of interest policy can serve as evidence that it was the corporation's regular practice to seek to identify and resolve potential conflicts. For instance, adherence to a conflict of interest policy could make the difference in a court determining whether the Business Judgment Rule defense was available to a corporate decision involving an insider, since the Business Judgment Rule only applies to decisions made by directors who made reasonable efforts to obtain all material information.

**Making a record of conflict disclosures and related party transactions.** Whenever a conflict of interest situation arises, the corporate minutes or other records should document the nature of the disclosure given regarding the conflict, as well as the board's proceedings to evaluate the relevant transaction in light of the conflict. In addition, related party transactions (such as purchase of property from an officer or director) may have to be disclosed in the notes to the corporation's audited financial statements, and in its annual tax filing (such as Form 990) to the IRS.

**Duty of disclosure.** The corporation should have a formal policy that requires its board members to annually disclose relationships that may present a conflict of interest or that take them out of the category of "independent" directors. The directors also should be required to update annual disclosures as changes occur during the year. Equally important is having a process whereby the board reviews and evaluates these disclosures so that board members are aware of relationships that may affect action taken by the board. Whenever a conflict of interest policy exists that includes a formal recurring disclosure process, it is now to be described on Form 990. Nonprofits also are required to disclose whether the board closely monitors these disclosures (*see Chapter 4, Taxation*). This process is also of growing importance under state law, and nonprofit corporations are subject to increasing scrutiny regarding their attention to potential conflicts.[30]

As noted above, many state nonprofit corporation statutes uphold the validity of a transaction authorized even when a director had an undisclosed interest, as long as the transaction was "fair" to the corporation. (Note, however, that in some states, such as California, fairness is only one of several factors—including disclosure—that must be satisfied in conflict situations.) Nonetheless, directors should be aware that *lack of disclosure of a conflict exposes both the affected director and the rest of the board, to greater risk.* In the event of litigation, the nondisclosing director, and, in some instances, even the disinterested directors who supported the transaction will have the burden of proving after the fact that the transaction was fair. Disclosure also enables the other members of the board to evaluate the proposed transaction not merely in terms of fairness, but also for its impact on the public image of the corporation.[31] Even if a matter involving a conflict does not result in litigation, in some cases, if the conflict is disclosed publicly, it may be a source of embarrassment due to the appearance of impropriety.

**Content of disclosure and participation in board discussions by interested director.** Generally, the disclosure of a conflict of interest should include the existence of the interest and its nature (e.g., those arising from financial or family relationships, or professional or business affiliations, etc.) and should be made in advance, before any action is taken by the board concerning the matter. It is generally prudent—and may be required by state law or the corporation's conflicts policy—that the interested director be absent from that part of the meeting when the matter is being discussed except when the director's information may be needed. A director having a conflict should make sure that his or her absence from discussion and abstention from a vote relating to it is duly noted in the meeting minutes.

In some cases, a director may have an interest in a transaction but be unable, because of duties running to others, to disclose the nature of the interest. In such a case, the director should at least state that such an interest exists, consider leaving the meeting, or at least abstain from the discussion and not vote on the matter. When the conflicting interest presents so difficult a problem that even the above measures are impossible, the director should consider resigning.

**Quorum and voting requirements.** State law and other applicable laws (as well as the corporation's bylaws or conflict of interest policy) may specify whether an interested director can be counted in determining whether a quorum exists at a meeting at which the board considers the conflict of interest transaction. Legal standards and corporate procedures may also address whether an interested director may vote on the transaction in which he or she has an interest. Generally, a director, even if interested, may be counted for the purpose of determining the presence of a quorum. Still, this director may not be permitted to vote, or the director's vote may not be allowed to be counted in determining whether there were sufficient votes to approve the transaction.

In some states, a transaction may not be approved by the board if too many directors have a conflict. For instance, some state nonprofit corporation laws do not recognize board approval as providing liability protection if there is only one noninterested director voting on the matter.[32] In this situation, the corporation needs to consider other alternatives, such as obtaining an outside opinion that the transaction is fair to the corporation. Given the uniqueness of how state law applies in such a situation, it is advisable to consult with counsel on the matter.

In addition, the use of a written consent to approve board action can present a problem when there is a conflict of interest transaction, given that states generally require unanimous consent of the directors.  In some states, however, the written consent does not require the signature of the interested director.[33]

**Action by board after discovering an undisclosed conflict.**  A board of directors that discovers that it has acted on a proposal in ignorance of an undisclosed interest should promptly reexamine the issue, with an appropriate record of such scrutiny.

## Corporate Opportunity

In certain circumstances, a director is obliged to treat a business opportunity as a "corporate opportunity" that must first be offered to the corporation before the director can take advantage of it outside of his role as a corporate director. The duty to treat a potential transaction as a corporate opportunity arises when a director, because of his or her position with the organization, learns of a prospective transaction or business opportunity that would be attractive to the director or the director's business apart from his role as a director, but that is also a transaction that would plausibly fall within the corporation's present or future activities. The requirement of a director's good faith, as well as other requirements such as those in the Model Act, generally requires that the director affirmatively present the opportunity to the board before participating in the transaction outside the corporation.[34]

Although legal requirements as to these transactions vary from state to state, directors should, for their self-protection, and as a matter of good corporate practice, make a clear record of this disclosure and request that the board's abstention (if any) from exercise of the opportunity be explicit and of record. Further, even if entering into such a transaction would not breach the director's duty of loyalty, the applicable director should consider any appearance of impropriety that could be created.

## Confidentiality

A director should not, in the regular course of business, disclose information about the corporation's legitimate activities unless they are already known by the public or are of public record.

In the normal course of business, a director should treat as confidential all matters involving the corporation until there has been general public disclosure or unless the information is a matter of public record or common knowledge. The individual director is not a spokesperson for the corporation and, thus, disclosure to the public (including the press) of corporate activities should be made only through the corporation's designated spokesperson, usually the chief executive or the board chair or, in large organizations, a public relations officer. The presumption of confidential treatment should apply to all current information about legitimate board or corporate activities.[35]

# Directors' Rights

As a corollary to all the previously described director duties, the director has rights appropriate to the discharge of such duties.

## Management Access

Within the bounds of reason, board members should feel free to contact the chief executive, the board secretary, or similar staff person, to obtain information needed to fulfill the director's duties. Board members should be more restrained in contacting other members of management and should be cognizant of management's role, of not interfering with it, and of not undercutting the chief executive or other officers. Requests for such access to information or management staff are most effective (for both management and the board) if requested through the board chair, at board meetings, or pursuant to committee work or other delegations of authority from the board. If directors also serve as volunteers or receive services from the organization, they should be especially careful when in those other roles to not make demands or requests of staff that would be inappropriate for other volunteers or clients of the organization. All board members should benefit from equal access to management staff and the information management can provide.

## Books and Records

A director has a right to inspect the corporation's books and records and to be provided with requested data derived from them. A board member may reasonably require that her or his accountant or attorney have access to such data. Any such request should be handled in a manner that does not unduly disrupt normal business operations.

## Notice of Meetings

All directors should be given ample advance notice of all board and committee meetings that they are expected to attend.

## Right to Dissent and to Have Dissent Recorded

There are two circumstances in which a director may register dissent regarding actions to be taken at a board meeting. First, any director may dissent from the holding of a board meeting for which the proper notice has not been given or other procedural requirements have not been satisfied. In this circumstance, the board member should state either upon arriving or prior to voting on a specific matter that he or she objects to the transaction of some or all business at the meeting, because of noncompliance with notice or other applicable procedures. If the director does not object, the director's presence at the meeting is deemed to be a waiver of any improper notice or other procedural requirement.[36]

Second, a director has the right not only to vote against any matter put forth for vote at a board meeting, but also to have the minutes of the meeting record that he or she dissented from the action approved by other members of the board.[37] This right is important in the event that the action is ever challenged. A director who voted against an action later found to be improper will not generally be subject to liability relating to this action, assuming no separate violation of fiduciary duty on the director's part (such as failure to disclose material information relating to the proposed matter to the other members of the board). However, the dissenting director needs to be able to prove, through the voting detail recorded in the meeting minutes, that he or she did, in fact, dissent.

## Minutes

All directors should be provided a copy of minutes of all meetings of the full board and any committee exercising board powers as soon as possible after each meeting. Except for the minutes of the executive committee, which generally acts in place of the whole board, and for the minutes of committees of which he or she is a member, a director usually will be satisfied with a review of only the summarized reports of committees that are submitted to the whole board. A review of other minutes, however, can be a useful way of keeping informed, and a director has a right to receive them on request. As noted above, a director should carefully review minutes as they become available to confirm their accuracy. The minutes are important for recording board action. In addition, the minutes become an important document if there is ever a question raised as to whether the directors carried out their fiduciary duties.

# When a Special Duty Applies: The Director with Knowledge of Illegal Activities

A director may not ignore what he or she believes or suspects to be illegal activity. When a director believes that an activity being engaged in by or on behalf of the corporation (whether or not clearly approved by the board of directors) may be illegal, he or she should proceed as follows:

First, contact the chief executive or board chair. If the subject activity is ongoing, or is about to take place, the board member should bring the issue to the attention of the chief executive or board chair with a demand for action or investigation; if the board chair fails to respond, the issue should go to the full board.

Second, dissent and consult with personal counsel. If, after a board discussion, an activity that appears to a director to be illegal is not repudiated, or if the activity is a past event that the director was previously unaware of, the director's dissent should be clearly recorded in the minutes. In addition, the director may wish to consult his or her own counsel to determine if further disclosure outside the corporation is required, or if she or he should resign.

## Ethics and Business Conduct Codes

Current views of good governance practice recommend that in addition to a conflict of interest policy, a nonprofit corporation have an ethics and business conduct code. Such a code should be applicable to directors, senior management, agents, and employees and should require a commitment to operating the entity in the best interests of the organization and in compliance with applicable law, ethical business standards, and the organization's governing documents. There is no standard form for such a code. Depending on the nature of the nonprofit, it may look to the type of code adopted by its for-profit counterparts in preparing its own code.[38]

# The Duty of Obedience

Courts occasionally have determined that there is a third fiduciary duty—the duty of obedience—imposed on directors of nonprofit corporations. This "duty" carves out the requirement that directors take action in a manner consistent with the purpose of the organization, as set forth in the corporation's organizational documents, such as the articles of incorporation. The duty of obedience also has been interpreted to require directors to comply with applicable state and federal laws that relate to the organization and the manner in which it conducts its business. Such duty is more frequently viewed as being encompassed under the duty of care and the duty of loyalty.

# When Is a Director of a Nonprofit Corporation Considered to Be a "Trustee" with Duties Beyond Those Normally Attributed to Directors?

Even if the governing members of a nonprofit corporation are referred to as a board of trustees, they are not subject to a different or higher standard of care compared to nonprofit boards of directors. The use of the word *trustee* to refer to a member of a nonprofit corporation's governing board does not in and of itself change the duties of the members of the board, which are the same as those described above for directors. Still, as noted below, in certain circumstances, a member of a nonprofit board (whether called a director, trustee, or other term) may legally be required to comply with the higher standards of a trustee.

## When a Director May Be Considered a Trustee

Persons who are considered trustees of a trust are subject to stringent standards of conduct. For instance, whereas most state nonprofit corporation laws treat director conflicts of interest as an issue to be dealt with by following certain guidelines and disclosures, the law of trusts generally regards a trustee's self-dealing as inherently voidable, regardless of motives or objective fairness. Furthermore, the trustee's power to delegate may be narrowly limited, much more so than a corporate director. Although the law does not consider a director of a nonprofit corporation to be a trustee in most situations, in some circumstances directors may be held to the generally higher trustee standards, such as in the following situations:

- An employer corporation maintains employee benefit plans, thereby triggering, in certain circumstances under both state and federal law, obligations analogous to those of a trustee with respect to such plans.
- A public benefit or religious corporation seeks to change its purpose or function, but public or community representatives challenge this action on the basis that the assets of these corporations are generally deemed to be held in trust for the purposes set forth in the corporation's governing documents, and that the proposed change is inconsistent with these purposes. In some states, the directors may not be permitted to effect the change in corporate purpose or use of corporate assets until approved by the attorney general, or by a court in a *cy pres* proceeding.

## When a Director or Trustee Is Not a Trustee under the Law

Some nonprofit corporations, particularly in the public benefit field, may call their directors *trustees* without intending to confer any special powers or impose any special duties in doing so. Directors of public benefit and religious corporations (this issue rarely arises for mutual benefit corporations) should make sure they understand under what circumstances they could legally be considered to be trustees. For example, funds held by a corporation in acknowledged trusts must be identified and treated separately on the corporation's balance sheets, and the board must see to it that an appropriate officer (and counsel and the corporation's accountant) is acquainted with the terms of the relevant trust instrument. In any other circumstance in which a board is faced with an assertion that it should be held to a trusteeship standard with respect to a certain matter, the matter should be discussed with the corporation's counsel, in order to give the board clarification of its role under the specific circumstances.

## The Impact of the Sarbanes-Oxley Act

In an attempt to prevent further erosion in investor confidence in the markets after the Enron and WorldCom scandals, Congress enacted the Sarbanes-Oxley Act of 2002. Only two provisions of Sarbanes-Oxley directly apply to nonprofit organizations. They relate to the penalties for obstruction of justice, including document destruction, and a prohibition on retaliation against whistleblowers.[39] Nevertheless, the concerns giving rise to Sarbanes-Oxley have some application in the nonprofit sector. This has resulted in recommendations relating to various "best practices" for nonprofit organizations. These recommendations are very similar to the recommendations set forth in this chapter and include the need for an independent board, certain committees (such as compensation committees, governance committees, and audit committees) and the need to have compliance programs and policies addressing such matters as whistleblower protection, document retention and destruction, conflicts of interest, and ethics.[40]

## Panel on the Nonprofit Sector

The Independent Sector established the Panel on the Nonprofit Sector to address various proposals that were being considered by the Senate Finance Committee. The Panel has issued several reports that contain recommendations for improving government oversight, including new rules to prevent unscrupulous individuals from abusing charitable organizations for personal gain. The Pension Protection Act of 2006 enacted many of these recommendations into law. The Panel also has focused on recommendations relating to self-regulation. In 2007, the Panel issued the *Principles for Good Governance in Ethical Practice: A Guide for Charities and Foundations*. The document sets forth thirty-three principles of sound practice that the Panel recommended should be considered by every charitable organization as a guide in determining how to strengthen its effectiveness and accountability. The thirty-three principles are organized under four main categories: (1) legal compliance in public disclosure; (2) effective governance; (3) strong financial oversight; and (4) responsible fundraising.[41]

*See the Suggested Questions and Checklist following the Endnotes below to review the issues discussed in this chapter.*

## Endnotes

1. *See generally*, Comment to Model Act § 8.30.
2. *See, e.g.*, People ex rel. Spitzer v. Grasso, 893 N.E.2d 105 (N.Y. 2008); California Nonprofit Integrity Act, CAL. GOV'T CODE §§ 12585, et al.
3. In determining the degree of care that a director should exhibit, the law generally sets forth an ideal, such as the care of "an ordinarily prudent person in a like position under similar circumstances" or the care that a person in a like position under similar circumstances reasonably believes is appropriate. *See* Model Act, § 8.30(b). In describing a director's standard of care, the Model Act eliminated the reference to an "ordinarily prudent person," a phrase that has a

special meaning under tort law, but may have a different meaning in the context of a director's duty of care.

The Model Act comment to § 8.30 states "[T]he combined phrase 'in a like position—under similar circumstances' is intended to recognize that (a) the nature and extent of responsibilities will vary, depending upon such factors as the size, complexity, urgency, and location of activities carried on by the particular nonprofit corporation, (b) decisions must be made on the basis of information known to the directors without the benefit of hindsight, and (c) the special background, qualifications, and management responsibilities of a particular director may be relevant in evaluating that director's compliance with the standard of care. Still, even though the combined phrase is intended to take into account the special background, qualifications, and management responsibilities of a particular director, it does not excuse a director lacking business experience or particular expertise from exercising the basic director attributes of common sense, practical wisdom, and informed judgment."

4.    *See, e.g.,* 18B Am. Jur. 2d Corporations § 1285; In re Acadia Dairies, Inc., 135 A. 846 (Del. Ch. 1927). Nonetheless, in at least one state, a nonprofit's articles or bylaws may allow a nonprofit corporation director to advance written consents or opposition to an action to be considered at a board meeting. *See* N.D. CENT. CODE § 10-33-40.

5.    Under the Model Act, the board of directors may remove a director who has missed the number of board meetings specified in the articles of incorporation or bylaws, if the articles or bylaws at the beginning of the director's current term provided that a director may be removed for missing the specified number of board meetings. § 8.08(c)(4).

6.    *See* CAL. CORP. CODE. § 5227 (no more than 49 percent of the board can be "interested persons" (i.e., any person compensated by the corporation within the past twelve months and any member of such person's family)). (Requirement does not apply to mutual benefit or religious corporations).

7.    *See* ABA Coordinating Committee on Nonprofit Governance, *Guide to Nonprofit Corporate Governance in the Wake of Sarbanes-Oxley* 26-28 (American Bar Association 2005).

8.    *See Guide to Nonprofit Corporate Governance in the Wake of Sarbanes-Oxley, supra note 7,* at 23-28.

9.    *See* Lawrence M. Braver and Charles F. Kaiser, *Tax-Exempt Health Care Organizations Community Board and Conflict of Interest Policy,* 1997 EO CPE Text (available at www.irs.gov/pub/irs-tege/eotopic00.pdf).

10.   *See* Model Act § 8.30(c).

11.   Comment 5 to the Model Act § 8.30 states, reliance on "a report, statement, opinion, or other information is permitted only if the

director has read the information, opinion, report, or statement in question, or was present at a meeting at which it was orally presented, or took other steps to become generally familiar with it."

12.  *See* Model Act § 8.30(f).

13.  *See* Model Act § 8.30(e).

14.  *See* Comment to Model Act § 8.01, Comment (stating that directors, although considered to "manage" the corporation, may delegate management authority to officers).

15.  In In Re Caremark International Inc. Derivative Litigation, 698 A.2d 959 (Del. Ch. 1996), the Delaware Chancery noted that a board's failure to assure that there was an adequate information and reporting system to provide senior management and the board with timely and accurate information regarding legal compliance might, in some circumstances, be viewed as a violation of a director's duty of care. *See also* Stone v. Ritter, 911 A.2d 362, 365 (Del. 2006).

16.  *See* Model Act § 8.12 (permitting resting of powers in a designated body); COLO. REV. STAT. § 7-128-101; GA. CODE ANN. § 14-3-801.

17.  *See* Model Act § 8.21; Iowa Code section 504.822.

18.  *See, e.g.,* GA. CODE ANN. § 14-3-821 (written consent by less than unanimous consent permissible if articles of incorporation or bylaws expressly permit such action); WIS. STAT. § 181.0821 (written consent by less than two-thirds of the directors then in office, if the articles or bylaws so provide, and if all directors receive notice of the text of the consent and its effective date and time); MINN. STAT. § 317A.239 (written consent by less than unanimous consent permissible if articles of incorporation expressly permit such action).

19.  *See, e.g.,* COLO. REV. STAT. § 7-128-202 (unless bylaws provide otherwise, consent may be transmitted or received by facsimile, e-mail, or other form of wire or wireless communication that provides the nonprofit with a complete copy of the document, including a copy of the director's signature).

20.  Directors also may have protection under state immunity statutes. *See Chapter 11, Director Liability: Risks and Protections.*

21.  *See* Oberly v. Kirby, 592 A.2d 445, 462 (Del. 1991) ("A court cannot second-guess the wisdom of facially valid decisions made by charitable fiduciaries, any more than it can question the business judgment of the directors of a for-profit corporation."). Although cases explicitly mentioning the Business Judgment Rule in a nonprofit context are few, the standards used by the courts in nonprofit cases are often clearly derived from the business context. *See, e.g.,* Beard v. Achenbach Mem. Hosp. Ass'n., 170 F.2d 859 (10th Cir. 1948).

22.  *See, e.g.,* Model Act §§ 8.30 and 8.31; IOWA CODE §§ 504.831 and 504.832. The Business Judgment Rule, as applied to business corporations, is discussed in detail in Stephen A. Radin, *The Business*

*Judgment Rule* (Aspen Law & Business, 6th ed., 2009). *See also* discussion in Jack B. Siegel, *A Desktop Guide for Nonprofit Directors, Officers, and Advisors,* 85 (John Wiley & Sons, Inc. 2006).

23.  *See* Lisa A. Runquist, *The Night the Sky Fell: Directors of Nonprofits Continue at Risk,* 15 Bus. L. News 15 (Spring 1994) (available at runquist.com), discussing the California Supreme Court's decision in *Francis T. v. Village Green Owners Association,* [42] Cal. 3d 490 (1986), holding that the Business Judgment Rule protection provided for under the California Corporations Code is not a bar to individual director liability for action taken as a board member, if the action created an unreasonable risk of personal injury to third parties. The case was brought by the owner of a condominium who was assaulted and robbed by an intruder, after the condominium board ordered the owner to stop using exterior lights she had installed outside her unit following numerous burglaries in the complex.

24.  *See* In re Walt Disney Derivative Litig., 906 A.2d 27 (Del. 2006).

25.  *See* Stern v. Lucy Webb Hayes Nat'l Training Sch. for Deaconesses & Missionaries, 381 F. Supp. 1003, 1012-1014 (D.D.C. 1974).

26.  *See* Manhattan Eye, Ear & Throat Hosp. v. Spitzer, 715 N.Y.S.2d 575 (N.Y. Sup. Ct. 1999); *see also* Deanna Bellandi, *The Watchdogs Are Biting: State Attorney General Asserting Authority over Not-For-Profit Hospital,* Modern Healthcare at 22 (January 29, 2001); and *Lawsuit Seeking to Preserve Acute Care Set for Trial on AG's Charitable Trust Claims,* BNA's Health Care Daily Report. (March 2, 2001); both discussing a Florida attorney general lawsuit against Intracostal Health Systems, a two-hospital nonprofit health system that had proposed to move all acute-care services out of a money-losing hospital and shift such services to its "sister" hospital three miles away.

27.  *See* California Nonprofit Integrity Act, Cal. Gov't Code §§ 12585, et al., which requires audited financial statements of certain charitable organizations with certain levels or assets or gross revenues to be made available for inspection by the public and the State Attorney General in the same manner as Form 990.

28.  *See* IRS, *Governance and Related Topics - 501(c)(3) Organizations,* http://www.irs.gov/pub/irs-tege/governance_practices.pdf; Lisa A. Runquist and Michael E. Malamut, *The IRS's New Regulation of Nonprofit Governance,* 18 ABA Bus. L. Today 29 (July/August 2009).

29.  *See* Model Act § 8.60. Under the laws of many states, a conflict of interest transaction need only be fair to the corporation at the time it was authorized or approved to avoid treatment of the transaction as void or a potential breach of the duty of loyalty by the conflicted director. *See, e.g.,* Ohio Rev. Code Ann., § 1702.301; Ky. Rev. Stat. Ann. § 273.219. Some state nonprofit laws, however, are more

stringent, with fairness to the corporation being only one of several elements necessary to avoid characterization of a conflict of interest transaction as void and one that may subject the interested director to liability. *See, e.g.,* CAL. CORP. CODE, § 5233(d)(2). In addition, under California law, if the director is interested, the transaction must be approved by the entire board and not just a committee of the board prior to the transaction being consummated.

30.  For example, the Massachusetts Attorney General recently criticized Suffolk University's failure to methodically review annual board disclosures. Letter from Commonwealth of Massachusetts, Office of the Attorney General to Members of the Board of Trustees, Suffolk University (July 9, 2009), www.mass.gov/ago/docs/nonprofit/suffolk-university-070909.pdf.

31.  *See* Linda Grant, *Acts of Charity: Furious Donors Blame a Lax Board after a Fund's Scandal Toppeled the Lavish-Living Hand of the United Way,* LOS ANGELES TIMES MAGAZINE 39 (September 13, 1992).

32.  *See* IOWA CODE § 504.833(4). The Model Act does not contain such a limitation. *See* Model Act § 8.60.

33.  *See, e.g.,* CAL. CORP. CODE § 7211.

34.  *See* Model Act § 8.70; Valle v. N. Jersey Auto. Club, 359 A.2d 504 (N.J. Super. Ct. App. Div. 1976).

35.  Some public benefit corporations face demands for open meetings of their boards; in some cases, mixed public-private activities may impose that duty. Such practices are infrequently required as a matter of law; however, if open meetings are adopted as a practice, specific rules as to confidentiality, whether or not legally mandated, should be developed.
     A somewhat different issue is raised by the many statutes governing condominiums, which require that all board meetings (with narrowly defined exceptions) be open to owners. *See, e.g.*, 765 ILL. COMP. STAT. 605/18.5(4). In such cases, of course, the board meets in the presence of those to whom it is accountable.

36.  *See* Model Act § 8.23.

37.  Otherwise, a director who is present at a board meeting at which action is taken may be presumed to have assented to the action. *See, e.g.,* Ill. General Not For Profit Corporation Act of 1986, 805 ILL. COMP. STAT. 105/108.65(b).

38.  *See Guide to Nonprofit Corporate Governance in the Wake of Sarbanes-Oxley, supra* note 7, at 41-42.

39.  *See* 18 U.S.C. §§ 1514A and 1519.

40.  *See Guide to Nonprofit Corporate Governance in the Wake of Sarbanes-Oxley, supra* 7, at 17-18.

41.  Panel on the Nonprofit Sector, *Principles for Good Governance and Ethical Practice: A Guide for Charities and Foundations* (October 2007).

# Suggested Questions for Directors Regarding Director Duties and Rights

(1)  How often does our board meet? Is this according to a regular schedule?

(2)  How frequently do I attend regular board meetings?

(3)  What information is given to me in advance of each board meeting? Is it relevant to decisions to be reached at the meeting?

(4)  Does the corporation make board materials available via a secure board governance website?

(5)  Am I satisfied with the information I have received? As to quantity? As to subject? As to timeliness? As to reliability? Is it too little? Is it more than I can really analyze between my receipt of it and the board meeting?

(6)  Is there any information submitted to me that I feel is incomplete or untrustworthy? How do I deal with this problem?

(7)  Who manages, in the day-to-day sense, the business of the corporation?

(8)  Do I have an interest—personal or business—that conflicts with the interests of the corporation?

(9)  Has a situation arisen under which I should disclose that interest?

(10)  Do I know of a conflict involving another director? Did the director disclose that problem?

(11)  Does our corporation have a policy on conflict disclosure? Is it in writing? Do we annually sign a disclosure statement relating to this subject?

(12)  Does the corporation have other policies and procedures that the Form 990 asks about?

(13)  What contact do I have with the chief executive of the corporation? Is it primarily at board meetings or do I have a close personal relationship that may affect my objectivity?

(14)  What contact do I have with subordinate staff members? Am I interfering in operations?

(15)  What notice is given as to board meetings? How and when is such notice given?

(16)  When do I receive the agenda and materials for board meetings? Do I have time to examine and consider them before voting on them? Do I, in fact, read them?

(17)  When do I receive minutes of prior board meetings? Do I read them? Do I communicate any corrections needed?  Do I see minutes or reports of committee meetings? When?

(18)   Do I know of illegitimate or illegal acts of the corporation or its officers? What should I do if I know of or suspect such acts have occurred or are occurring?

(19)   Was I chosen to serve on the board as a representative or delegate of a particular constituency? What am I expected to do for that constituency?

# Checklist: Duties and Rights of Nonprofit Corporation Directors

*Note:*   For simplicity, these and other chapter checklists describe a corporation having a chair, who presides over the board of directors; a chief executive, who may be a staff person; an executive committee; a governance/nominating committee; and an audit committee. (We recognize, however, that in many smaller and other nonprofits, these committee functions may be performed by either the executive committee or the board as a whole.) We also assume a legal counsel—someone, paid or unpaid, having primary responsibility for the corporation's legal affairs. Many corporations, especially larger nonprofits, may have other committees established for specific purposes, such as establishing executive compensation; monitoring compliance with legal requirements; and overseeing investments and other financial matters.

| Subject | Review By | How Often | Comment |
|---|---|---|---|
| **The Board's Record of Service** | | | |
| 1. What is the record of each director's attendance at board meetings? | Chair, chief executive, governance/ nominating committee | Before submission of nominations for election; from time to time during year | Regular attendance serves to maintain an active board of high morale. |

| Subject | Review By | How Often | Comment |
|---|---|---|---|
| 2. What members of the board have missed half the meetings during last twelve months? | Chair, chief executive and governance/ nominating committee | Before submission of nominations for election; from time to time during year | If the number is large, see below. |
| 3. Does the corporation have, or should the board consider a provision in the bylaws or a written board policy for removal of a director who fails (without adequate excuse) to reach a minimum record of attendance? | Chair, chief executive and governance/ nominating committee | Whenever there is review of bylaws | Sometimes the simple proposal of such a bylaw or bylaw provision will trigger appropriate resignations. Even if actual removals are accomplished by requested resignations, a bylaw provision or a director's signed acknowledgement of attendance and other expectations may be desirable, and in some states, required if a director is to be removed for attendance reasons. |
| 4. How many board meetings took place in the last twelve months? Were all the meetings called for in the bylaws actually held? | Chair and chief executive | At least annually | The optimum number of board meetings is to be determined by needs, but a quarterly meeting schedule is often appropriate for an operating organization. |

| Subject | Review By | How Often | Comment |
|---|---|---|---|
| 5. Is there any feeling on the part of the members of the board that this number of meetings is inadequate for effective oversight of the corporation's business? | Chair and board | Annually | This question is closely related to the committee structure of the corporation. |
| 6. Should the number of meetings be reduced? | Chair and board | Annually | It is good practice to periodically evaluate if the board's meeting schedule, agenda structure, length, and location are most conducive for effective board deliberations. |
| 7. Would more adequate oversight be obtained by delegating more duties to committees? | Chair and board | Annually | *See Chapter 3, Committees and Advisory Bodies.* |
| 8. How many directors have contributed funds to the corporation? Have all done so? What is the average? | Chief executive and governance/ nominating committee | Annually, and before any reelection or renomination of directors | It is recommended that a charitable nonprofit corporation be explicit with board members and board candidates regarding any expectations for director philanthropy supporting the corporation. |

| Subject | Review By | How Often | Comment |
|---------|-----------|-----------|---------|
| 9. What has been the attendance record of the members of the corporation's committees? | Chief executive and governance/nominating committee | Annually, if committees are elected or appointed on a schedule, before such election or appointment | Attendance records at committee meetings should be part of director's record reviewed for any reelection decision. |
| **The Board's Procedures** | | | |
| 1. What material is distributed *in advance* of board meetings? | Chair and chief executive | As a general matter, periodically by chair; as to particular meetings, chief executive | Materials should include at minimum the certain standard items, such as financial statements, prior board and committee minutes, and summary data on company operations. |
| Does it include: | | | |
| a. Minutes of the last meeting and committee meetings? | Full board | All regular meetings | Always |
| b. Current financial statements? | Full board and audit committee | All regular meetings | Always |

| Subject | Review By | How Often | Comment |
|---|---|---|---|
| c. Current reports of committees? | Full board | At each meeting of board | Committees should report in writing, as well as orally, The committee's prior meeting minutes may suffice as the written portion of the report. |
| d. Summaries of board actions or decisions that will be requested? | Full board | Before each meeting | All directors should be urged to consider identified board actions prior to the meeting. In addition to this summary, relevant documents should be provided for the directors' advance review to the extent practicable. |
| e. Copies of resolutions proposed for adoption? | Full board | Before each meeting | Having resolutions distributed in advance enables the board to focus on the precise matters to be considered by the board and results in increased efficiency. |

| Subject | Review By | How Often | Comment |
|---|---|---|---|
| **The Corporation's Policies on Conflicts** | | | |
| 1. Do we have a conflicts policy that requires all directors and officers to execute an annual disclosure? | Full board | Annually | IRS Form 990 and governance authorities indicate an expectation that directors and officers are subject to conflicts disclosure requirements. |
| a. Has the corporation's conflict of interest policy been recently reviewed for substantive content and compliance with current governance standards? | Legal counsel and audit committee; then full board | Annually | Periodic review by the full board is recommended. |
| b. Were board disclosure statements in fact provided to all directors? | Audit committee | Annually and at point at which each new director joins board | Disclosure statements should be made every year. |
| c. How does the corporation deal with conflicts that arise between the execution dates of a regular conflicts disclosure? | Chief executive reporting to board | As often as conflicts arise; review of totality annually | Full and prompt reporting is essential when the conflict applies to a specific matter before the board or a board committee, or may create an appearance of impropriety. |

| Subject | Review By | How Often | Comment |
|---|---|---|---|
| 2. Was there a meeting at which a director disclosed a conflict of interest regarding a decision? | Legal counsel and audit committee | The disclosure should precede or be simultaneous with the decision | Corporate minutes should record the disclosure and how the conflict was handled. |
| a. Was there a vote on the issue to which the director had a conflict? | Legal counsel and audit committee | As often as this disclosure occurs | Corporate minutes should record whether the subject director voted or recused himself from voting or discussion. |
| b. If so, was there a quorum (as defined by the statute of incorporation) for this vote? | Legal counsel and audit committee | At meeting in question | State statutes vary as to whether a recused director is counted for purposes of quorum and voting. |
| c. Was there a vote of an adequate number of disinterested directors with the requisite quorum? | Chair, legal counsel | At meeting in question | The conflicted director should not vote on the subject transaction or decision. |

# Chapter 3:
## Committees, Advisory Bodies, and Officers

# Chapter 3
# Committees, Advisory Bodies, and Officers

*The directors of a nonprofit corporation will frequently discharge their duties through committees composed, wholly or in part, by members of the board. The directors should understand what functions can be delegated to committees, what responsibilities the board has concerning committee activities, and the degree to which directors can rely on information provided by committees. The directors should understand the difference between committees of directors and certain kinds of advisory or auxiliary boards or other bodies composed of nondirectors. In addition, officers serve an important role in carrying out the directions of the board of directors. As a result, it is also important to understand the role of officers.*

## Board Committees: Introduction

Committees are usually necessary for the efficient discharge of the board's work.[1] Indeed, many boards would find it impossible to discharge their responsibilities without the use of committees. A director should understand the different types of committees available to the corporation, and the extent to which the board may delegate authority to committees to act on behalf of the board. For example, in some states, only board members may serve on a committee that has board-delegated powers. The purpose, powers, and limitations of any committee should be clearly stated in the corporation's bylaws or by resolution recorded in the minutes of the board. These documents should define the membership, term of office, and method of appointment.

# Advisory and Auxiliary Bodies: Introduction

In contrast to board committees, advisory or auxiliary boards, councils, or other bodies will often include nondirectors (they may also include former directors) and largely work independently of the board. These boards may provide additional support to the corporation's mission and provide useful insight to the corporation's board. Directors should be aware, however, that such advisory boards and auxiliary groups may be regarded by the public as agents of the corporation. Board members should make sure there are effective procedures both for exercising oversight for advisory and auxiliary boards and for directing these boards to report back periodically to the corporation's board concerning their activities and recommendations.

# The Types of Board Committees

For analysis in this *Guidebook,* we divide board committees into two categories:

## Special Committees

These committees are temporary or *ad hoc* groups established for a limited purpose. Most special committees will be created by board resolution as the need arises, and are often limited in their duration.

## Standing or Permanent Committees

These committees are permanent, and may be described or provided for in the corporation's bylaws or board resolutions. Standing committees may make recommendations, oversee operations, and study specific areas of activity. Depending on the bylaws or resolutions creating them, they may have power to bind the corporation. This power may be extensive (as in the case of executive committees) or fairly limited.

A common standing committee is the executive committee, which generally has extensive power to act on behalf of the corporation between board meetings. Other common standing committees include: a governance/nominating committee; finance committee; audit committee; compensation committee; compliance committee; investment committee; personnel/human resources committee; planning committee; public relations committee; programming committee; and capital campaigns and grants committee. Although the circumstances of each nonprofit will dictate what kinds of standing committees are appropriate, most nonprofit corporations should, at a minimum, consider the merits of a governance/nominating committee and an audit committee. (For further discussion of common standing committees, see the section *"Descriptions of Common Standing Committees"* below.)

# Special Committees

Special committees are appointed by a board of directors to perform limited functions.

## Purposes of Special Committees

Special committees can be either advisory—with no power to bind or act for the corporation—or created for a certain purpose with limited powers. The board of directors may, from time to time, create committees to investigate or recommend actions of a special nature. Special committees may be formed to negotiate the purchase of a building, plan a reception, approve drafts of documents, evaluate a major transaction, assess the fairness to the corporation of a transaction between the corporation and a director or officer, or for some similar purpose. They also may be asked to represent the corporation in dealing with another group or meeting.

Special committees also can be delegated special powers to act as agents or to act in place of the board in appropriate situations. For instance, the corporation's bylaws or an applicable law may require the delegation of decision-making authority to a committee of "disinterested directors" to decide sensitive issues involving other board members or key management, such as indemnification, compensation arrangements, or conflict of interest transactions.

## Special Committees of Nonboard Members

Of course, a board of directors may, at any time, retain persons, entities, or organizations to investigate a problem and report on it, or to serve as agents of the corporation in some matter. Thus, even a committee of total outsiders, named to perform some specific function, can be formed at the discretion of the board of directors, except that in most states, the board may not delegate any board-level power to such nondirector committees. For further discussion on committees comprised of non-board members, see the section "Advisory and Auxiliary Bodies" below.

The board should note, however, that even when a special committee has either no authority, or strictly limited authority to bind the corporation, parties outside the corporation may be entitled to rely on the *apparent* authority of the committee, and both the committee and the board should be alert to this risk.

# Standing Committees: General Issues

Most nonprofit corporations find it necessary, in order to fulfill their duties, to have permanent standing committees of the board.

## Board Use of and Reliance on Committees

The board of directors may discharge its duties for a particular class of issues through a committee created to assemble information and make decisions or recommendations concerning such specific corporate activity. A board member who does not serve on a specific committee is entitled to rely on such a committee in the normal course of business, unless the director has some reason to know that the committee's action is deficient.[2]

## Committee Creation: Bylaw Description or Board Resolution

Because the work product of the committee can form part of the record of the board's action in regard to an issue, the committee's formation, purpose, and authority to act on behalf of the corporation should be stated in detail in the bylaws or in the board resolution creating the committee. In addition, the bylaws or resolution should describe the process for appointing committee members and the committee chairs. Often, these appointments occur by board action. Some states prohibit committees from appointing their own members.[3] Directors should recognize that in a dispute concerning a committee's purpose and the scope of its duties, the resolutions and minutes recording the committee's creation may be examined long after their adoption.

## Committee Exercise of Board Authority

Committees empowered to exercise board authority in a wide scope of activities must, first of all, be formed consistent with applicable provisions of the corporation's articles of incorporation and bylaws and the state nonprofit corporation law. Under the Model Act, executive or other committees may be authorized to exercise the board's authority in general or specific respects, except that the board may not delegate to committees the authority to take certain actions defined by law, such as approving the distribution of assets, or amendment of the corporation's bylaws.[4]

## Committee Size

As with the board itself, committees should be selected and managed to maximize the efficiency of the directors in discharging their duties. In general, smaller groups are more efficient—three to seven is an optimal size—and large committees can be unwieldy. Awarding committee memberships as "perks" or to assuage egos is a sure prescription for poor performance. Still, the committee must have enough people to carry out its purpose and to provide representation from all whose concerns are to be examined in the committee's work. As is frequently the case in the nonprofit field, there may be a conflict between the corporation's need for diversity in committee membership and its need for efficiency in its operations. The bylaws or the resolution appointing the committee should specify the size of the committee, by requiring a particular number or by setting forth a permissible range.

## Conflicts of Interest

All standards regarding directors' duty of loyalty and conflicts of interest apply to members of board committees (see the section *"Conflict of Interest: General Principles"* in *Chapter 2, Duties and Rights of Nonprofit Corporation Directors*). Indeed, they apply with somewhat greater force, since a conflict involving a single member of a small committee may affect whether a director not serving on that committee may reasonably believe that the committee's recommendations merit confidence.

# Descriptions of Common Standing Committees

## Executive Committee

Many nonprofit corporations will find that the efficient discharge of their work requires the creation of an executive committee able to exercise, between board meetings, most of the power the board could exercise.

Nonprofit corporations often find it expedient to have an executive committee. Most executive committees are composed of directors of the corporation who also are officers, and perhaps also a small number of other directors. The purpose of an executive committee is to create a group that is able to act for the board between its regular meetings and in situations in which an assembly of a quorum of the board would be impractical or impossible. Such an executive committee, in an organization of more than purely local nature, should generally consist of directors geographically close to the corporation's center of operations, except to the extent others are able to participate effectively long-distance, through telephone conferences or similar communications equipment. At each board meeting, the board should be informed of any actions taken by the executive committee since the last meeting.

If the executive committee exercises a substantial amount of the power of the board, the board as a whole should periodically evaluate whether the board is meeting its fiduciary obligations through such delegations, and whether the board effectively oversees and has the opportunity to provide input regarding executive committee decisions. The board also should review the amount of board-level power that the executive committee typically delegates to the corporation's chief executive or other officers (apart from any such officer's role as a director or executive committee member) to ensure that board power is not routinely exercised by officers rather than the board and its committees. As noted in the section *"Committee Exercise of Board Authority"* above, the board should be aware that state law generally places limits on the powers that a nonprofit board may delegate to an executive or other committee.

A large board that delegates a significant amount of power to its executive committee also should periodically evaluate whether the corporation would benefit from having a smaller board that meets more frequently, thereby enabling the full board to participate in many decisions typically handled by the executive committee. Nonetheless, for many nonprofits, the use of the executive committee mechanism may be an appropriate and efficient use of board resources, by identifying board representatives who are able to make decisions when needed on the board's behalf.

An executive committee should never be a "super" board. As with all committees, the executive committee reports to the board; the board does not report to the executive committee. Assigning duties regarding matters to be approved by the executive committee before being brought to the full board can disenfranchise the rest of the board.

In recent years there has been decreased reliance on an executive committee by some nonprofits. This may be due to the enhanced ability to communicate offered by the Internet and the ubiquity of cell phones, which make it easier than in the past to obtain participation from the full board on matters needing to be addressed between board meetings. Still, an executive committee can be useful for some nonprofit organizations, especially those with large boards. In addition, nonprofits may find executive committees useful to make final decisions on matters previously approved by the board subject to the final determination of certain issues (such as final terms on a large transaction) or to handle matters when it is not feasible to convene all of the board by phone or web access.

## Governance/Nominating Committee

Good corporate practice suggests the appointment of a governance/nominating committee to strengthen the corporate mission, increase board effectiveness, and identify board candidates having the range of qualities desired for an effective board.

### *Importance of governance/nominating committees*

A governance/nominating committee is almost always a standing committee, yet is rarely regarded as a body whose diligence or negligence is legally reviewed. Nevertheless, the process used to determine board nominations obviously is of great importance to the corporation's future and its ability to carry out the corporation's mission. The board of directors has a duty to ensure that a governance/nominating committee is organized and operated in a manner that is likely to generate quality candidates for open board positions.

A nonprofit corporation's mission may require racial and gender diversification or other specific qualifications in the corporation's governing body. Similarly, certain diversity, qualifications or status among the corporation's board may be necessary in order to be considered for government and other funds. Even apart from such specific demands, the governance/nominating committee should formalize and develop procedures for determining who should have positions on the board itself and on committees. The presence of a governance/nominating committee also helps to ensure that important board decisions regarding the selection of directors (and perhaps also officers and committee members) will not be handled on a default basis by management alone.

## *Developing criteria for board nominees*

The governance/nominating committee should define explicit criteria and qualities for board membership, and have the full board approve the list. Such criteria may include knowledge of the corporation's business or industry and purpose/mission; skills needed on the board (e.g., legal, financial, fundraising); association or familiarity with the corporation's constituencies; prior successful board experience; evidence of commitment to the corporation's mission; experience with facing similar challenges as those currently facing the corporation; and the ability to satisfy the time commitment required for board service. The governance/nominating committee also may identify personal qualities desirable for board members, such as good listening skills, ability to effectively (and diplomatically) articulate views contrary to those of other board members, and willingness to support board decisions in which their views are in the minority.

## *Other powers: recommendations for removal of directors, board size, and composition and functions*

The governance/nominating committee also may have responsibility for recommending removal of a director prior to the expiration of a director's term of office, based on inappropriate acts or the director's inattention to his duty.

The committee (or other board committee) also should have other functions, including reviewing the board structure and operations to determine their effectiveness. This review should include a determination of whether there is a culture that supports collegiality, civility, openness, and respect for the board's decisions. In addition, the committee should be involved in evaluating the optimum size of the board, the age profile of board members, the merits of inclusion (or exclusion) of management officers on the board, and the types and functions of board committees, as well as reviewing and making recommendations on the corporation's governing documents.[5] The results of any such review and recommendations should be presented to the full board for consideration and action.

## *Composition*

Ideally, the governance/nominating committee should be composed of directors who do not participate in management and are free of relationships, both business and personal, that could interfere with their exercise of independent judgment. This will help provide both the appearance and the reality of objectivity. In addition, it may be prudent to rotate the members of the committee from time to time. A compromise should be reached between the need to draw on the corporation's present activities, history, and experience, and the need for fresh insights into the corporation's present and future mission.

# Audit Committee

Good corporate practice and some state laws require an organization with significant financial resources to have a committee to review and guide accounting and audit practices.[6] Such a committee should be comprised solely of nonmanagement directors. An independent audit committee can help ensure the financial integrity of the corporation and strengthen the board's ability to exercise its oversight function by reviewing the audited financial statements and hearing reports from auditors first-hand, rather than simply reviewing digested material prepared by management.[7] Some nonprofit organizations maintain a finance committee and an audit committee that do not have overlapping membership. In at least one state, the audit committee must be different from the finance committee, which would generally be the committee regularly reviewing the draft financial statements through the year and providing regular guidance.[8]

An audit committee has responsibilities concerning the corporation's auditing, accounting, and control functions. Depending on the size and activities of the nonprofit, the organization may hire an outside accounting firm to compile, review, or audit the corporation's financial books and records. Federal and state laws or regulations may require a formal audit by a certified public accountant.[9]

The audit committee serves as a liaison between the corporation and the outside accountants. In order to retain objectivity of the audit process, employees of the corporation, even if serving on the board of directors, should not be members of the audit committee. Thus, it is optimal for the audit committee to be composed entirely of independent directors. In addition, to be able to evaluate the financial matters related to the corporation effectively, each audit committee member should be, or be willing to become, financially literate, including the ability to read and understand the corporation's financial statements and the kind of financial issues the corporation typically faces.[10]

The audit committee's duties usually include choosing services needed in financial management, reviewing reports and determining adequate procedures and controls, reviewing financial performance, and approving the annual budget for submission to the board (unless there is a separate finance committee, in which case the finance committee may have some of these duties). Sometimes a review of legal compliance is included within the duties of an audit committee. Any additional duties should be undertaken with caution, for if the committee becomes involved in operational matters, it may jeopardize its essential independence from management. In order to adhere to the proper limits, the duties delegated to the committee should be spelled out very specifically, after consultation with and the concurrence of the outside accountant. This definition of duties can be accomplished either by bylaw provisions or board resolution.

With a need of the board of directors to review the Form 990 prior to filing, the audit committee might be an appropriate committee to be delegated the responsibility for such an in- depth review (with the full board being given an opportunity to review the Form 990 after the audit committee's in-depth review).

## Compensation Committee

It is useful for many nonprofit corporations to establish compensation committees to evaluate the appropriateness of compensation for the chief executive and other key individuals and to assure that compensation decisions are tied to the executives' performance in meeting predetermined goals and objectives.[11]

A nonprofit board should consider whether it should have a standing compensation committee. Whether a separate committee is formed for this function or it is assigned to another committee, it is recommended that the committee be composed solely of independent persons. In addition, the corporation should clearly organize the review of staff qualifications and compensation, and, in particular, the compensation of the chief executive and other key employees. Since such a task involves the receipt and evaluation of confidential and sensitive data, it should be assigned to a separate standing committee, if the size of the board is large enough to make this possible.

The entire board should be aware of the total compensation package for the chief executive and for other key individuals. In order to avoid conflicts of interest, however, approval of such compensation may need to be delegated to a committee. (As noted in the section *"Procedures for Establishing Reasonableness"* in *Chapter 4, Taxation,* the IRS's excess benefit rules provide a presumption of reasonableness if certain financial transactions with insiders (known as "disqualified persons") are approved by disinterested members of a board or board committee, and certain other procedures are followed.) Still, in at least one state, conflicts of interest involving the board must be approved by the full board and not just a committee of the board.[12]

## Investment Committee

For nonprofit corporations that maintain an endowment or significant cash reserves, good corporate practice (and the demands of the Uniform Prudent Management of Institutional Funds Act), suggests appointing an investment committee.

The Uniform Prudent Management of Institutional Funds Act (UPMIFA), which has been adopted in most states, provides rules governing the investment of a charity's assets. UPMIFA, which replaced the Uniform Management of

Institutional Funds Act (UMIFA), provides more specific guidance than UMIFA with regard to prudence in investments and the expenditure of endowment funds.  UPMIFA also eliminates a floor on spending by providing that an institution may appropriate for expenditure or accumulate so much of an endowment fund as the institution determines to be prudent for uses, benefits, purposes, and duration for which the endowment fund is established.  A more detailed discussion regarding the standards under UPMIFA are described in *Chapter 10, Investments and Expenditure of Endowment Funds.*

## Compliance Committee

Nonprofit corporations also may need a committee that is assigned compliance oversight.  This responsibility might be delegated to a nominating/governance committee, an audit committee, an executive committee, or a separate compliance committee.  The committee with the compliance responsibility should regularly review the compliance programs established for the corporation, which should include policies addressing issues to mitigate legal and operational risks.  It is important that any staff assigned compliance responsibilities in the corporation have direct access to the committee that is assigned compliance oversight.  Where the corporation uses a committee to oversee compliance, it is still important for the full board to be involved in compliance matters.  As a result, there should be regular reporting to the full board regarding compliance matters.

# The Composition of a Committee

The appropriate composition of a committee will depend on the type of committee involved. Executive committees may be composed primarily of directors who are also officers; in contrast, governance/nominating and audit committees should consist primarily or entirely of nonofficer directors.

The Model Act requires that all committee members be members of the board of directors.[13] Some state statutes permit nondirectors to serve on committees, including, committees that exercise board-delegated authority; however, board members must still comprise a majority of such committees.[14] The extent to which a committee should consist solely or predominantly of directors, or may be appointed without any directors at all, depends on the purpose of the committee and the authority given it. Advisory committees may be comprised of few, if any, board members, if appropriate under the circumstances.

# Committee Procedures, Minutes, and Reports

The procedures, records and operations of committees should be as clearly defined as those of the board itself.

The distinction between the board of directors' procedures and those of a committee will depend somewhat on the size of the corporation and the individual committee. The committees of large nonprofit boards may be of substantial size and therefore require, for orderly and efficient procedure, a degree of formality that would be inefficient (and possibly ridiculous) in smaller committees. The need for formality is increased if the directors are not routinely acquainted with each other, and the board or committee meetings may be the only occasion when any interpersonal contact is achieved. In these situations, meetings conducted according to fairly structured rules may be necessary. Nonetheless, committees may provide a more flexible way for the board to fulfill specific functions.

Committee members are entitled to notices of meetings, quorum requirements, access to records, clear resolutions in the event of controversy, and a right to record dissent. Informality of discussions should not amount to or imply an infringement of the committee members' rights in this regard.

All committees should maintain minutes of meetings and other records appropriate to their purposes. The more a board relies on a committee in the discharge of the board's duty of care, as in reliance on the judgment and actions of an investment committee, the more this committee should maintain fully detailed minutes and records, and make regular reports to the board. Executive committees and other standing committees should submit minutes to the board in detail roughly comparable to those of the board itself. On the other hand, it may be sufficient for the board to require that a special committee prepare only a report.

# Advisory and Auxiliary Bodies

## Use of Advisory and Auxiliary Bodies

A frequent device used in nonprofit corporations is to appoint one or more advisory or auxiliary boards, councils, or committees, composed of community leaders, volunteers, other supporters, and community representatives. These bodies differ from board committees in generally including in their membership nondirectors, and in lacking the ability to exercise power on behalf of the board.

These advisory and auxiliary bodies also are distinguished from committees in that they may be more involved in activities supporting the organization and less involved in governance matters.

Establishing advisory and auxiliary bodies may be useful in enabling a nonprofit board to enlist the interest and input of individuals who would be too numerous or too busy to serve on the board directly. For example, a public benefit corporation may use an advisory council as a mechanism for involving the community leaders who are unable to give the time commitments necessary for board service, but whose insights and names will aid the organization in fundraising or political arenas. In some cases, an advisory board may be advantageous for start-up nonprofits, as a means to assure donors and the community that the actions of the new organization are subject to some form of independent review. Advisory boards also may be established in connection with a merger or consolidation of nonprofit organizations, allowing the new organization to take advantage of the continued contributions and insight of persons who formerly served as directors of one of the merged organizations, while keeping the consolidated board to a manageable size. Advisory or auxiliary bodies having either indefinite or limited duration may prove useful in a variety of other circumstances. Despite the usefulness of advisory or auxiliary groups, the board should be aware of legal implications of creating and maintaining such groups.

## Legal Status of Advisory and Auxiliary Bodies

First of all, corporate law, in general, does not give an advisory or auxiliary body any particular status (unless it is a separately incorporated auxiliary) and its members do not have the same legal duties, responsibilities, and powers that have been outlined in this *Guidebook* as applicable to the board of directors. For that reason, the board of directors should make sure there exists some document (whether titled charter, bylaws, regulations, or other name) outlining the purposes and powers of the advisory or auxiliary group, and indicating the group's legal relationship to the establishing organization.

At the same time, any group or individual publicly acknowledged to be connected with the corporation in some manner can, in some circumstances, be considered an agent of the corporation. Thus, the advisory or auxiliary group's actions, even if unauthorized, could be found to be binding against the corporation. Because the group's advisory or unofficial status may not be clear to the public, statements or actions of such a group or individual may, at least in the public's eye, be attributed to the board of directors or the corporation. In addition, members of such a group may face the same kinds of conflicts of interest experienced by directors. None of these problems are insoluble, but they do call for scrutiny and attention.

# Relationship of Board to Advisory Bodies

With respect to advisory bodies, the board should recognize that, having purported to seek advice, the board then has at least a moral obligation to give this advice at least some measure of consideration, perhaps through a formal process followed at the board or committee level. Directors should further recognize that, unlike the regular committees of the board whose efficient functioning may lessen the burdens of the board, an advisory body may increase those burdens by placing on the board an obligation to review its recommendations.

# Relationship of Board to Auxiliary Bodies

With respect to auxiliary bodies, the board should exercise some level of oversight, since the auxiliary will be acting publicly in the name of the corporation or the institutions it operates. If the auxiliary functions as a division of the nonprofit, the chief executive or other corporate officer should oversee the auxiliary and report to the board regarding auxiliary operations. In addition, the corporation should establish a mechanism for periodically recognizing the contributions made by the auxiliary group. The board or a committee also should afford the auxiliary periodic opportunities to report on its activities, and give or seek advice relating to the operations of the corporation or the auxiliary.

# Scope of Activity of Advisory and Auxiliary Bodies

When creating an advisory or auxiliary body, the board must first define the purposes of the group and determine how the board of directors will exercise oversight of the group's activities. Second, the role of the group in relation to the corporation's staff should be defined in the same documents and decisions that create the group. Advisory and auxiliary board or committee members should not be allowed to demand more staff time than is appropriate to the group's role. Moreover, particularly when the advisory or auxiliary group relates to a successful or growing function, the board should be alert to the danger that the group and its related staff may develop a level of independence that fails to recognize that the group is still ultimately subject to the board's control. While such events are not unknown, they can be avoided through appropriate structuring of the group at the outset and continued oversight thereafter.

## Limitations on Rights of Members of Advisory and Auxiliary Bodies and Liability Protection

The bylaw or board resolution creating the advisory or auxiliary body should designate the criteria for membership, the term for which such members are appointed, and the power of some corporate officer, director, or the board itself to remove members of the advisory or auxiliary group. In general, the members of an advisory or auxiliary group have no vested right to serve, no immunity from removal, and no right to renewal of appointment. The board should be careful, however, to make sure that no resolutions or communications imply the creation of such rights. It is also prudent for the board to address whether (and the extent to which) conflicts of interest policies apply to members of advisory and auxiliary bodies. In addition, as part of the board's review of its directors and officers (D&O) insurance, indemnification rights, and other liability protections (see the discussion in *Chapter 11, Director Liability: Risks and Protections*), the board should determine what protections can and should be afforded to advisory and auxiliary group members. Assuming that advisory and auxiliary bodies have no delegated board authority, members of such bodies should not be subject to the fiduciary duties imposed on the nonprofit corporation's board of directors.

# Designated Bodies

For some nonprofits, certain of the responsibilities normally vested with the board of directors or the members may be vested with a different person or group. This can arise, for instance, in the situation of certain religious organizations in which a church authority has certain approval requirements relating to the operations of the organization. The Model Act defines a "designated body" broadly to include a person or group (other than a committee of the board of directors) that has been vested by the articles of incorporation or bylaws with powers that otherwise would be required to be exercised by the board or the members.[15]

Under the Model Act, if a designated body is created, to the extent the powers of a board of directors are vested with the designated body, the rights, duties, and liabilities of the board of directors or directors individually also apply to the designated body and to the members of the designated body individually. In addition, to the extent that the powers, authority, or functions of the board of directors have been vested with a designated body, the directors are relieved from their duties and liabilities with respect to such powers, authority, and functions.[16] Similarly, to the extent the rights of members have been vested with a designated body, the members are relieved from responsibility with respect to those rights and obligations.[17]

# Officers: Introduction

Nonprofit corporations typically have officers who are delegated responsibilities by the board of directors either through the articles of incorporation, bylaws, or board resolution. The officers are selected in accordance with the terms of the articles of incorporation and bylaws. Normally, the board of directors elects the officers, but in some nonprofit organizations, the members elect the officers. Traditionally, officer positions have included the chair, one or more vice chairs, a treasurer, and a secretary. The name of the officer positions are generally not mandated, and the position of chair is sometimes referred to as president or some other name. Regardless of the names of the officers, it is important to recognize that these individuals are officers of the corporation as a whole and not just officers of the board, even though some may be referred to as "board officers" as opposed to "staff officers."

## Officer Responsibilities

In general, the officers have the responsibility for implementing the directives of the board of directors. Still, board officers may not be involved in the day-to-day operations of the organization where there is a staff with a chief executive (who is generally an officer) that assumes this responsibility. Nevertheless, officers are accountable to the board of directors, which can involve reporting back to the directors as to the activities of the organization.[18]

An individual may be both an officer and a director; however, it is important to identify his or her role at any given time. In the role of an officer, the individual is implementing the activities approved by the board of directors and reports to the board of directors. In the role as a director, the individual, along with the rest of the board, supervises the entire operation of the corporation.[19]

# Officer Positions

## Chair and Vice Chair

The chair is often delegated the responsibility of chairing or running the meetings of the board of directors. A chair also can be given the responsibility of chairing any meeting of the members. In addition, the chair, in some states, can be given authority to appoint committees as well as have signing authority on behalf of the organization. Although the bylaws should provide a description of the responsibilities of the chair, some of the duties of the chair may not be specified. In this situation, it is prudent for the board to consider amending its bylaws to reflect the chair's actual responsibilities.

Although not addressed in the articles of incorporation or bylaws, the chair plays an extremely important role in institutional dynamics. A chair needs to take a leadership role in the organization and understand and be responsive to the views and expectations of other board members and to work with them to enhance their effectiveness.[20] The chair, in conjunction with the chief executive, must establish the direction of the board's work. He or she also must take steps to ensure that the board is functioning properly in a collegial atmosphere. It is important that the chair and chief executive regularly communicate regarding matters affecting the organization.

As noted above, in the situation where there is a chief executive, it is not expected that the chair will be involved in the day-to-day operations of the organization and can be criticized for micromanaging if attempts are made to have this involvement. A position description for the board chair can be very helpful to ensure that this role is filled appropriately and expectations are met.

A vice chair position often exists in order that there is an individual available to act as the chair in the event the chair becomes unable to serve. Organizations differ on whether a vice chair will automatically ascend to the chair position. The key is that this individual is able and willing to serve in the chair role if necessary.

## Treasurer

A treasurer is often delegated various responsibilities relating to the financial affairs of a nonprofit corporation. This can include responsibility for maintaining all monies and securities of the corporation, keeping full and accurate records and accounts in books belonging to the corporation, depositing funds in the name of the corporation with banks designated by the corporation, and preparing the corporation's financial statements.

Small nonprofit organizations may often have a board member serve as treasurer, even if the actual financial functions are handled by a staff member. For nonprofit corporations with large budgets, it is generally not feasible for a board member serving in the treasurer role to be able to perform all of the designated functions of treasurer. Nonprofit organizations with a full-time chief financial officer or controller often designate this person as the organization's treasurer, or in some cases, the assistant treasurer.

## Secretary

The position of secretary often includes the responsibilities of keeping and maintaining minutes of meetings and maintaining the corporate records for the organization.  Similar to the situation with the treasurer, in smaller nonprofit organizations—and some larger organizations—a board member may serve in the secretary role.  In these cases, it is often beneficial to have a staff member serve as assistant secretary to perform certain of the duties relating to the secretary. In larger nonprofit organizations, an executive such as the chief governance officer or the general counsel serves as secretary of the organization.  This individual has the responsibility not only to  maintain the corporation's minutes and other governance books and records, but also to  attest to board and corporate authority matters for governmental filings, banking resolutions, and  Secretary's Certificates required in connection with transactions with third parties.

## Standards of Conduct for Officers

The standard of conduct for officers is similar to the conduct imposed on directors discussed in *Chapter 2, Duties and Rights of Nonprofit Corporation Directors*; however, the application of this standard in the role of a director serving as an officer can differ.  For instance, an officer's ability to rely on others in meeting the duty of care may be more limited, depending on the circumstances of the particular case, than the scope of reliance permitted for a director.  This is because of the obligation the officer may have to be more familiar with the affairs of the nonprofit corporation.[21]  In addition, officers have a duty to inform a superior officer, the board of directors, or a committee regarding information they know about the affairs of the nonprofit corporation that are material to the superior officer, board, or committee.[22] The liability protections that are available to directors (described in *Chapter*

*11, Director Liability Risks and Protections*) also generally apply to directors serving in officer roles.

*See the Suggested Questions and Checklist following the Endnotes below to review the issues discussed in this chapter.*

## Endnotes

1. *See* Jack B. Siegel, *A Desktop Guide for Nonprofit Directors, Officers, and Advisors: Avoiding Trouble While Doing Good* 31 (John Wiley & Sons 2006).

2. *See* Model Act §§ 8.30 (e) and (f). *See also* the section *"Reliance"* in Chapter 2, *"Director Duties and Rights."*

3. *See, e.g.,* Illinois General Not for Profit Corporation Act of 1986, 805 Ill. Comp. Stat. 105/108.40.

4. *See* Comment to Model Act § 8.25.

5. Some state statutes specifically provide for a governance/nominating committee. *See* 15 Pa. Cons. Stat. § 5725(e). *See also* ABA Coordinating Committee on Nonprofit Governance, *Guide to Nonprofit Corporate Governance in the Wake of Sarbanes-Oxley* 28-34 (American Bar Association 2005).

6. *See, e.g.,* California Nonprofit Integrity Act of 2004, Cal. Gov't. Code §§ 12585-12589.

7. Under the California Nonprofit Integrity Act of 2004, audited financial statements are required of nonprofit organizations that receive or accrue gross revenues of $2 million in any fiscal year.

8. *See* California Nonprofit Integrity Act of 2004, *supra* note 6.

9. *See Guide to Nonprofit Corporation Governance in the Wake of Sarbanes-Oxley* 28-34, *supra* note 5.

10. *See Guide to Nonprofit Corporation Governance in the Wake of Sarbanes-Oxley* 31, *supra* note 5.

11. *See Guide to Nonprofit Corporate Governance in the Wake of Sarbanes-Oxley* 35-37, *supra* note 5.

12. *See* California Nonprofit Integrity Act of 2004, *supra* note 6.

13. *See* Model Act § 8.25. (Still, nondirectors may serve on advisory committees under the Model Act).

14. *See, e.g.,* 805 ILCS § 105/108.40.

15. *See* Lizabeth A. Moody, Forward to Model Act, at xxiii (American Bar Association, 2009).

16. *See* Model Act §8.12(a).

17. *See* Model Act §8.12(b).

18. *See* Lisa A. Runquist, *The ABCs of Nonprofits* 22 (American Bar Association 2005).

19.    *See* Runquist, *The ABCs of Nonprofits* 23, *supra* n. 17.

20.    *See* Cheryl Sorokin, Judith A. Cion, Jeannie Carmedelle Frey and Richard Sevcik, Eds., *Nonprofit Governance and Management* 18 (American Bar Association 2011).

21.    *See* Model Act § 8.42(a) and Comment to Model Act § 8.42.

22.    *See* Model Act § 8.42(b).

# Suggested Questions for Directors Regarding Committees, Advisory Bodies, and Officers

(1)    What committees does our board have? What powers does each committee have?

(2)    Is there an executive committee? What are the limitations on its power to act?

(3)    Do we have a governance/nominating committee?

(4)    Who monitors the corporation's accounting and financial reports? Is there an audit committee? Who serves on it?

(5)    Is there a committee that reviews executive performance and compensation?

(6)    If the corporation has investments, does it have or need an investment committee?

(7)    Is there a committee responsible for legal compliance? If not, how does the corporation address compliance matters?

(8)    How do committees report to the board?

(9)    What auxiliary groups or advisory boards are associated with the corporation? What are their relationship to the corporation? How does the board monitor and recognize the activities of these groups?

(10)    Is there a person or group that has been vested with the rights and responsibilities of the board of directors or members under the articles and bylaws? If so, what are these rights and responsibilities?

(11)    What are the officer positions in the organization and what are the responsibilities of the officers?

(12)    Are any of the officer positions to be held by nonboard members?

# Checklist: Committees and Advisory Bodies

Note: For purposes of simplicity in these checklists, we describe a corporation with a chair, who presides over the board of directors; a chief executive, who may be a staff person; an executive committee; a governance/nominating committee; and an audit committee. (We recognize, however, that in many smaller and other nonprofits, these committee functions may be performed by either the executive committee or the board as a whole.) We also assume a legal counsel—someone, paid or unpaid, having primary responsibility for the corporation's legal affairs. Many corporations, especially larger nonprofits, may have other committees established for specific purposes, such as reviewing staff performance, fixing compensation, monitoring compliance with legal requirements, and periodic review of bylaws.

| Subject | Review By | How Often | Comment |
|---|---|---|---|
| 1. What are the committees of the corporation? | Chair, chief executive, full board | Annually | A review of bylaw provisions relating to committees should be performed simultaneously. |
| 2. Which committees have power to bind the corporation? | Chair, chief executive, full board | Annually | The board should periodically review whether it is delegating too much, or too little, authority to committees. |
| 3. Which committees, with or without power to bind the corporation, deal with major parties or interests outside the corporation? | Chair, chief executive, full board | Annually | Even committees or committee members without *actual* authority to bind the corporation could have *apparent* authority in the view of outside parties. |

| Subject | Review By | How Often | Comment |
|---|---|---|---|
| 4. Which committees simply report or advise the board? | Chair, chief executive, full board | Annually | The board should periodically review the use and usefulness of advisory committees. |
| 5. Do we have a governance/ nominating committee? | Chair, chief executive, full board | Annually, in preparation for annual meeting; before each meeting at which a vacancy is to be filled | An effective governance/ nominating committee must discuss board evaluation and board needs with the full board prior to its annual meeting. |
| 6. Do we have a compensation committee? If not, who determines compensation? | Chair/chief executive/full board | Annually | Compensation committee or other committee or full board should review executive compensation annually. |

| Subject | Review By | How Often | Comment |
|---|---|---|---|
| 7. Should there be provisions limiting the number of consecutive terms a director may serve? Or a maximum age for directors? | Governance/ nominating committee, reviewing proposed changes with legal counsel, and reporting to board | Probably every three or four years | Governance/ nominating committee should, as a regular function, analyze years of service of each director, maximum age, and average age of board. No bright-line tests apply to all cases, but decisions on these issues (including the decision to make no changes) should be conscious. |
| 8. What committee reviews staff compensation? | Chair, chief executive, full board | Annually | This function should be formally assigned even if no separate compensation committee is created. |
| 9. Does the committee that decides compensation matters report to the board in executive session? | Chair, chief executive, full board | Annually | Discussion of staff salaries should always be held outside of the presence of staff, without need for a special resolution to that effect. |

| Subject | Review By | How Often | Comment |
|---------|-----------|-----------|---------|
| 10. Does the corporation have or need an investment committee? Is the corporation subject to the Uniform Prudent Management of Institutional Funds Act? | Chair, chief executive, chief financial officer, and full board | Every two or three years | The board should periodically review and assure that investment committee members understand their responsibilities. |
| 11. Does the corporation have a committee responsible for oversight of legal and operational compliance matters? | Chair, chief executive, and full board | Every two or three years | Even where there is a committee assigned the responsibility of overseeing compliance matters, there should be regular reporting to the full board on these matters. |

| Subject | Review By | How Often | Comment |
|---|---|---|---|
| 12. Do the responsibilities of the officers as described in the articles of incorporation or bylaws accurately reflect the responsibilities being carried out by the officers? | Chair or chief executive; governance/ nominating committee | Annually in all cases; always before notice goes out of meeting to elect officers. | Many public benefit corporations have bylaws describing as "chair" an uncompensated person who presides over the board. In many nonprofits, the chief executive's functions are not described in bylaws if he or she is not the president or other corporate officer.  If the chief executive is not described in the bylaws,  this person may not be an officer. |

# Chapter 4:
## Taxation

# Chapter 4
# Taxation

*A director should understand the basic application of federal, state, and local tax law to the corporation. This chapter outlines the principal federal income tax issues of the more common nonprofit corporations.*

## Introduction

A director should have a general understanding of the tax status of the corporation. The director should know, for example, if the corporation is exempt from federal income tax, and if so, under what section of the Internal Revenue Code (the Code); if the corporation is exempt from local real estate or other taxes; and, in a general way, what is required to maintain these exemptions.

Taxation is a technical field, and a director's obligations do not require a detailed knowledge of the various tax statutes and regulations. Most nonprofit corporations have, or should consider having, their tax reporting handled by outside professionals, either accountants or attorneys. The function of the board, in oversight of these persons, is part of the oversight that the board exercises generally. Moreover, the reader should be aware that federal tax law and the interpretation of its provisions is subject to change; therefore, while the issues discussed here are areas requiring a director's attention and are likely to remain relevant to the operations of tax-exempt corporations, specific rules may change over time.[1]

The subject is a broad one, but this chapter will outline only the principal federal income tax issues of the more common nonprofit corporations. And, despite the importance of local tax issues, space constrains us from addressing state and local tax law. Still, directors must understand that federal tax-exempt status does not automatically confer exemption from state and local taxes.[2]

## Qualifying for Exemption from Federal Income Tax

Most nonprofit corporations are exempt from the federal income taxes applicable to corporations. Still, corporations do not automatically qualify for exemption from federal income taxation simply because they are nonprofit. Nonprofit status is primarily a state law organizational construct; federal tax exemption is based on federal law.

A director should not assume that because the corporation is nonprofit it is exempt from any income tax whatsoever. Tax-exempt status is a privilege, not a right, which is conferred on an organization that meets and continues to meet certain requirements set out by the Code. Other than churches and very small organizations, organizations seeking exemption under Code § 501(c)(3), described in this chapter, must obtain IRS approval of their applications for exemption. The IRS lists a series of tax-exempt organizations in IRS Publication 557, *Tax-Exempt Status for Your Organization*, along with brief descriptions defining their activities.[3] This list is set forth in *Appendix A* of this *Guidebook*.

A director should understand that exemption from federal income tax does not necessarily permit donors to the corporation to deduct gifts to it. The Code permits donors to deduct gifts to tax-exempt corporations *only* if the corporation qualifies under § 501(c)(3). Payments to other types of tax-exempt corporations may be deductible by the donor only if the payment qualifies as a trade or business expense. Although the ability to attract tax-deductible charitable contributions is essential for many organizations, it is not a primary or significant source of income for others. Directors should periodically evaluate whether the corporation is qualified under the appropriate category, or whether conversion to a different category or creation of an affiliate of a different category should be considered.

## Corporations Exempt from Tax under § 501(c)(3)

Most public benefit and religious corporations, and any such corporation wishing deductibility of gifts as charitable contributions, will seek exemption under § 501(c)(3).

For a corporation to be exempt under § 501(c)(3), it must be organized and operated exclusively for charitable, religious, educational, literary, or scientific purposes.[4] These general categories conform roughly to traditional state law trust and corporate definitions of "charity." Code § 501 also contains additional specific requirements for certain types of § 501(c)(3) organizations, such as hospitals, child care providers, and credit counseling organizations.

## Particular Advantages of § 501(c)(3) Status

In addition to exemption of the corporation itself from most federal income taxes, § 501(c)(3) organizations enjoy certain unique advantages. Contributions made to them are tax-deductible by the contributors, up to the limits imposed by Code § 170(b).[5] In addition, some § 501(c)(3) corporations may finance their exempt activities by issuing tax-exempt bonds, enabling these organizations to lower their borrowing costs. Other benefits may include exemption from state real property and sales and use taxes and reduced postal rates for mailings.

## General Requirements

To achieve and maintain exemption under § 501(c)(3), the corporation must comply with explicit restrictions. With limited exceptions, the IRS must approve an application for exemption, as described in more detail in the section *"Obtaining Tax-Exempt Status"* below.

In order to be tax-exempt under § 501(c)(3), a corporation must be *organized and operated* exclusively for exempt purposes. This is called the "organized and operated" test for obtaining and maintaining exempt status. The requirement that the corporation be "organized" exclusively for exempt purposes means that the articles of incorporation (and any amendments thereto) must contain appropriate restrictions on the corporation's purposes, activities, and use of assets, including ultimate disposition of assets upon a dissolution of the corporation. A director should bear this in mind in considering any amendments to the articles. It is not sufficient that the corporation merely operate in an appropriate manner.

In addition, in order to maintain tax-exempt status, an organization must not allow any net earnings to inure to private individuals, as described in the section *"Limitations on Private Benefit and Private Inurement"* below. It also must not carry on substantial activities to influence legislation and must not participate, *in any way,* in any political campaign, as described in the sections *"Limitations on Lobbying"* and *"The Absolute Prohibition on Political Campaign Activities"* below.[6]

## Limitations on Unrelated Business Activities

The conduct of unrelated business activities may not disqualify an otherwise exempt § 501(c)(3) corporation if the unrelated activities do not constitute the organization's primary purpose; however, the corporation may be taxed on income from the unrelated activity.

A § 501(c)(3) corporation may engage in some activities that are not related to its exempt purposes. For example, the corporation may own property that it leases to commercial tenants when the property is not needed by the corporation, or it may use its staff and resources to provide for-profit consulting services to generate income. Such activities will not disqualify the corporation from tax-exempt status so long as the corporation's unrelated activities do not constitute the corporation's primary purpose.

Income derived from certain unrelated activities may be subject to federal tax. See the discussion in the section *"Unrelated Business Income"* below.

## Limitations on Private Benefit and Private Inurement

A § 501(c)(3) corporation must not be operated for the benefit of any private individual. A § 501(c)(3) corporation is not operated for charitable purposes if it serves a private interest. This is the general standard applicable to all charitable corporations and simply incorporates into the Code the trust law standards of a charity. Further, in order for the corporation to be recognized as a § 501(c)(3) organization "no part of the net earnings of" a corporation may inure "to the benefit of any private shareholder or individual."

Private benefit or private inurement may occur, for example, when a § 501(c)(3) corporation pays for goods or services in sums in excess of their fair market value, when assets of a corporation are given to or used for the benefit of an individual who gave less than fair consideration for the same, or when an individual or corporation is paid by the exempt organization in excess of reasonable compensation or on a percentage of the tax-exempt organization's net income. Private inurement relates to a benefit conferred on an "insider" of the organization, such as a director or officer. A director should understand that a non-fair-market-value transaction with such a person may jeopardize the continuing tax-exempt status of the organization. As discussed below in the section *"Intermediate Sanctions: Excise Tax on Public Charities' Excess Benefit Transactions,"* the payment of other than fair market value for items or services may also raise excess benefit transaction excise tax issues.

## Limitations on Lobbying

A corporation will not qualify as a § 501(c)(3) organization if it devotes a substantial part of its activities to lobbying, propaganda, or attempting to influence legislation. "Legislation" generally refers to acts, bills, resolutions, or similar items passed or proposed to be passed or acted on by a legislative body, including treaties. In contrast, regulations adopted or other actions taken by executive or judicial or governmental administrative bodies (e.g., school boards, zoning boards, housing authority, and water districts) are not considered legislation and therefore not subject to the lobbying limits. This includes lobbying certain government officials and grass roots lobbying. Section 501(h) of the Code provides a helpful alternative safe harbor for certain corporations that wish to regularly engage in some lobbying. Although § 501(h) clarifies the scope of permitted activities, it can impose strict penalties on the corporation and its directors if these safe harbor dollar limits are exceeded.

Lobbying means issue advocacy, not political campaign activity. A common (but not absolute) rule of thumb is that a nonprofit corporation will not be considered to be engaging in substantial lobbying if *less than 5 percent* of its activities are devoted to this activity. Whether or not more than 5 percent constitutes a substantial amount of activities is determined based on all the facts and circumstances.

Certain qualifying organizations may file a special election under § 501(h) of the Code to allow them to spend up to a specified dollar amount (which may represent a larger percentage of total activities) for lobbying without fear of adverse tax consequences from such activities. While persistent lobbying in excess of that permitted by § 501(h) will lead to a loss of both the protection of the § 501(h) safe harbor and a loss of the corporation's basic tax exemption, isolated instances of lobbying in excess of permissible amounts will not cost the organization its tax-exemption. Instead, an excise tax will be applied against the organization. *In addition, penalty taxes may be imposed on any officer, director, or responsible employee of the organization* involved in the excessive lobbying activities. In some cases, the definition and measurement of lobbying activities will be easier than in others; for instance, as discussed in *Chapter 6, Nonprofits on the Internet: Fundraising, Selling Goods and Services, Lobbying, and Other Activities*, lobbying activities on the Internet pose challenging questions both for tax-exempt organizations trying to comply with § 501(h) and the IRS.

## The Absolute Prohibition on Political Campaign Activities

A § 501(c)(3) corporation is strictly prohibited from supporting, participating in, or intervening in any election for public office.

A § 501(c)(3) corporation will lose its tax-exempt status if it participates or intervenes in a political campaign on behalf of, or in opposition to, a candidate for public office, through financial support, endorsements, or other actions directly or indirectly advocating the election or defeat of a candidate. In addition, it will be subject to an excise tax of 10 percent of the political expenditures. Unlike the restrictions on lobbying, the prohibition on political activities is absolute, and applies to any such activities, no matter how small. There are *severe penalties imposed on the corporation and, in some instances, its directors*, if prohibited political activities continue.[7]

# Special Rules Relating to Public Charities and Private Foundations

The Code classifies certain § 501(c)(3) organizations as "private foundations," in contrast to "public charities," the latter being the term commonly used to refer to those § 501(c)(3) organizations that are not private foundations, although this term does not appear in the Code. A director should understand that all § 501(c)(3) corporations are treated as private foundations unless they can demonstrate that they meet one of the definitions of a public charity, as described below. The principal difference is that private foundations receive most, if not all, of their support from one or a few persons whereas most public charities have a broad base of support.

Private foundations are subject to various restrictions and excise taxes not applicable to other § 501(c)(3) corporations (commonly referred to as public charities). Unlike most public charities, private foundations are subject to a requirement to distribute a minimum annual amount of funds. Since private foundations are subject to greater restrictions and certain excise taxes not applicable to public charities, a § 501(c)(3) corporation should make sure that the classification of the organization as a public charity or private foundation is properly determined and maintained. This issue is generally addressed when the public charity or private foundation is organized and during the IRS exemption application process and can be updated with the IRS as necessary. This *Guidebook* gives this question only a brief overview.

## Definition of Public Charity

A corporation can avoid the additional taxes and restrictions imposed on private foundations if it falls within one of the enumerated types of organizations classified as public charities as listed in IRS Publication 557. Typical public charities include churches, schools, and hospitals. A corporation not falling within one of the categories listed in IRS Publication 557 may still avoid classification as a private foundation if it qualifies as a "publicly supported" charity or a "supporting organization," (e.g., it has a broad base of public support or is to provide support to another public charity). To qualify as either type of organization, certain specific tests must be met.

An organization is considered a publicly supported charity if it meets one of two tests: (1) a substantial part of the support the organization receives is in the form of contributions from publicly supported organizations, governmental units, or the general public (e.g., a human services organization whose revenue is generated through widespread public fundraising campaigns); or (2) no more than one-third of the support received by the organization is from gross investment income and more than one-third of the organization's support is received from contributions, membership fees, and gross receipts from activities related to its exempt functions (e.g., a membership-fee organization, such as a parent-teacher organization).

Supporting organizations are charities that carry out their exempt purposes by supporting other exempt organizations, usually other public charities. An important aspect of a supporting organization is the strong relationship with an organization it supports, which enables the supported organization to oversee the operations of the supporting organization. The supporting organization is classified as a public charity, and may be funded by a small number of persons in a manner similar to a private foundation. An example of a supporting organization is an organization that provides essential services for hospital systems. Similar to other charitable organizations, a supporting organization needs to be organized and operated exclusively for purposes described in § 501(c)(3).

A supporting organization must have one of three kinds of relationships with the supported organization(s), identified by the IRS as "Type I, Type II, or Type III" relationships. Type I supporting organizations are operated, supervised, or controlled by the supported organization. Type II supporting organizations are supervised or controlled in connection with the supported organization. Type III supporting organizations are operated in connection with the supported organization. Given that the Type III relationships are less formal than a Type I or Type II relationship, Type III organizations also need to meet other requirements (known as the responsiveness and integral part tests) that are designed to ensure that the supporting organization is responsive to the needs of a public charity and that the public charity oversees the operations of the supporting organization. Finally, the supporting organization may not be controlled directly or indirectly by disqualified persons. Additional information discussion can be found in IRS Publication 557 and the IRS's website, www.irs.gov.

# Restrictions and Taxes on Private Foundations

"Private foundations" refer to organizations that are tax-exempt under § 501(c)
(3) and characterized under § 509(a) of the Code as a private foundation,
rather than a public charity. In general, a nonprofit will be considered a private
foundation if it does not meet the test for a "public charity." Private foundations
generally are subject to a 2 percent excise tax on their net investment income
(including capital gains). Private foundations are also subject to several other
restrictions that may result in various taxes and penalties, including:

- restrictions on self-dealing between private foundations and their substantial contributors and other individuals described as "disqualified persons,"
  including their directors and trustees (and directors' or trustees' family
  members and owned entities);
- minimum requirements for distribution of income and principal for charitable purposes, as described below;
- a potential tax upon termination of private foundation status;
- a potential excise tax on noncharitable grants;
- a potential excise tax on jeopardy investments; and
- restrictions on excess business holdings.

## *Self-dealing rules*

The prohibitions on self-dealing reach a broad range of transactions between
a private foundation and a "disqualified person," including:

- the sale, exchange, or leasing of property;
- the lending of money or other extensions of credit;
- the furnishing of goods, services, or facilities;
- the payment of unreasonable compensation or expenses;
- the transfer to, or use by or for the benefit of, a disqualified person of the
  private foundation's income or assets; and
- payments to government officials.

In determining whether a transaction is restricted or prohibited by the self-
dealing rules, it does not matter whether the transaction results in a benefit
or a detriment to the private foundation or whether the transaction is "fair."
(In this respect, the self-dealing prohibitions differ from the intermediate
sanctions imposed on public charities.) An act of self-dealing includes both
direct and indirect transactions between a private foundation and a disqualified
person. The Code does, however, permit certain exceptions to the self-dealing
rules, including, for example, the payment of reasonable compensation. *Any
transaction between a private foundation and a disqualified person should be
reviewed by counsel or an appropriate committee to ensure the self-dealing rules
are not violated.* Violations of the self-dealing restrictions may result in severe
penalties and substantial legal complications.

### Distribution requirements

A private foundation must distribute annually a minimum amount for charitable purposes, which is roughly 5 percent of the fair market value of its noncharitable (e.g., investment) assets. The required distribution may take the form of a direct payment for charitable purposes, such as payment of expenses incurred in conducting a charitable activity, an acquisition of assets to be used in performing the organization's exempt purposes, or a contribution to another charitable organization.

If a private foundation satisfies its distribution requirements by making charitable contributions to other § 501(c)(3) exempt organizations, the foundation's responsibilities may not end at the time the contribution is made. Except where the contribution is made to a public charity or to certain operating foundations, the private foundation must take steps to ensure that the contribution is, in fact, subsequently used by the receiving organization to accomplish exempt purposes. Some private foundations, in very limited circumstances, may avoid this requirement.

### Limitation on excess business holdings

The Code imposes limitations on the ability of a private foundation to hold an ownership interest in another business entity, such as a corporation or a partnership.

### Liability of foundation managers

Excise taxes generally are imposed against a private foundation that violates any of the private foundation rules. In some cases, moreover, excise taxes may be imposed against "foundation managers," substantial contributors to the foundations, and, with respect to self-dealing, other "disqualified persons." Persons considered foundation managers include officers, directors, or trustees of a private foundation, and employees of the foundation who have authority or responsibility over the matter resulting in the tax.

# Section 501(c)(4) Organizations: Civic Leagues and Social Welfare Organizations

A nonprofit corporation operated exclusively for the promotion of social welfare may seek exemption under § 501(c)(4). Exemption under this section will not confer charitable contributions deductibility for donors to the corporation, but may enable it to avoid the restrictions of private foundation status, and the restrictions on lobbying and political activity.

A nonprofit corporation that is operated exclusively for the promotion of social welfare may qualify as a § 501(c)(4) organization and thus be exempt from federal income tax. In addition to the lack of deductibility as charitable contributions, contributions or dues paid to a § 501(c)(4) corporation are subject to the same tax treatment limitations as discussed with respect to trade organizations in the section *"Tax Treatment of Contributions or Dues to a § 501(c)(6) Corporation"* below.

## Definition of Social Welfare

A corporation is operated exclusively for the promotion of social welfare if it is operated primarily to further the common good and general welfare of the people of a community, such as by bringing about civic betterment and social improvement, and no part of its net earnings inures to the benefit of any private shareholder or individual. In addition, a § 501(c)(4) corporation must benefit the community as a whole. Thus, a corporation will not qualify under § 501(c)(4) if its activities benefit only its membership or a select group of individuals. Still, the group benefitted may be a smaller segment of the public than is required for exemption under § 501(c)(3). Examples of the types of organizations that may qualify for § 501(c)(4) status are civic associations and volunteer fire companies, or organizations engaged in crime prevention.

A § 501(c)(4) corporation may not, as its primary activity, conduct a business with the general public in a commercial manner.

## Comparison of § 501(c)(3) and § 501(c)(4) Exemption Status

Although the requirements for § 501(c)(3) and § 501(c)(4) appear to be similar, a corporation may more easily satisfy the requirements of § 501(c)(4). First, it may benefit a smaller or more specific group or community than would qualify a corporation for charitable status under § 501(c)(3). Second, a § 501(c)(4) organization may engage in a greater amount of social activities, a greater amount of lobbying activities, and some, as opposed to no, political activities.

Note, however, that § 501(c)(3) status is preferable to § 501(c)(4) status if tax-deductible contributions or tax-exempt financing is important to the organization. Still, § 501(c)(4) status may be more advantageous if:

- lobbying will be a substantial part of the corporation's activities;
- freedom to support or oppose candidates for public office is sought; or

- the organization would be subject to the restrictions imposed on a private foundation (as discussed above) if the organization were exempt under § 501(c)(3).

Still, if an organization was once exempt as a § 501(c)(3) organization, but has lost its exemption because of lobbying or political campaign activities, it cannot then convert into a § 501(c)(4) organization.[8]

# Section 501(c)(6) Organizations

Nonprofit business leagues, chambers of commerce, trade associations, boards of trade, and professional football leagues may qualify as § 501(c)(6) organizations.

## Requirements for Exemption

A § 501(c)(6) corporation is an association of persons having a common business interest. Its purpose is to promote this interest; therefore, no part of the net earnings may inure to the benefit of any private shareholder or individual (such as members). These corporations must improve the business condition of the industry in general, rather than benefiting individual members by supplying these members with such things as management services, or improving the economy and convenience of conducting individual businesses. The corporation may satisfy this requirement if, as a whole, it represents all components of an industry or line of business within a particular geographic area. The corporation generally may not, however, be in competition with another group within the same industry or line of business, although members within the corporation may compete with each other.

Certain examples of common activities that may affect a corporation's compliance with § 501(c)(6) are worth noting. On the one hand, activities such as conducting an advertising campaign to promote an industry (rather than particular individuals) and publishing a trade publication for the benefit of an industry generally are considered activities that promote a particular line of business and, hence, are permissible activities. On the other hand, activities such as operating a real estate multiple-listing service and supplying management services and supplies to members have been found to benefit the members individually, rather than promote the industry or line of business as a whole. A § 501(c)(6) corporation may engage in some business activities that do not promote an industry or line of business, subject to the rules relating to unrelated business income (UBI) discussed in the section *"Unrelated Business Income"* below, so long as these activities are not substantial.

## Tax Treatment of Contributions or Dues to a § 501(c)(6) Corporation

As a general rule, contributions or dues payable to a § 501(c)(6) organization may be deductible as trade or business expenses except to the extent they are used to:

(a)    participate in a political campaign on behalf of any candidate for public office;

(b)    engage in certain types of lobbying; or

(c)    attempt to influence legislation that is not of direct interest to the taxpayer's business.

A § 501(c)(6) organization that incurs lobbying or political expenditures is required to notify its members of a reasonable estimate of the portion of their dues allocable to those expenditures, which are nondeductible to the members. If the organization fails to provide this notice, or otherwise elects not to provide it, the organization is required to pay a proxy tax based on the amount of the expenditures.

Contributions to § 501(c)(6) organizations cannot be deducted as charitable contributions.

## Obtaining Tax-Exempt Status

With few exceptions, most § 501(c)(3) corporations must obtain IRS recognition of tax-exempt status; they hold this status only when and if such recognition is valid and applicable. Other tax-exempt organizations (i.e., § 501(c)(4), § 501(c)(6) and other corporations qualifying for exemption under § 501(c) of the Code) should consider obtaining IRS recognition to ensure their tax-exempt status, but generally are not required to do so.

If a corporation is, in fact, organized and operated in accordance with the applicable requirements to qualify for tax exemption under § 501(c) of the Code, the corporation may claim tax-exempt status without the need for an IRS ruling to that effect, *unless* exemption under § 501(c)(3) is sought. Section 501(c)(3) corporations generally are required to obtain recognition of their tax-exempt status from the IRS as a condition to the tax exemption.

Organizations apply for tax-exempt status under Section 501(c)(3) by submitting an application on IRS Form 1023. Section 501(c)(3) corporations that are not subject to the application requirement are (1) churches and certain other church-related corporations, and (2) corporations (other than private foundations) normally having annual gross receipts of not more than $5,000. In addition, certain corporations do not have to apply directly to the IRS for recognition of exemption under § 501(c)(3), because they are covered by a group exemption letter issued to a central organization. Other corporations should consider obtaining IRS recognition to ensure their tax-exempt status.

# Unrelated Business Income (UBI)

Any exempt corporation may be subject to a tax on UBI, if it regularly carries on a trade or business that is unrelated to its exempt purpose. If its unrelated business activities are more than insubstantial, the corporation may lose its tax exemption.

The Code permits an exempt organization to engage in some activities that are not related to its exempt purposes. These activities are permissible so long as the exempt corporation's unrelated activities remain insubstantial when compared to the corporation's exempt activities. Whether an activity is considered substantial is based on all the facts and circumstances, including the amount of income derived from the activity and the expenses and staff time devoted to it. No one factor is controlling.

The Code imposes a tax on income generated from the conduct of an "unrelated trade or business," generally at standard corporate tax rates, and organizations must report this income on IRS Form 990-T. Certain passive types of investment income, such as rents, dividends, and interest, are generally excluded from taxation.

If the corporation conducts unrelated activities, a director should have a basic understanding of the types of activities that produce UBI to ensure that the organization's unrelated business activities do not become substantial and that procedures are in place to monitor and properly report these activities to the IRS.

## Definition of Unrelated Trade or Business

An *unrelated trade or business* is any trade or business that is *regularly carried on, the conduct of which is not substantially related to the corporation's exempt purposes.* For example, a tax-exempt corporation may sell advertising in its otherwise educational publications.

An activity is *regularly carried on* if the activity is conducted with the frequency and continuity comparable to commercial activities of for-profit ventures.

An activity is *substantially related* (i.e., not unrelated) to the corporation's exempt purposes if it contributes importantly to the accomplishment of the corporation's exempt purposes other than through producing income. The need for the funds generated by the activity does not make it substantially related.

The Code excludes several types of activities from the definition of *unrelated trade or business.* An activity will not be treated as an unrelated trade or business if:

- substantially all of the work is performed by volunteers;
- it is carried on primarily by a § 501(c)(3) organization for the benefit of its members, students, patients, officers, or employees;
- it consists of selling merchandise, substantially all of which has been donated;
- it relates to the distribution of low-cost articles in connection with charitable solicitations; or
- the business consists of a legal bingo game, in a state where bingo games are ordinarily not conducted on a commercial basis.

## Types of Income Excluded from UBI

The Code excludes the following types of income from UBI unless this income is debt-financed:

- dividends, interest, payments with respect to securities loans, and annuities;
- royalties;
- most rents from real property;
- insubstantial rents from personal property when leased with real property; and
- gain from the sale of capital assets.[9]

In addition, certain research income is excluded from UBI.

## Use of a Taxable Subsidiary

As noted above, an exempt corporation may conduct an insubstantial amount of unrelated activities itself. It is not necessary to establish a separate taxable corporation for these activities. Still, an exempt corporation may choose to create a taxable subsidiary through which to conduct unrelated activities, especially if these activities would otherwise become substantial and thereby jeopardize the corporation's exempt status, or for nontax reasons, such as the desire to limit the corporation's liabilities.

If a taxable subsidiary is formed, the subsidiary itself will be taxed on the income from the activities, but dividends paid by the taxable subsidiary to the exempt parent generally will not be subject to UBI. Still, the tax-exempt parent of a taxable subsidiary should be aware that for all such subsidiaries in which the parent nonprofit holds more than a 50 percent ownership interest, the tax-exempt corporation's receipt of rent, royalties, interest, and other types of income from the subsidiary may be taxable as UBI. (This is in contrast to the usual rule, under which a tax-exempt corporation's receipt of rent, royalties, interest, and similar kinds of "passive" income is not taxable as UBI, provided that such income is received from an entity unrelated to the tax-exempt corporation.)

Another possible option for a nonprofit needing a separate business organization for liability purposes is the organization of a single member limited liability company. For tax purposes, this entity can be treated either as a corporation or a single member "disregarded entity." In most cases, the nonprofit decides to have the limited liability company treated as a "disregarded entity" with the parent being taxed as a sole proprietor for income tax purposes. The disregarded entity's activities, revenues, and expenses are treated as those of the nonprofit and reported on its Form 990. Thus, this approach does not address the issue of "too much" UBI.

The use of a subsidiary requires careful tax planning as, in general, decisions made in the process are usually irrevocable. For example, future transfers of property from a taxable subsidiary to the exempt corporation and the eventual liquidation of the subsidiary may result in certain adverse tax consequences. For further discussion of issues to be considered by tax-exempt corporation directors regarding use of taxable subsidiaries, see *Chapter 5, Creation of For-Profit Subsidiaries and Joint Ventures*.

# Advertisements vs. Sponsorship Acknowledgements

### *Acknowledgements vs. advertisements*

Directors of tax-exempt entities should understand the difference, both in terms of donor deductibility and UBI treatment, between revenues received from sponsors for which the tax-exempt organization provides public acknowledgement and revenues received in exchange for advertising.

Revenues received from corporate sponsors who are then publicly acknowledged by the tax-exempt organization—in a statement that recites only basic and "fact neutral" information about the sponsoring organization, such as its name, contact information, logo, or slogan—are generally deductible by the sponsor as a tax-exempt contribution. Provided the event being sponsored is substantially related to the tax-exempt corporation's purposes, such revenues would not be subject to taxation as UBI. In contrast, revenues received by a tax-exempt corporation for advertisements—such as an ad for a dance apparel store in the program for the annual recital of a local ballet school—would be considered payment for advertising and not be deductible as a charitable contribution by the apparel store.[10]

Some distinguishing characteristics of advertising are that it presents advantages of a product or urges purchase of a product. In this example, if the apparel store also underwrote a portion of the recital costs, and was acknowledged as a corporate sponsor in that regard, the store could deduct the portion of its payment to the school that exceeded the regular cost of the ad. In such a case, the payment by the sponsor may not be considered fully tax-deductible as a charitable contribution. Moreover, depending on the context (e.g., was the payment made in connection with an activity that is "regularly carried on" by the organization, or was it for a discrete event, such as the annual recital?), the money the sponsor paid for advertising may be considered taxable UBI to the exempt organization.

### *Different treatment of advertisements in periodicals*

If advertising revenue is considered taxable as UBI to the tax-exempt organization, the amount of UBI tax payable will depend on whether or not the ad revenue was generated from an advertisement in a periodical publication, such as a monthly newsletter or magazine, or in a nonperiodical publication. Ad revenue that is UBI will be taxed at a lower rate if the ad appeared in a periodical. Still, in some cases, it is difficult to determine whether a publication is a periodical for which the lower UBI tax calculation would apply. The general rule is that advertising within material that appears on a regular periodic schedule, within a standard format, is likely to be considered a periodical, whereas material that appears perennially with regular updates (like a brochure) would not.

# Special Reporting Requirements

## Noncharitable Contributions

The director must understand that exemption from federal income tax does not necessarily mean that donations to the corporation are deductible as charitable contributions. If deductibility is not available, the corporation must disclose this fact—including disclosures on dues statements.

Any tax-exempt corporation or political organization that is not eligible to receive charitable contributions—i.e., any corporation other than a § 501(c)(3) corporation—is required to disclose to its donors "in a conspicuous and easily recognizable format" in all fundraising solicitations, whether in written or printed form, by television or radio, or by telephone, that contributions to it are not deductible as charitable contributions for federal income tax purposes.[11] A dues statement or solicitation of a § 501(c)(4) or § 501(c)(6) organization counts as a fundraising solicitation for this purpose.

## Charitable Contributions

Any contribution to a charitable organization of $250 or more may only be deductible as a charitable contribution to the donor if the donor receives contemporaneous substantiation from the charitable organization as to the receipt of the donation.

While technically a charitable organization is under no requirement to provide substantiation of a charitable contribution of $250 or more to a donor, the fact that the donor will not receive a charitable contribution deduction without this substantiation imposes a practical requirement on the charity to provide the information. In general, the charity should supply the substantiation contemporaneously with the receipt of the contribution and, additionally, describe the property donated and state whether any goods or services were provided in connection with the contribution. Detailed guidance concerning the substantiation requirements is contained in IRS Publication 1771.

Special guidelines apply to donations of motor vehicles, boats, or airplanes if the claimed value exceeds $500.[12]

## Charitable Contributions in Return for Items of Value

If a donor receives an item of value in return for a contribution to a § 501(c)(3) corporation, the Code requires that the donor's deduction be limited to the difference between the amount contributed and the fair market value of the goods or services received by the donor. For example, if a donor contributes $100 and receives a ticket to a symphony concert or a dinner that would normally cost $60, the donor is entitled to deduct $40. In addition, the Code requires that the charity receiving the contribution (provided the contribution is in excess of $75) provide substantiation to the donor estimating the fair market value of the goods or services received in return for the contribution.

Failure to make this disclosure could result in fines against the charity.[13]

## Disclosure of Annual Returns and Exemption Applications

Both annual information returns and IRS exemption applications must be made available by the tax-exempt organizations for public inspection or in copy form.

Tax-exempt corporations must make their annual tax information returns (IRS Form 990 and, for § 501(c)(3) organizations, Form 990-T) and their IRS exemption applications (e.g. Form 1023 for § 501(c)(3) organizations), including all submissions and correspondence, available for public inspection at their principal offices and at all regional offices. (The corporation may, however, withhold the names and addresses of its contributors if it is a public charity and may also withhold any information in the exemption application relating to trade secrets, patents, processes, or styles of work, if the IRS determines that public disclosure of this information would adversely affect the organization.)

These organizations also are required to provide copies of the returns to individuals requesting them, but may charge the requestor reasonable copying fees. Organizations that post copies of their tax returns, exemption applications, and related documents on the Internet (whether on their own website or a compilation site such as GuideStar), are relieved of the obligation to provide physical copies of the documents to requesting individuals. See the section *"Sales of Goods and Services"* in *Chapter 6, Nonprofits on the Internet* for further discussion of Internet postings of Form 990s.

Corporation personnel who have a duty to comply with the public inspection requirements and fail to comply may be subject to penalties. Criminal penalties may be imposed on any person who willfully and knowingly furnishes false or fraudulent information.

# Intermediate Sanctions: Excise Tax on Public Charities' Excess Benefit Transactions

The IRS may impose an excise tax on "disqualified persons" who engage in "excess benefit transactions" with § 501(c)(3) public charities, § 501(c)(4) corporations, and § 501(c)(29) consumer-operated and -oriented plans (CO-OPs). In addition, the IRS may impose an excise tax on any "organization manager" of such a tax-exempt organization that knowingly approved the excess benefit transaction. The IRS may impose "intermediate sanctions" for transactions that previously could have been punished only with revocation of an organization's tax-exempt status.

Section 501(c)(3) organizations that are private foundations are subject to the range of restrictions and taxes described in the section *"Restrictions and Taxes on Private Foundations"* above. The intermediate sanctions for excess benefit transactions impose taxes that are similar to the private foundation self-dealing taxes, but apply to § 501(c)(3) public charities, § 501(c)(4) corporations, and § 501(c)(29) CO-OPs. One significant difference, however, is that intermediate sanctions are imposed only on transactions that are not at fair market value (hence the term "excess benefit" transactions), while the private foundation self-dealing rules apply to any covered transactions whether or not at fair market value. Another difference is that the excise tax is imposed on the amount constituting the "excess benefit" whereas, the self-dealing tax is based on the entire amount involved.

## Potential for Imposing Intermediate Sanctions

Every member of a board of directors of a § 501(c)(3) public charity or § 501(c)(4) organization should be aware of the possibility of financial sanctions that could be imposed on board members, officers, and related persons as a result of transactions that the IRS determines provide "excess benefits" to a related ("disqualified") person.

An excess benefit transaction is a transaction, such as the payment of compensation or the transfer of property, in which a disqualified person receives more than fair market value from the exempt organization or pays the exempt organization less than fair market value for property or services received. The tax imposed on the disqualified person is 25 percent of the excess benefit amount. If the excess benefit transaction is not corrected (for example, through repayment), a second-tier tax of 200 percent of the excess benefit amount can be imposed.

The IRS defines the term *disqualified person* as any person who, at any time during the five-year period ending on the date of the transaction, was in a position to exercise substantial influence over the organization's affairs. The term also includes family members of an individual described in the previous sentence and any entity in which disqualified persons in the aggregate control 35 percent of the voting interests. For most § 501(c)(3) and § 501(c)(4) organizations, disqualified persons includes directors/trustees, officers, and "substantial contributors" to the organization. Disqualified persons will include top-management employees. Whether a person has substantial influence over the organization's affairs, however, is a facts and circumstances test. Accordingly, the definition is potentially much broader than the aforementioned categories. For example, it may include substantial contributors, founders, and others.

## Taxes on Directors, Officers, and Other Managers

In addition to imposing an excise tax on disqualified persons who engage in excess benefit transactions, the IRS has the authority to impose excise taxes on "organization managers" who knowingly approved an excess benefit transaction. An organization manager includes any officer, director, or trustee of an applicable tax-exempt organization, or any individual having the powers or responsibilities similar to those of officers, directors, or trustees of the organization. The tax is 10 percent of the excess benefit amount, up to a collective maximum of $20,000 per transaction.

## Procedures for Establishing Reasonableness

In determining whether there is an excess benefit transaction, the reasonableness of compensation and the fair market value of transactions are determined under existing tax law standards. Still, there is a rebuttable presumption of reasonableness if the transaction with a disqualified person is approved in advance by an independent board or committee, comprised of individuals without a conflict of interest, who obtained and relied on appropriate objective data as to comparability, and documented the basis for their determination contemporaneously in the minutes of the relevant board or committee meeting.

If the procedures for the rebuttable presumption are met, the burden of proof is on the IRS to demonstrate unreasonableness. Even without the presumption, benefits provided to disqualified persons are not excess benefit transactions if it can be demonstrated that they are part of a fair market value exchange of goods or services. In this connection, however, payment of personal expenses and benefits and non-fair-market-value transactions benefiting disqualified persons can only be justified as reasonable compensation for services if it is clear that the organization intended and made the payments as compensation for services at the time the payments were made.

Form 990 requires information with regard to excess benefit transactions. In addition, an exempt organization's reimbursement of expenses incurred by a disqualified person paid under an arrangement that is a "nonaccountable plan" is treated as an "automatic" excess benefit transaction without regard to whether the economic benefit is reasonable, any other compensation the disqualified person may have received is reasonable, or the aggregate of the reimbursements and any other compensation the disqualified person may have received is reasonable.[14]

The enactment of intermediate sanctions does not alter the actual standards of conduct for tax-exempt organizations; instead, it simply provides another mechanism for IRS enforcement of existing standards. In particular, the intermediate sanctions legislation does not eliminate revocation of exempt status as a penalty for organizations that commit egregious or repeated violations of the laws governing exempt organizations.

A full discussion of the excess benefit transaction excise tax is beyond the scope of this publication. Nonetheless, § 501(c)(3) and § 501(c)(4) organizations are encouraged to consult with their legal advisers to establish procedures that will protect parties with whom the organization deals, and its directors/trustees, officers, and other organization managers, from the potential imposition of significant personal excise taxes.

# Governance and IRS Form 990

Directors of tax-exempt organizations should know that IRS Form 990 is a disclosure document and has extensive reporting requirements that require organizations to make more intrusive inquiries into the personal and business dealings of directors and between and among directors, their family members, and businesses. The reporting requirements are complex, and the exempt organization must spent significant time and effort to collect, review and analyze the information and track these relationships across affiliates.

The disclosure approach of the Form 990 means that a significant amount of information is to be available to the public about governance operations and board relationships. Certain of the questions require disclosure of complex and indirect relationships that may not be well understood by the average reader.

Governance-related disclosures can be found on the Form and on certain of the related schedules to the Form. Part VI of the core form contains questions on the governing body and management, governance policies, and disclosure practices. (There are also questions in other parts of the Form 990 that relate to governance issues, including Part VII (compensation) and Part XII (financial statements and reporting).) Questions in Part VI cover board size and structure, conflicts of interest management, trustee independence, intra board relationships, audit committee practices, conflicts of interest management, governance policies, and how key corporate and financial documents are disclosed to the public. Additional discussion of governance questions that must be addressed in Form 990 can be found in the section "*Discharging the Duty of Care: Some Practical Suggestions: Form 990 Governance Focus Areas*", at *Chapter 2, Duties and Rights of Nonprofit Corporation Directors.*

## IRS Governance Guidelines

Although the Code does not itself mandate governance requirements for tax-exempt organizations, the IRS believes that well-governed organizations are more likely to be tax compliant. Therefore, the IRS has designed questions on the Form 990 to elicit information about governance practices. Form 990 requests information on practices or policies that are not required by federal tax law. Still, good governance and accountability practices provide safeguards that the organization's assets will be used consistently with its exempt purposes. This is a critical tax compliance consideration, especially for organizations that are subject to private benefit, excess benefit, and private inurement prohibitions.[15] Moreover, although there are no right or wrong answers to the questions asked in Part VI of Form 990, the responses may be significant not only to the IRS, but also to donors, grant-makers, rating agencies, state regulators, community stakeholders, and the press. Further discussion on the types of policies covered by the Form 990 is in *Chapter 2, Duties and Rights of Nonprofit Corporation Directors.*

The most current and complete explanation of the IRS position on governance of charities is evident in Form 990, as explained in more detail in the Form 990 Instructions and in the IRS's website educational materials.[16]

## Conflict of Interest Disclosures

In addition to the governance-related disclosures discussed above, the specific details of interested party transactions that meet certain thresholds must be disclosed on the Form 990, including the names of the interested persons (whether director, family member, or related entity, and the dollar amount and description of the relationship).

## Independence

The Form 990 Instructions contain a definition of "independence" that is substantially different from prior IRS interpretations of how an exempt organization should evaluate the independence of its board members. One key difference is that Form 990 independence requires that the trustee have no "interested party transaction" (as defined under the Instructions) with the tax-exempt organization. Thus, the IRS has linked conflict of interest matters to independence for purposes of the Form 990 reporting.

"Independence" for Form 990 reporting purposes requires satisfaction of *all three* of the following during the tax year:

1.   The director was not compensated as an officer by the organization or an affiliate,

2.   The director was not an independent contractor who received more than $10,000 from the organization or an affiliate, AND

3.   Neither the director nor a family member, directly or indirectly, was involved in an interested party transaction with the organization reportable on the Form 990, schedule L (which requires reporting of any excess benefit transaction with an insider (in IRS terms, a "disqualified person"); any loans to or from an interested person; grants or other assistance benefitting an interested person; or other business transactions involving any interested person).

# IRS Revocation of Tax-Exempt Status

The Pension Protection Act of 2006 (PPA) imposed a requirement on most tax-exempt organizations to file an annual information return or notice (Form 990, Form 990EZ, or Form 990N) with the IRS. For small organizations, the law imposed a filing requirement for the first time in 2007. Under the law, tax-exempt status is automatically revoked for any organization that fails to file the required return or notice for three consecutive years.

As a result of the PPA, thousands of organizations have automatically lost their tax-exempt status because they did not file legally required annual returns or notices for three consecutive years. A list of the automatically revoked organizations is maintained on a searchable database maintained on the IRS website at www.irs.gov. The effective date of the automatic revocation for an organization that does not file a required annual return for three consecutive years is the filing due date of the third year's return. The consequence of loss of tax exemption is that there is income tax on earned income, there is a requirement to file a Form 1120 for a corporation or Form 1041 for a trust, no deductions are permitted for donors and there is possible liability for sales tax, property tax and other types of taxes that were based at least in part on the organization's federal tax-exempt status.

For organizations that have had their tax-exempt status automatically revoked, the organization may seek reinstatement. An organization must apply to have its tax-exempt status reinstated even it was not originally required to file an application for the exemption. An organization also may request reinstatement back to the date of automatic revocation by showing "reasonable cause" and filing the application for reinstatement within a certain time period.

# Conclusion

It is important that a director of a nonprofit organization understand the nature of the organization's federal tax-exempt status and the fundamental limitations on these organizations. For Section 501(c)(3) organizations, this includes a basic understanding of private inurement and private benefit, intermediate sanctions, and the lobbying and campaign activity rules. It also is important that a director understand the importance of Form 990 and be involved in reviewing it annually.

*See the Suggested Questions and Checklist following the Endnotes below to review the issues discussed in this chapter.*

# Endnotes

1. Our discussion, even of these limited areas, is based on the law as it stood when this chapter was written. The Code is usually amended in some manner with each session of Congress, and the IRS periodically issues new rulings and interpretations that change the general understanding of tax law provisions. As a result, some statements contained in this discussion may be incomplete or inaccurate when they meet the reader's eyes. Nonetheless, the issues addressed are permanent.

2. Although many states rely on federal tax-exempt status in determining exemption from state income tax, some require separate filings. In addition, the requirements for exemption from real property and sales taxes typically may be more stringent than those in federal tax law. Generally, only certain § 501(c)(3) organizations (and usually not all of them) will qualify for these exemptions, but the criteria vary from state to state.

3. As shown in the list provided in Appendix A, § 501(a) of the Code recognizes a series of tax-exempt organizations, but the list includes some entities that are outside the focus of this *Guidebook.* Three significant types of tax-exempt organizations not included in the Appendix A are trusts held under qualified pension plans, state and local government instrumentalities, and political organizations.

4. An organization also may qualify under § 501(c)(3) if it is organized for testing for public safety; fostering national or international amateur sports competition (if no part of its activities involve providing athletic facilities or equipment); or preventing cruelty to children or animals.

5. The limits on deductibility imposed by § 170(b) range from 20 percent to 50 percent of an individual contributor's income. A discussion of these limits is outside the scope of this *Guidebook*. See, however, *IRS Publication 526, Charitable Contributions.*

6. These requirements are set forth in detail in IRS Publication 557. The requirements are also explained on the IRS website, www.irs. gov, at the "Charities and Non-Profits" tab. The IRS has developed an educational tool called *"Life Cycle of an Exempt Organization,"* which lays out, by topic area, the regulations applicable to these organizations and other compliance matters.

7. Churches are not exempt from challenge when they engage in political activities; despite the general reluctance of most government officials to challenge actions of religious organizations, the IRS has not hesitated in this regard. *See, e.g.,* Branch Ministries v. Rossotti, 211 F.3d 137 (D.C. Cir. 2000), *aff'g* 40 F. Supp. 2d 15 (D.D.C. 1999) (revoking the tax-exempt status of Branch Ministries, Inc. dba the Church at Pierce Creek.).

8. *See* I.R.C. § 504(a).

9. I.R.C. § 514 provides a special exception for real property acquired by certain "qualified organizations," including educational institutions and pension trusts. However, interest, rents, royalties, and annuities paid by controlled for-profit subsidiaries to their exempt parent generally will not be excludable from income. To the extent that income is excluded from UBI, any related deductions also are excluded from the computation of tax.

10. *See* I.R.C. § 513(i).

11. I.R.C. § 6113. The rule does not apply to (a) organizations with annual gross receipts of $100,000 or less, or (b) any letter or telephone call if the communication is not part of a coordinated campaign soliciting more than ten persons during the calendar year.

12. *See* IRS Publication No. 4302 and IRS Publication No. 4303.

13. IRS Publication 1771 provides a good summary of the IRS position on this issue.

14. *See* Reg. 53.4958-4(c)(1).

15. Redesigned Form 990 FAQs, at www.irs.gov/charities.

16. The IRS's website has extensive compliance materials for tax-exempt entities at www.irs.gov/charities.

# Suggested Questions for Directors Regarding Taxation

(1)   Is the corporation on whose board I serve exempt from federal income taxation?

(2)   If it is, under what section of the Code is it exempt?

(3)   If it is exempt under § 501(c)(3), is it a private foundation?

(4)   If it is a private foundation, do I understand the special limitations that status imposes? Do the board and staff understand them?

(5)   If we aren't exempt under § 501(c)(3), do we make clear to our donors that they cannot deduct their contributions to us?

(6)   Who prepares our tax returns (Form 990)? What is the process for the board review of Form 990? Have they been filed each year?

(7)   What were the corporation's activities and mission as described to the IRS in applying for an exemption ruling? Is this description still an accurate portrayal of what we do?

(8)   Do I know how much lobbying activity we have engaged in? How much are we allowed under our particular exemption?

(9)   Has the organization made an election with the IRS under § 501(h) for its lobbying activities? If so, are the organization's lobbying expenditures below the permitted dollar limit?

(10)  If we are exempt under § 501(c)(3), do I understand the scope of activities covered by the absolute prohibition on campaign activity by the organization?

(11)  Has the board put procedures in place to ensure that transactions potentially subject to intermediate sanctions are reviewed and documented to the extent it determines appropriate?

(12)  What activities, if any, of our corporation may result in UBI?

(13)  Who on our staff monitors UBI tax matters? Do our independent accountants do so?

# Checklist: Taxation

*Note:*    For purposes of simplicity in these checklists, we describe a corporation with a chair, who pre-sides over the board of directors; a chief executive, who may be a staff person; an executive committee; a governance/nominating committee; and an audit committee. (However, we recognize that in many smaller and other nonprofits, these committee functions may be performed by either the executive committee or the board as a whole.) We also assume a legal counsel—someone, paid or unpaid, having primary responsibility for the corporation's legal affairs. Many corporations, especially larger nonprofits, may have other committees established for specific purposes, such as reviewing staff performance, fixing compensation, monitoring compliance with legal requirements and periodic review of bylaws.

| Subject | Review By | How Often | Comment |
|---|---|---|---|
| 1. If our corporation is exempt from federal income tax, under what section of the Internal Revenue Code is it exempt? | Legal counsel | Upon organization; Annually | Whole board should understand basic nature of the corporation's specific exemption. Information on this subject should be in the director's manual. |
| 2. If it is exempt under Section 501(c)(3), is the corporation a private foundation, a private operating foundation, or a public charity? | Legal counsel, then full board | Upon organization; Annually | Board should understand the privileges or limitations imposed by the applicable provisions of the Code on the corporation's particular type of activity. |

| Subject | Review By | How Often | Comment |
|---|---|---|---|
| 3. If the corporation is exempt under Section 501(c)(3) or Section 501(c)(4) and is not a private foundation, has the corporation established procedures to identify potential excess benefit transactions and obtain the rebuttable presumption of reasonableness where appropriate? | Chief executive, legal counsel | Annually | Boards should determine the level of scrutiny that will be applied to various types of transactions depending on the likelihood that the party is a disqualified person and the significance of the transaction. |

| Subject | Review By | How Often | Comment |
|---|---|---|---|
| 4. If the corporation is exempt under Section 501(c)(3), have we engaged in activities that are limited (lobbying) or prohibited (campaign activity) by virtue of our 501(c)(3) status?  Has the organization made an election to have its lobbying activities covered by Section 501(h) of the Internal Revenue Code? | Legal counsel, then full board | Annually, and during discussion of any major change in contemplated political activities | This is a field of tax law with frequent new interpretations. Section 501(c)(3) organizations should closely monitor activities to ensure compliance. For instance, as discussed in Chapter 6, *"Supervision of Internet Activities,"* whether links from a tax-exempt organization's website to an organization that engages in substantial lobbying activity constitutes lobbying by the organization is an issue the IRS is reviewing. |

| Subject | Review By | How Often | Comment |
|---|---|---|---|
| 5. If the advocacy activities of the corporation are restricted but not prohibited (as in the case of lobbying), have we compared the actual activities undertaken with the restrictions of applicable tax law? | Chief executive, legal counsel | Annually | If these activities are substantial and continuing, the corporation's books should be organized to quantify them. The board should also ask the chief executive or legal counsel to determine if anyone associated with the organization is required to be registered as a lobbyist. |
| 6. If our corporation is exempt from federal income tax, has the board reviewed Form 990? | Legal counsel, then full board | Annually | Form 990 requires the organization to describe the board's involvement in the review of the Form 990. |
| 7. If our corporation is exempt from federal income tax, do we have all of the policies identified in Part VI of Form 990? | Legal counsel, then full board | Annually | Part VI of Form 990 asks whether the corporation has certain written policies and procedures. Although it is not a legal requirement, adoption of many of these policies may be beneficial to the organization. |

# Chapter 5:
## Creating For-Profit Subsidiaries and Joint Ventures

# Chapter 5
# Creating For-Profit Subsidiaries and Joint Ventures

*The board of a nonprofit corporation may decide that the corporation's mission and goals would be served by engaging in an activity that does not easily fit within the corporation's current structure. If this activity is one that is typically engaged in by nonprofit organizations, the board may establish a nonprofit subsidiary or affiliate. However, if the activity is one that will generate taxable income, or is typically conducted by for-profit rather than nonprofit organizations, the board may consider establishing a for-profit subsidiary, or entering into a joint-venture arrangement with a for-profit entity. Set forth below is a summary of many of the issues that a nonprofit board should consider before establishing a for-profit subsidiary or entering into a joint venture with a for-profit organization.[1]*

## Engaging in New Activities

A nonprofit, tax-exempt corporation may find that in order to fulfill its corporate mission, it would be useful to engage in an activity that is outside the general range of activities for which it was organized and is operated. For example, a health care corporation or museum may desire to operate a wellness center or a community organization may find it has an opportunity to buy used computers and resell them to low-income residents. Similarly, a corporation that owns and operates low-income housing may desire to provide housing management services to similar corporations. The revenues derived from these activities may be of a kind not generally treated as exempt from taxation. Nevertheless, the nonprofit's board may believe that engaging in the activity will further its exempt purposes. When a corporation's board considers engaging in such a nonexempt activity, the directors should keep the following considerations in mind:

# Furthering Exempt Purposes

Generally, the nonexempt activity should only be engaged in if it is consistent with the corporation's mission and exempt purposes. The organization could jeopardize its tax exemption if a substantial amount of its activity is deemed to be "unrelated" to the corporation's tax-exempt purpose. In the IRS's view, an activity is treated as unrelated to a § 501(c)(3) corporation's tax-exempt purposes unless it is "substantially related" to such exempt purposes, by "contributing importantly" to the accomplishment of the exempt purposes.

# UBI

If the nonexempt activity is unrelated, in the IRS's view, to the corporation's exempt purposes, the revenue from the activity may be subject to taxation as unrelated business income (UBI) and reported on Form 990-T, which is a publicly available document. However, some forms of unrelated revenue are exempted from taxation, including most forms of investment income and passive income. In addition, revenues derived from unrelated activities that are performed entirely by volunteers; are primarily conducted for the benefit of members, students, officers, or employees; or involve resale of primarily donated items are also exempt from tax.

# Substantiality of Nonexempt Activity

An unrelated, nonexempt activity may be conducted within the corporation as long as it would not constitute a "substantial" part of the organization's overall activity. As a rule of thumb, an activity is likely to not be considered substantial if revenues from the activity are less than 10 percent of the organization's overall revenues—although higher percentages may be permitted in certain circumstances, and lower percentages are recommended for tax-exempt corporations classified as "supporting" organizations under § 509(a)(3) of the Internal Revenue Code (the Code).

# Advantages of Establishing Separate For-Profit Subsidiaries

If a proposed nonexempt activity is of a kind that is likely to be viewed by the IRS as unrelated to the corporation's purposes, the board may decide to place the activity in a separate, for-profit subsidiary, rather than maintaining it within the corporation's structure. Some of the factors that nonprofit boards tend to weigh in favor of establishing a for-profit subsidiary include the following:

(1)    The amount of the unrelated activity, or the income generated by it, could become substantial and thus threaten the corporation's tax-exemption if conducted within the corporation.

(2)    The nonexempt activity requires a substantial devotion of management time and attention, or requires a significant number of employees.

(3)    The activity entails a level of business risk that should be segregated, to the extent possible, from the assets or endowment of the charitable organization.

(4)    The management of the activity requires a kind of expertise not generally present in the corporation's management officers or board.

(5)    It will be easier to recruit management staff for the nonexempt activity if the activity is contained in a separate organization rather than within the confines of the nonprofit corporation.

(6)    The nonexempt activity is best performed in a corporate environment that is less hierarchical, or otherwise distinct from that of the nonprofit.

(7)    The board prefers that the revenues and expenses of the nonexempt activity not be reflected on the income statements and balance sheet of the exempt corporation. (Note, however, that most often an organization owning a majority of the stock of a subsidiary must include the subsidiary's financial statements in its own consolidated financial statement and the Form 990 requires additional disclosure of subsidiaries).

(8)    It is considered desirable or necessary to be able to offer stock or stock options to senior management or other employees associated with the nonexempt activity, in order to recruit and incentivize the performance of these employees. Still, it is important to understand that there can be private benefit concerns regarding issuing stock to insiders.

Once the board has decided to establish a for-profit subsidiary, it will need to decide on the type of new entity, how the new entity will be organized, and the extent and nature of control that the nonprofit corporation will exert over the for-profit.

# Type of Organization

A nonprofit establishing a for-profit subsidiary can choose among several different types of corporate entities. These include, among others, a business corporation, limited liability company (LLC), and limited partnership. A limited liability company is often attractive because of the pass-through tax treatment given to it and the flexibility in its structure.

# Directors or Managers

If the nonprofit owns more than 50 percent of the for-profit, it usually will have the power to elect a majority of the for-profit entity's directors or managers. The board of the nonprofit should determine who will serve as the new entity's initial board of directors or managers, and whether certain director or manager positions should be filled, ex officio, by persons who hold certain officer or director positions with the nonprofit. For instance, the board of the nonprofit could specify that its chair, chief executive and/or chief financial officer will serve ex officio on the for-profit corporation's board, or that one or more of the nonprofit's board members also will serve on the for-profit entity's board. If the new entity is a limited liability company, it also may be member-managed, which would mean the nonprofit's board would, in effect, be making the management decisions for the entity.

# Officers

Depending on the activities of the for-profit, the nonprofit parent may desire to have some degree of overlap between the officers of the nonprofit and its for-profit subsidiary. For instance, when organizing the for-profit subsidiary, the parent nonprofit board may require the subsidiary's bylaws, operating agreement, or other governance document to provide that the chief executive of the nonprofit will serve, ex officio, as the chair of the for-profit subsidiary. This will ensure that the chief executive of the nonprofit parent is kept informed regarding all material operational issues affecting the subsidiary. Alternatively, the nonprofit, as shareholder or member, can elect directors of the subsidiary who will appoint officers acceptable to the nonprofit.

## Other Oversight Mechanisms

The parent board should evaluate what other mechanisms it will use to oversee the operation of the subsidiary. In addition to any director and officer overlap between the parent nonprofit and the for-profit subsidiary, the parent board should determine how often it wishes to receive reports on the subsidiary's operations, and then incorporate such reports on the parent board's agenda. The board also may wish to provide for member or shareholder approval or veto power over significant corporate actions—such as the adoption of budgets. The board should be aware of which corporate actions (such as merger, substantial asset sale, and dissolution) typically require approval by a majority or higher percentage of members or shareholders.

With any subsidiary, it is important to observe certain formalities relating to the exercise of the powers or management of the subsidiary. If the parent company does not do so, the debts, obligations, or other liability of the subsidiary can become the liability of the parent company through a doctrine called "piercing the corporate veil." The doctrine of "piercing the corporate veil" is well-established. In the corporate realm, the disregard of corporate formalities can be a key factor in the piercing analysis. For LLCs, which are less formal, the failure to follow corporate formalities may not be decisive. Still, other factors allowing a piercing, such as a disregard by entity's owner of the entity's economic separateness from its owners, can lead to a piercing of the veil.

## Tax Implications

Any revenue generated by the for-profit subsidiary, if it is a corporation, will be subject to taxation at the corporate level, although dividends to the tax-exempt shareholder would frequently be tax-exempt in its hands, similar to other passive income. (See the discussion in the section *"Types of Income Excluded from UBI"* in *Chapter 4, Taxation.*). Any losses experienced by the for-profit corporation may be offset by the gains from that corporation's other activities. Section 512(b)(13) of the Code provides special rules with respect to any interest, annuities, royalties, or rent paid from the for-profit subsidiary to its tax-exempt parent.

## Other Organizational Issues

Nonprofits that establish a subsidiary will generally find that it is most appropriate to establish this entity under the laws of the state in which the nonprofit is itself incorporated. However, nonprofit corporations may sometimes find it useful to take advantage of favorable provisions in the business entity laws of another state, by forming the subsidiary under the laws of such other state, and registering the subsidiary as a foreign corporation, LLC, or other type of entity doing business in the nonprofit corporation's state. The nonprofit corporation's legal counsel can assist the board and officers in assessing whether the use of a foreign entity offers any significant advantages to offset the administrative inconveniences of organization under a different state.

# Creating Joint Ventures with For-Profits

Nonprofit, tax-exempt corporations may also find it useful in certain circumstances to enter into joint ventures with individuals or for-profit entities. The nonprofit board should make sure that the joint venture is not structured or operated in a manner that would constitute an undue benefit to its for-profit partner or other for-profit entities.[2] A tax-exempt corporation that is a prospective partner in a joint venture (whether organized as an LLC, partnership, or corporation) must take care to structure the joint venture, and the nonprofit's role in it, in a manner that minimizes the risk that the nonprofit's participation might put the organization's tax-exemption in jeopardy or generate unexpected UBI.

Even if the tax-exempt corporation's participation in a for-profit joint venture is only a small part of the tax-exempt's total activities, the tax-exempt should exercise a level of control over the venture's operational issues that will assure that the venture operates in furtherance of the tax-exempt organization's charitable purposes. This is particularly true in the case of joint ventures structured as partnerships or LLCs. With such "pass-through" entities, the IRS attributes the acts of the partnership (or LLC) entity as being the actions of the joint-venture partners.[3] To evaluate whether a tax-exempt corporation's participation in the joint venture is in furtherance of tax-exempt purposes, the IRS will look at such issues as:

(1)   Does the nonprofit appoint a majority of the joint-venture's governing body?

(2)   Does the nonprofit have a veto power over significant for-profit venture actions?  Does the nonprofit have the ability to affirmatively require the venture to take action?

(3)   Will a for-profit entity (whether a partner, a partner's affiliate, or unrelated third party) manage the operations of the joint venture? If so, what is the term of the management contract? How are the management fees determined?

(4)   Do the governing documents of the joint venture explicitly provide that the joint venture will be operated consistently with the charitable purposes of the tax-exempt partner? Does the tax-exempt partner have the ability to require the joint venture to put charitable purposes ahead of economic objectives?

(5)   Will the compensation paid to the joint venture's officers and vendors (especially the for-profit partner or any affiliate) be reasonable in light of the services or goods provided?

(6)   Will the joint venture use space financed by tax-exempt bonds? If so, have the implications of such "bad use" on the tax exemption of the bonds been considered?

# Joint Venture Policy

Joint ventures involving tax-exempt organizations have become a focus of the IRS and information regarding joint venture activities is required to be disclosed in the Form 990. Form 990 requires information with regard to whether or not a nonprofit has invested in, contributed assets to, or otherwise participated in the joint venture or similar arrangement with one or more taxable entities within the past taxable year. A "yes" response requires the organization to state whether it has adopted a written policy or procedures requiring the organization to evaluate its participation in joint venture arrangements and has taken steps to safeguard the organization's exempt status with respect to such arrangements. The type of joint venture policy contemplated by the Form 990 should describe the type of activities subject to the policy. It also should require the organization to take steps to ensure that participation in the joint venture is in furtherance of tax-exempt purposes with an evaluation of the factors described above.

In addition, a policy should require that any joint venture be in writing and include the following minimum requirements: (1) with respect to any "whole operation" joint venture (i.e., a joint venture in which the nonprofit contributes essentially all of its assets to the enterprise), the nonprofit maintains control of the joint venture through majority voting rights and/or veto powers; (2) with respect to an ancillary joint venture (i.e., a joint venture in which a portion of the nonprofit's resources are contributed), the nonprofit maintains control over tax-exempt aspects of the joint venture and voting and ownership interests in the joint venture that are consistent with contributions; (3) any dealings between the parties to the joint venture must be at arm's length and for fair market value; (4) the joint venture must give priority to the nonprofit's tax-exempt purposes over maximization of profit for the participants of the joint venture; and (5) activities that would jeopardize the nonprofit's tax-exempt status are prohibited.

# Taxation of Joint Venture Revenue

Any income generated by the joint venture will be subject to tax at the joint venture level, if the joint venture is a "regular" (or C) corporation. However, joint ventures structured as tax pass-through entities—that is, partnerships and LLCs—will not be taxed at the entity level. If the joint venture is appropriately structured to further the purposes of the tax-exempt partner, the tax-exempt organization's share of joint venture revenue (that is, LLC/partnership revenue allocations) should be exempt from taxation, and not treated as UBI. Joint venture interests in S corporations present special issues. Although S corporations are generally pass-through entities, the Code specifically provides that all of an exempt S corporation shareholder's allocated income is UBI.

The UBI rules are complex. As an illustration, joint venture income that is passive (such as rents, royalties, and interest) would not ordinarily be taxed to the nonprofit when "passed through." However, any otherwise nontaxable joint venture income will be taxed to the nonprofit (at least in part) if the venture is debt-financed or if the nonprofit acquired its joint venture interest with debt. Any nonprofit contemplating a joint venture with for-profit entities should thoroughly explore the structure with tax counsel. (See the section *"Unrelated Business Income"* in *Chapter 4, Taxation.*)

*See the Suggested Questions and Checklist following the Endnotes below to review the issues discussed in this chapter.*

# Endnotes

1.    For a detailed discussion of legal issues that arise in partnerships and joint ventures involving nonprofit corporations, *see* Michael I. Sanders, *Joint Ventures Involving Tax-Exempt Organizations* (John Wiley & Sons, 3d ed 2007).

2.    The IRS is giving increasing scrutiny to nonprofit joint ventures with private individuals or for-profit entities. *See* I.R.S. Rev. Rul. 98-15, 1998-1 C. B. 718; Rev. Rul. 2004-51, 2004-1 C.B. 974.

3.    *See* Redlands Surgical Servs. v. Commissioner, 113 T.C. 47 (1999), *aff'd per curiam*, 242 F.3d 904 (9th Cir. 2001).

# Suggested Questions for Directors Regarding For-Profit Subsidiaries and Joint Ventures

(1)    Is the corporation contemplating engaging in any new business activities or joint ventures?

(2)    If so, is this activity substantially related to the corporation's nonprofit purposes?

(3)    Do we know if the new activity or joint venture will generate UBI?

(4)    What are the reasons for or against putting a new activity in a taxable subsidiary, or conducting it with another party through a joint venture, rather than conducting the activity through a division within the corporation?

(5)    If the board wants to establish a subsidiary involved in taxable activities, what will be the form of the subsidiary? Who will serve as the subsidiary's officers and directors/managers? How will the nonprofit parent board exercise oversight on the subsidiary?

(6)    In what state should a subsidiary or joint venture be established?

(7)    For joint ventures to be engaged in by a tax-exempt nonprofit, what controls has the organization put into place to assure that the venture operates in furtherance of the nonprofit partner's charitable purposes?

(8)    How will the joint venture be organized (general partnership, LLC, corporation, etc.)? What are the advantages of this form over another alternative?

(9)    Will the joint venture use space that was financed by tax-exempt bonds?

(10)   Who would be part of the organization's proposed joint venture? Will this party provide goods or services to the joint venture? What controls are in place to assure that the other joint venturer does not profit from the venture at the expense of the venture or the nonprofit partner?

# Checklist: For-Profit Subsidiaries and Joint Ventures

*Note:*    For simplicity, these and other chapter checklists describe a corporation having a chair, who pre-sides over the board of directors; a chief executive, who may be a staff person; an executive committee; a governance/nominating committee; and an audit committee. (We recognize, however, that in many smaller and other nonprofits, these committee functions may be performed by either the executive committee or the board as a whole.) We also assume a legal counsel—someone, paid or unpaid, having primary responsibility for the corporation's legal affairs. Many corporations, especially larger nonprofits, may have other committees established for specific purposes, such as establishing executive compensation; monitoring compliance with legal requirements; and overseeing investments and other financial matters.

| Subject | Review By | How Often | Comment |
|---|---|---|---|
| 1. Are there any new taxable activities planned by the corporation that might be best conducted through a subsidiary or joint venture? | Full board and chief executive | At least annually | The chief executive should recommend, and the board should decide, if any such activities should be kept within the corporation or placed in a separate entity. |
| 2. For existing subsidiaries and joint ventures, how often is the board apprised of financial and business issues for these entities? | Full board and chief executive | At least quarterly, with detailed reviews at least annually | |
| 3. Are the activities and organizational form of existing subsidiaries or joint ventures consistent with the organization's nonprofit purposes? | Full board, chief executive, legal counsel | At least annually | The board should monitor the evolution of such affiliates' activities to ensure consistency with the organization's purposes. |

| Subject | Review By | How Often | Comment |
|---|---|---|---|
| 4. How much UBI, if any, have subsidiaries or joint ventures generated for the nonprofit? | Full board, chief financial officer | At least annually | |
| 5. Does a joint venture partner provide management or other services or goods to the joint venture? If so, does this partner derive any revenues in excess of those that would be paid to an unrelated party on an arms'- length basis? | Full board, chief executive, chief financial officer | Quarterly, with detailed reviews annually | Management contracts with for-profit joint venture partners are subject to close scrutiny for private inurement and other tax-exemption concerns. |
| 6. Does the corporation have a joint venture policy? | Full board, governance/ nominating committee, chief executive | At least annually | Form 990 asks for information regarding joint ventures. |

# Chapter 6:
## Nonprofits On The Internet:  Fundraising, Selling Goods And Services, Lobbying, And Other Activities

# Chapter 6

# Nonprofits on the Internet: Fundraising, Selling Goods and Services, Lobbying, and Other Activities

*Nonprofit corporations are subject to various state and federal requirements depending on their activities. These include, for example, requirements relating to fundraising, lobbying and political activity, intellectual property, sales tax, and privacy. With many of these activities being conducted through the Internet, it is necessary to not only be aware of the legal requirements relating to these activities, but also to the requirements relating to use of the Internet. Although the law generally applicable to the particular issue continues to apply, the actual application of the law to activities on the Internet continues to evolve.*

*Lawmakers, regulators, and judges across the country are in the process of determining how various laws written for the traditional economy fit the virtual world of the Internet. Although this chapter is designed to alert nonprofit corporation directors to some of the major legal implications of certain activities and the involvement of the Internet in these activities, specific statements may become inaccurate, or less accurate, over time. (For instance, it can be expected that the IRS will continue to make, and periodically revise, pronouncements on many of the topics discussed below.) Nonprofit boards should make sure that their corporation's activities, including those conducted through the Internet, are reviewed by legal counsel on a regular basis, to ensure compliance with changing legal standards.*

# Potential Hazards and Benefits of Using the Internet

The Internet offers a highly convenient and cost-effective tool for communicating a nonprofit corporation's purposes and conducting some of its activities. Still, use of the Internet may implicate a number of legal issues applicable to nonprofit corporations generally. Some of the more significant of these general laws are discussed below. Although it may be unlikely that any one nonprofit would simultaneously (if ever) encounter all of the issues discussed below, a broad range of potential issues is presented here to alert directors to the wide variety of legal issues that could be raised by different forms of Internet activity.

# Fundraising

## Charitable Solicitation Registration Requirements

### General rule

Most states and many local governments require nonprofit organizations and their fundraisers to register before soliciting contributions in that jurisdiction. These jurisdictions have regulations relating to telephone, mail, and other types of solicitations from organizations that are not physically located in the solicitation area.[1] A majority of the states that require charitable solicitation registration accept the Unified Registration Statement form for charitable solicitations, which was developed to ease the burden on charitable organizations of filling out multiple different registrations forms. Many of these states require state-specific appendices to be submitted with the United Registration Statement.

Related to state registration requirements, a number of states require certain information to be disclosed by charitable organizations on written solicitations, prior to conducting telephone solicitations, upon confirmation of a gift or pledge, and when receipting gifts.[2] These disclosure requirements are intended to protect donors from fraudulent organizations soliciting funds through the use of false or misleading information. Each state's requirements differ and the definitions of "solicitation" can be quite broad, capturing any direct or indirect request or invitation to contribute.

### *Application to the Internet*

Most jurisdictions are still determining what constitutes sufficient presence over the Internet to require registration under the jurisdiction's charitable solicitation laws. Any organization that raises funds over the Internet should be sure that it keeps abreast of the evolving standards that apply to such fundraising.

The Internet allows nonprofits to communicate with a large audience of potential new donors, generally at less expense than traditional fundraising methods. Many nonprofits have identified this opportunity and developed websites that describe their organizations' purposes, activities, upcoming events, contact information, and more. They also may include statements that directly solicit contributions. For example, some nonprofits provide a form on their websites that enables donors to make contributions on-line, using their credit cards.

It is unlikely that most jurisdictions will require registration of nonprofit organizations that only maintain a passive web page and merely provides information on the organization without requesting donations. In contrast, registration may be required if a nonprofit actively solicits donations by e-mail to persons located in the jurisdiction or permits donors to make contributions by providing their credit card numbers on the organization's website. The registration requirements are less clear for nonprofits that provide the opportunity for donations to be made over the Internet via their website, but which do not otherwise actively solicit donations in specific jurisdictions.

Directors should expect both that the rules in this area will continue to be refined, and that different jurisdictions may take different approaches. Accordingly, directors should periodically check with counsel whether the organization's website or other Internet activity subjects it to the charitable solicitation laws of different jurisdictions—both in and out of the United States.

The National Association of Attorneys General (NAAG) and the National Association of State Charity Officers (NASCO) issued a set of principles relating to regulation of charitable solicitations over the Internet called the "Charleston Principles."[3] Under these principles, an organization should register with the state if (1) it is domiciled in the state; (2) its non-Internet activities require registration; (3) it specifically targets persons physically located in the state for solicitation; or (4) it receives contributions from persons in the state on a repeated and ongoing basis or a substantial basis through its website. Although these principles are not legally mandated, they can serve as very useful guidance as to the expectations of state attorneys generals.

Questions that are likely to be relevant to the issue of whether an organization's Internet activities are deemed to make it subject to regulation in a particular jurisdiction include the following:

> (1)    Must individuals take the initiative to go to the organization's website, or does the organization contact prospective donors (such

as through e-mail) and request that they log on to the website and make a donation?

(2)   Does the organization's website have a mechanism for corresponding (by e-mail or regular mail) with persons who express an interest in the organization after visiting the website?

(3)   Does the organization's website have a mechanism for accepting contributions by donors who provide credit card information?

(4)   How much money is raised in a particular jurisdiction through Internet activities?

It is advisable to review the applicable disclosure statement requirements to determine whether they may apply to online-giving web pages or other Internet solicitation content, even if the organization is not required to register with the state.

## Acknowledging Donors' Contributions

### *General rule*

Federal tax law requires a donor contributing $250 or more to a charitable corporation to obtain a written receipt for the contribution before filing a federal income tax return in order to claim a charitable contribution deduction for the donation.[4] Similarly, charitable organizations that receive contributions of more than $75 in connection with the provision to the donor of a certain amount of goods or services—such as a seat at a table for a charity dinner (quid pro quo contributions)—must provide the donor with a written statement estimating the deductible portion of the contribution, above the value of the goods or services the donor received.[5] These requirements apply regardless of whether the contribution is made in person, over the telephone, through traditional mail or over the Internet. See the section *"Charitable Contribution"* in *Chapter 4, Taxation.*

### *Application to the Internet*

Charitable corporations that allow contributions to be made over the Internet should be sure the corporation has a system in place for acknowledging such contributions that complies with current IRS acknowledgement requirements. An acknowledgment provided by e-mail, or that can be provided off the organization's website, will satisfy this donation acknowledgement requirement.[6]

# Allowing Other Organizations to Raise Money for the Corporation

## *General rules*

**Registration requirements.** A nonprofit organization may use an individual or other organization to generate donations. Such an individual or group may need to register under the charitable solicitation rules of the jurisdiction in which donations are solicited. A nonprofit organization should ensure that any third party with which it contracts for these services is properly registered, given that the third party may create a compliance risk for the nonprofit organization. To protect against such a risk, a nonprofit organization may require in its contract with a third party that the third party indemnify the nonprofit organization for any damages (including penalties) incurred by the organization as a result of the third party's failure to comply with the applicable registration laws. The ability to terminate the contract immediately without any penalty in the event of a third party's failure to comply with the registration laws also helps protect the nonprofit organization.

**Fundraiser as agent of the tax-exempt corporation.** If the individual or group is not itself tax-exempt, the fundraiser must qualify as an agent of the tax-exempt entity in order for the donor's contribution to be tax-deductible. If the fund-raiser is considered the organization's agent, contributions to such an agent are deductible in the same way that direct contributions are deductible. In contrast, if a non-tax-exempt fundraiser is not the agent of a tax-exempt organization, contributions to the fundraiser will not be tax-deductible to the donor.

**Fundraising resulting from sales by taxable entities; commercial co-ventures.** Another way that a tax-exempt organization may raise funds is through an arrangement to receive a percentage of the sales of goods sold by a taxable entity to supporters of the tax-exempt organization. For instance, a taxable entity may volunteer, or agree, to make donations to the tax-exempt entity based on purchases made by organization supporters on a certain day or during some other time period. Similarly, for-profit stores may sell to nonprofits coupons or "scrip" for store products, at a discount to face value.

Under such an arrangement, for example, a local grocery store may agree with a tax-exempt preschool to honor coupons for groceries bought by the school's supporters. Such coupons may be purchased at a discount by the school, and resold at face value to school supporters. The net income made from the sales is generally not considered unrelated business income (UBI), if the coupon sales are not an activity "regularly carried on" by the school, or if it is carried on by volunteers. Still, the payment for such purchases or scrip is not deductible by the purchasers as tax-exempt contributions.

Under other arrangements between a for-profit merchant and a nonprofit corporation, a merchant (such as a credit card company) may pay to a nonprofit institution (such as a nonprofit college) a percentage of sales made by a credit card depicting the college, its name, and logo. In these cases, the percentage of sales payments may be eligible to be treated as a royalty for the use of the institution's name and image, and not taxed as UBI. As noted in the section *"Types of Income Excluded from UBI"* in *Chapter 4, Taxation,* royalties for use of an intangible (such as a corporation's name or logo) are generally considered exempt from treatment as UBI; however, if such payments were instead to be characterized as payment for a service (i.e., the referral of customers), then this income would be considered UBI.

These arrangements, which can benefit both the tax-exempt organization and the for-profit merchant, are commonly referred to as "commercial co-ventures," "charitable sales promotions," or "cause-related marketing," and can be subject to state charitable fundraising and solicitation laws. Some of these laws require that the charitable nonprofit have control over the fundraising activity and that the agreement between the parties include certain requirements protecting the nonprofit as well as consumers. In addition, one or both of the parties involved in the arrangement may be required to register with the states where the offers are being made.

### *Internet applications*

The Internet has spawned a number of creative fundraising mechanisms. Directors of nonprofit organizations that receive donations through websites maintained by for-profit entities should obtain legal advice regarding whether the contributions were generated in a manner consistent with IRS rules on deductibility.

**Websites acting as agents of tax-exempt organizations.** Some websites purport to raise funds for many charities at once. They are promoted as offering donors convenience and detailed information about potential donees. Some such donation websites are not themselves operated by tax-exempt charitable organizations, so contributions made through these sites are not deductible by donors unless the donation website operator is an agent of the nonprofit. Nonprofit boards should ensure that the terms of any agreement they enter with a donation website operator establishes an appropriate agency relationship if users of the site are going to be promised deductibility for their contributions.[7]

On a more fundamental level, nonprofit boards should establish a mechanism for evaluating when and whether to allow such donation websites to serve as their fundraising agents. For instance, before granting permission to a donation website to use the corporation's name, the charity should investigate the history of the website, its operators, and its operations. Other questions to ask include:

- If the website deducts an administrative fee before passing on the donations, is the fee reasonable?
- How long does it take for the site to process donation payments and then make payments to the nonprofit?

- Does the site pass through the name and contact information of the donor so that the donation may be appropriate receipted?
- How does the website company retain and use donor information for its own or other purposes?

**Fundraising through sales by for-profit entities: Internet merchant affiliation and charity malls.** Certain Internet sites have programs under which a tax-exempt organization receives a payment as a result of sales made by the for-profit over the Internet. In exchange for this payment, the nonprofit generally either provides a link from its website to that of the participating for-profit, or the for-profit refers to the participating nonprofit on its own website and promises to donate money to support its mission.[8] As discussed above, the structure of these programs can have different UBI implications. Moreover, the IRS has questioned whether the payment by a vendor of a percentage of sales from customers referred by a tax-exempt organization to the vendor's website can ever be considered "substantially related" for UBI determination purposes.[9]

A unique on-line variant of the merchant affiliation model is a website that brings together consumers, for-profit retailers, and nonprofit corporations in a program that is similar to affinity credit cards. Visitors to such a charity mall website designate a preferred charity and then shop at affiliated on-line retailers through links on the charity mall's website. For each item a shopper buys through the charity mall, the retailers donate a specified percentage of the purchase price to the shopper's preferred charity through the charity mall operator.

Because shoppers initiate these donations and charities are therefore not involved in sales that are unrelated to their exempt purposes, it is generally believed that charities can treat the money they receive through charity malls as donations and not UBI. Still, donors should generally not be able to deduct donations attributable to purchases they make through charity malls because they receive items of equal value in return for their payments to retailers.

Some Internet charity mall operators claim that their programs have a special structure that allows donors to deduct donations. In these programs, when a donor makes a purchase through the charity mall, the operator offers the donor a rebate on the purchase. The operator holds the rebate in an account for the donor, and the donor has the option to either receive the money or donate it to the charity through the operator. Because the donor has the choice to keep or donate the rebate, the IRS allows the donor to claim a charitable contribution deduction.[10] Before participating in a charity mall, or if a nonprofit learns that a charity mall is making donations to its organization an option for mall-site shoppers, the nonprofit should investigate the operations and operator of the charity mall to make sure that it will not be associated with a questionable program or group.

# Corporate Sponsorship vs. Advertising

## General Rules

### Acknowledgements vs. advertisements

The distinction between sponsorship acknowledgements and advertisements may be subtle. Simple references to an organization sponsor by name, address, and phone number would generally be characterized as acknowledgements, and the funds paid by the sponsor in connection with the activity with which the acknowledgement is associated would be considered a tax-deductible contribution. In contrast, references to a sponsor's products or services that include an endorsement or statements about the relative quality of the sponsor's goods or services would be likely treated as advertisements (at least to the extent of the fair market value of comparable ads provided by the tax-exempt organization).[11] In addition, the money paid to the for-profit may be considered taxable UBI to the nonprofit, if paid in connection with an activity that is "regularly carried on."(See the section *"Advertising vs. Sponsorship Acknowledgements"* in *Chapter 4, Taxation.)*

### Different treatment of advertisements in periodicals

As noted in the section *"Advertising vs. Sponsorship Acknowledgements"* in *Chapter 4, Taxation,* payments received for an individual ad placed in a nonprofit's periodical publication will be subject to less UBI tax than an ad placed in a nonperiodical. However, it may sometimes be difficult to determine whether a publication is a periodical for which the lower UBI tax calculation would apply. The general rule is that material that appears on a regular periodic schedule, in a standard format, is likely to be considered a periodical, whereas material (such as a brochure) that is continuously available but subject to updating from time to time, is not likely to be considered a periodical.

## Internet Applications

### Acknowledgements vs. advertisements

For-profit companies may be interested in appearing on a nonprofit corporation's website as a sponsor or as an advertiser. As noted above, if the information about a for-profit company that appears on a nonprofit corporation's website is considered a sponsorship acknowledgment ("The maintenance of XYZ Charity's website is made possible through the support of Acme Widget and Gizmo Corporation, located at 1200 Main Street."), payment made by the sponsor is likely deductible as a charitable contribution, and the revenue received from the for-profit corporation in connection with the posted message would not be subject to tax. However, if the information about a for-profit corporation that is posted on the nonprofit corporation's website is considered an advertisement ("Need widgets or gizmos—fast? Call Acme Widget and Gizmo Corporation, a full-service provider of widget and gizmos since 1999, at area code 222-333-9999, or order on-line at www.widgetsnow.biz."), the revenues received from the for-profit corporation in connection with this information will be subject to taxation as UBI.

Because of the novel nature of certain Internet applications, the acknowledgement/advertisement distinction is not always obvious. For example, the IRS has indicated that a simple displayed link to a sponsor's website is not an advertisement, even though an individual who clicks on the link will then be presented, through the for-profit's website, with information on the company's products and services and how to purchase them. In contrast, the IRS also indicated that a banner on a nonprofit organization's website that displays a for-profit organization's website, but does not provide a link to the for-profit's website, may be considered an advertisement if the banner reference shows information about the for-profit entity's product.[12]

The IRS has solicited comments on the significance of links in the preamble to the proposed regulations on corporate sponsorship, which were originally published in the spring of 2000.[13] The regulations make clear that an acknowledgment of a sponsor may include the street address of the sponsor's place of business and telephone number.[14] A link is essentially an Internet address combined with a tool the user may employ, solely at the user's discretion, to go to the linked site. There appears to be no basis for treating the link differently than a street address or telephone number.

### Internet periodicals

Whether material containing advertisements published by a nonprofit corporation on the Internet can be considered a periodical for purposes of more favorable UBI tax calculation rules can be a difficult determination. The IRS has indicated that the UBI rules for periodical advertising income will not be available for Internet advertisements run by a nonprofit unless the advertisement appears in on-line materials that are "prepared and distributed in substantially the same manner as a traditional periodical," with an editorial staff, marketing program, and budget that is independent of the administration of the rest of the organization's website.[15] Under these rules, an advertisement that appears on a nonprofit website would not generally be considered to be "published in a periodical," even if the website is periodically updated.

# Association (Links) with Taxable Entities

## General Rule

Tax-exempt corporations may lose tax-exempt status by promoting, or appearing to promote, private interests of individuals or taxable entities, except as incident to the tax-exempt organization's purposes.

## Internet Applications

### *Website links with websites of taxable organizations*

The nature of the Internet is to create easy-to-use links between otherwise unrelated material. Corporate sponsors and other for-profit companies may wish to establish links with a tax-exempt corporation's website (either by placing a link on the for-profit's website to the nonprofit's site, or having the nonprofit's site contain a link to the for-profit corporation's website). While a link to a for-profit corporation on a tax-exempt corporation's website may take up very little space, the existence of the link can create the impression that the tax-exempt corporation supports or is involved with some or all of the activities described on the for-profit corporation's website. Further, links to the sites of corporate sponsors may (or may not) be deemed to be advertisements subject to taxation as UBI. (See the section *"Corporate Sponsorship vs. Advertising"* above.)

Tax-exempt organizations maintaining websites are well advised to develop a policy for determining which linkage requests it will honor and which it will reject.

Nonprofit boards should consider several issues as they develop and apply their linkage policies.[16] The policy should include a procedure for screening proposed links to ensure that they further the nonprofit's charitable purposes and satisfy its requirements for exemption. For instance, tax-exempt organizations should reject requests by political candidates to establish links with particular campaign sites, to avoid the appearance of making political endorsements and protect their tax-exempt status.

When a link goes to a site maintained by another nonprofit, the linkage policy also should provide for an evaluation of the § 501(c) status of the proposed linking organization, to assess the potential for attribution of the linking organization's activities to the nonprofit. For example, if the website of a nonprofit that works to preserve wetlands contains a link to an environmental advocacy group that conducts substantial lobbying, should the existence of the link cause the advocacy group's lobbying to be attributed to the nonprofit?

(See further discussion of this issue in the section *"Implication of Links to Lobbying Organization Websites"* below.)

In addition, a linkage policy should include a procedure for responding to the discovery of links on a for-profit corporation's website to the nonprofit's site that were created without the nonprofit's permission. If the linking organization would not meet the approval requirements set forth in the established policy, the nonprofit may want to have communications to record the fact that the nonprofit on the destination end of the link does not approve or condone what the linking organization is saying or doing, and, if appropriate, requests that the link be removed.

# Lobbying

## General Rule

As noted in the section *"The Absolute Prohibition on Political Campaign Activities"* in *Chapter 4, Taxation*, organizations that are exempt from federal income taxation under § 501(c) are prohibited from devoting more than an "insubstantial" part of their activities to lobbying. To avoid the subjective vagaries of what insubstantial may mean—for instance, as determined by percentage of organizational revenue, percentage of volunteer time or other resources, or the impact of the activities conducted—tax-exempt organizations (other than churches and other religious organizations) may take advantage of the election under § 501(h) of the Code. This Code section provides objective measures for determining permissible levels of lobbying, based on the organization's annual spending on its exempt purposes, and with different limits for "grassroots" and "direct" lobbying.  As such, the election can be extremely beneficial to a nonprofit corporation by providing a mechanism for calculating a specific "safe harbor" maximum dollar amount that the corporation may spend on lobbying activities. (For more information about the § 501(h) election, see the discussion in the section *"Limitations on Lobbying"* in *Chapter 4, Taxation*.)

## Internet Applications

### Benefits of § 501(h) Election
The Internet provides great potential for a nonprofit to increase the scope and effectiveness of its lobbying activity while satisfying the IRS limitations

on lobbying by tax-exempt corporations. Lobbying activity can be conducted over the Internet (through websites and electronic mail) at a very low cost, especially compared to the cost of traditional mail or personal lobbying visits. For example, legislative alerts or calls to action can be posted at the organization's website, referenced by links to other sites, and/or e-mail communications can be sent directly to the nonprofit corporation's list of supporters. The time and economic costs of these communications are typically trivial compared to mail or traditional broadcast mechanisms. As noted in the section *"Lobbying: General Rule"* above, the amount that a nonprofit can spend on lobbying is limited to an insubstantial amount. Tax-exempt corporations that would like to maximize the potential for lobbying using the Internet (alone or in conjunction with more traditional lobbying activities), while not jeopardizing their tax-exempt status, may wish to make the election permitted under § 501(h). (See the section *"Limitations on Lobbying"* in *Chapter 4, Taxation.*)

### Allocation of costs of e-mail and website postings

Despite the fact that lobbying through e-mail or website postings can save considerable expense over traditional mail or fax communications, it is currently unclear how costs should be allocated for such Internet lobbying activities. Making an appropriate allocation of costs of Internet lobbying is essential to ensure that the nonprofit does not exceed the applicable spending limit if a § 501(h) election has been made (or remains within the insubstantial range for organizations that have not made the § 501(h) election). Costs to be allocated may include hosting and maintaining websites. Until the IRS provides specific guidance in this area, nonprofits should consult with their accountant regarding appropriate measures of the cost of these activities.

### Implications of links to lobbying organization websites

Tax-exempt nonprofits should exercise caution before creating or permitting links on the nonprofit's website to a website for a lobbying organization. It is not yet clear under what circumstances, and to what extent, a link on a nonprofit organization's website to the website of an organization that engages in lobbying would be considered lobbying by the nonprofit. It can be expected that the IRS will be taking positions on this issue in the future; therefore, directors of nonprofits for whom this issue may be relevant should make sure that the organization routinely receives updated advice in this area.

# Political Activity

## General Rule

As noted in *Chapter 4, Taxation"* tax-exempt organizations are prohibited from supporting candidates for political office or otherwise intervening in political campaigns. (See the section *"The Absolute Prohibition on Political Campaign Activities"* in *Chapter 4, Taxation.*)

## Internet Applications

### *Implications of links to political campaigns or candidates' websites*

Tax-exempt nonprofits should not create or permit links on the nonprofit's website to websites for selected political campaigns or candidates for political office. In some instances, providing strictly nonpartisan information, including links to sites maintained by all the candidates in a race, may be consistent with federal tax law requirements, but a nonprofit should get legal advice before pursuing such an approach. The IRS has stated that a website link may violate the ban on political campaigning depending on the content of the linked site.[17]

# Avoiding Copyright and Trademark Infringement

## General Rule

Like other entities, nonprofit corporations should take appropriate steps to safeguard any intellectual property (such as copyrights, trademarks, and service marks) developed or owned by the corporation, while ensuring that its activities and those of its employees and agents do not infringe on the intellectual property of others. Thus, it should place copyright symbols and notices as appropriate on original written material, and use trade/service mark symbols and notices wherever such marks are used.

## Internet Applications

### *Protection of the nonprofit's copyrights and trademarks on the Internet*

If a nonprofit corporation intends to post material that it has developed and copyrighted on its website, it should also post notices to site visitors that inform them of the copyright status and the corporation's intent to pursue those who violate its copyright. The corporation also should consider providing copyright notices at the bottom of each screen.

The organization should take similar steps to protect its trademarked names and logos, especially if these are highly valued assets. Technological advances are likely to bring improved methods to assist a nonprofit corporation in protecting its trademarks and logos for this purpose; therefore, the nonprofit board should make sure that intellectual property protection mechanisms are periodically evaluated to take advantage of such improvements.

### *Avoiding infringement of the copyrights and trademarks of others*

Directors of a nonprofit organization should make sure that the corporation's employees and volunteers who engage in Internet activity on behalf of the corporation understand that certain activities, when done on the Internet, may constitute infringement of another organization's copyright or trademark, although an analogous "physical world" activity does not raise infringement issues. For example, whereas clipping a newspaper article from an actual newspaper and posting it on an office bulletin board would not generally be deemed to be copyright infringement, cutting the article electronically from an electronic copy of the paper and posting it on a page of the corporation's website without proper authorization may well constitute copyright infringement.[18]

# Sales of Goods and Services

## General Rules

### *Sales in stores or through catalogues, sales tax, and foreign business registration requirements*

Some nonprofit organizations, such as museums, maintain stores in which goods related to the nonprofit corporation's activities can be purchased. Others sell products through catalogues. Whether the sale of such goods constitutes an unrelated trade or business is generally assessed on an item-by-item basis, with sales of certain items being deemed "related" (and therefore not treated as UBI) and others being "unrelated" (with revenues from such items taxable as UBI). In addition, if the nonprofit transacts business in states other than the state in which the nonprofit is incorporated, the nonprofit may be required to register in such other states as a foreign corporation doing business in the state.

In general, such stores are required to collect and remit state and local sales and use taxes on their product sales. State and local sales and use taxes also must be collected and remitted on catalog sales, *if* the seller has a physical presence in the states to which the items are shipped. As a practical matter, a catalog seller may be required to collect and remit such taxes for the states in which it or any of its property is located, and in any state in which its employees or representatives engage in business on its behalf.

### Auctions and trade shows

Many § 501(c)(3) corporations raise money through annual charity auctions. Charities that conduct traditional auctions generally do not pay UBIT on the income they receive from donors, provided that the auction is not "regularly carried on" or the auctioned items are all donated. Similarly, trade organizations (such as the ABA) that are exempt from federal taxation under § 501(c)(6) of the Code may raise money through trade shows that coincide with one or more meetings of the organization's membership. The trade organization receives revenue by renting space to exhibitors and receiving underwriting contributions from corporate sponsors. As with charitable auctions, such trade show revenue is generally not treated as subject to taxation as UBI, since it is not regularly carried on.

### Sales of mailing lists

In contrast to sales of goods or services to supporters and others, many nonprofits raise money through the sale of their mailing lists. The value of these lists may be enhanced if the nonprofit also collects demographic information on its membership. Nonprofits may choose to sell mailing lists only to other nonprofits, or to both nonprofit and for-profit entities. Typically, the sale of mailing and membership lists is taxable as UBI. In addition, states may impose restrictions on sales of mailing lists by nonprofit organizations. However, even if not required by law, to preserve member goodwill, many organizations give their members the opportunity to opt out by requesting that their information not be sold to other organizations.

# Internet Applications

Many nonprofit corporations have begun to take advantage of the Internet's wide range of business opportunities. The descriptions that follow address some of the legal implications of several such opportunities.

### On-line stores

Many nonprofits have established on-line stores or virtual storefronts, through which they sell merchandise and services from their websites. For example, a museum that operates a physical gift shop also might operate an on-line store to allow visitors to its website to purchase the same merchandise over the Internet. Even a nonprofit that does *not* also operate a physical store might raise money and promote its visibility by selling books it publishes over the Internet. In comparison to the overhead needed to maintain a physical store or catalogue operation, the low-overhead costs of maintaining a sales location on the web will enable many more nonprofits to sell goods and services in this fashion.

**UBI issues.** Just as is the case for physical stores or catalogue sales, a nonprofit organization's revenue from the sale of goods or services over the web will generally be determined to be (nontaxable) related revenue or (taxable) UBI, on an item-by-item basis. Directors of nonprofit corporations selling an extensive array of goods and services over the Internet should make sure that, just as for traditional store and catalogue sales, the nonprofit has an accounting system that tracks sales revenue and UBI status on an item-by-item basis.

**Sales tax issues.** The state and local sales tax treatment of Internet sales is currently similar to that of catalog sales (described in the section "*Sales in Stores...*" above), such that sales taxes for Internet sales are generally not required to be collected and paid except in states in which the organization has some form of physical presence. Directors of nonprofit corporations that are selling goods and services over the Internet will need to stay informed as to how the sales tax debate is resolved to determine what, if any, sales taxes they may be responsible for collecting.

While the standards in this area are still evolving, directors should be aware that making Internet sales to buyers located in other states or abroad may expose the corporation to potential tax liability in these other jurisdictions. However, if an organization is otherwise subject to sales tax liability (for example, in the jurisdictions in which it has physical locations), it cannot avoid paying taxes for Internet sales to persons residing in these areas. A good number of states have participated in the Streamlined Sales Tax Project, which has been developing uniform standards and definitions for collecting sales tax, and has approved software from certain vendors to ease the collection burdens on sellers. Information on the model statutes that have been developed and the progress in getting the statutes adopted in various states is available at www.streamlinedsalestax.org.

**Whether Internet sales activity constitutes doing business in a state, requiring registration as a foreign corporation.** Currently, the law is unclear as to whether reaching a state through the Internet—rather than through physical presence—will cause a nonprofit corporation to be doing business in that state. However, if a nonprofit corporation finds that it is transacting business in one or more states in which it is not incorporated, it should obtain legal advice regarding whether registration is required in at least those states. Failure to register as a foreign corporation doing business in another state when required may prevent a corporation from availing itself of legal process against the state's residents, and could result in the imposition of other sanctions.

**Secure payment methods.** In traditional store and catalogue settings, most individuals assume the security of credit card and other personal information provided in connection with a purchase. Security is still a significant issue in Internet sales transactions, given the possibilities of hacker theft of credit card numbers and other concerns regarding the transmission of one's personal information across the globally linked Internet. Accordingly, a nonprofit corporation engaging in Internet sales transactions should take care to verify that it has appropriate security measures in place to avoid liability from allowing unauthorized access to this information. These security measures should be frequently reviewed and improved as both security technology and hacker capabilities evolve.

### *Charity auctions*

Online charity auctions are an increasingly popular means of fundraising for nonprofits. Some nonprofit organizations administer the auctions themselves, while others rely on an outside provider. As noted above, charities that conduct traditional auctions generally do not pay UBIT on the income they receive from donors, because the auction is not regularly carried on and/or involves the sale of donated items. In contrast, however, many online charity auctions may not be held only once or a few times a year; because of the ease of setting up online auctions, some nonprofit organizations may hold them frequently, such as once a month, or even maintain a continuous auction, with a differing array of products available to be bid on. Some such auctions, especially those held frequently, may be more likely to include purchased merchandise as well as donated merchandise. If both of these factors are present in online auctions conducted by a nonprofit, the revenues from such auctions may be taxable to the organization as UBI.

Even if an online auction is held only once a year, nonprofit organizations may encounter UBI issues if, due to unfamiliarity with the Internet environment, they rely on an outside provider to conduct their auctions. If the organization does not retain the primary responsibility for publicity of the auction and otherwise maintain certain controls to ensure that the auction is properly conducted as a fundraising event for IRS purposes, the auction revenues may be treated as UBI.[19]

### *Virtual trade shows*

Some trade associations have organized online virtual trade shows that are modeled on a traditional trade show format. The trade association may rent "display space" on its own site or may simply provide multiple links on its site to the websites of various vendors, or "virtual exhibitors." Some trade associations sponsor year-round virtual trade shows, while others plan virtual trade shows to coincide with their organizations' regular annual shows.

Directors of nonprofit corporations should be aware that although, as noted above, income from traditional trade show activities is generally not subject to tax as UBI, virtual trade shows raise a number of UBI issues. Although the IRS has not yet provided official guidance in this area, the UBI treatment of income from virtual trade shows is likely to depend on whether a trade organization can demonstrate that its on-line activities are substantially similar to those of a traditional trade show. For example, because a traditional trade show is a finite event, it is unlikely that income from a year-round virtual trade show would be excluded from UBI treatment.[20]

### *Sale of e-mail addresses and other electronically gathered information*

Just as many nonprofits have found that there is a market for their member/subscriber mailing and other information, nonprofit organizations have discovered that they may earn money from the sale of e-mail addresses or other data on supporters that can be mined by other organizations. The sale of e-mail addresses and the sale and maintenance of other electronically gathered information raises donor privacy issues. Although many privacy issues also are present in the non-Internet context, individuals may have greater sensitivity about information that is gathered through Internet communications compared to more traditional means.

Local, state, and federal legislators are in the process of reviewing the need for legislation to protect individual-specific information gathered online. While federal law generally does not currently protect such information, the Federal Trade Commission (FTC) recommends that nonprofits that gather donor information using the Internet establish a policy regarding the privacy of donor information and post it on their websites. The FTC has developed four "fair information practices," which would require nonprofits to:

(1)   notify donors regarding what personal information they are gathering, how it is used, and with whom it will be shared;

(2)   offer donors the option of directing that their information not be shared with third parties;

(3)   provide donors with information regarding the security measures that protect their information; and

(4)   allow donors to access their information, to review and correct it.[21]

Since the public is increasingly concerned with consumer and donor privacy issues, legislators are likely to respond by developing new laws and regulations in this area. (See further discussion of Internet privacy issues in the section *"Protecting Electronic Records Information"* below.) Directors of nonprofit corporations should consult with legal counsel on a regular basis to ensure that their practices involving donor information are in compliance with changing legal standards.

### *Unsolicited Commercial E-mails*

Federal law sets forth specific requirements for the content of unsolicited e-mails containing a commercial message.[22] Under the CAN-SPAM Act, a commercial message is a message that has as its primary purpose a commercial advertisement or promotion of a product or service. Messages that have a primary purpose relating to a specific transaction or relationship between the sender and consumer are exempt from the CAN-SPAM Act's requirements.

In order to be a transaction or relationship message, the primary purpose of the e-mail must be to do one of the following: (1) facilitate, complete, or confirm a commercial transaction previously agreed to by the e-mail recipient; (2) provide warranty, product recall, safety, or security information for a product purchased by the e-mail recipient; (3) provide certain information regarding a subscription, membership, account, loan, or similar ongoing relationship; (4) provide information regarding an employment relationship or related benefit; or (5) deliver goods or services that the e-mail recipient is entitled to receive as a result of a previously agreed upon transaction.[23]

Any person, including nonprofit organizations, that initiates commercial e-mail messages is required to comply with the CAN-SPAM requirements. These requirements include, among other things, a prohibition on deceptive subject headings in e-mails, the need for accurate information on the sender and the subject matter of the communication, the ability of e-mail recipients to opt-out of receiving commercial e-mails, which includes a clear and conspicuous notice of a right to "opt-out" of receipt of the e-mails, clear identification of the commercial nature of the e-mail, and the sender's valid physical postal address.[24] From a compliance standpoint, a nonprofit that is sending commercial messages should limit such messages to those persons who have affirmatively agreed (or opted-in) to receive such e-mails.

# Posting Information Returns and Exemption Applications on the Internet

## General Rule

Federal tax law requires tax-exempt organizations to provide copies of their exemption applications and three most recent information returns (Form 990s) to anyone requesting them in person or in writing.[25]

## Internet Application

Tax-exempt organizations can be relieved of the requirement to physically provide copies of their exemption applications and Form 990s if they post these documents on the organization's website or another site collecting similar applications and returns.[26] The organization must provide the web address where the documents can be found to anyone who asks for it. Organizations electing this web-posting option should be careful to post a return identical to what was filed with the IRS (although confidential information may be excluded to the same extent as for 990s provided to the public by more conventional means). Having the return available on another site, such as www.guidestar. org—which posts all Forms 990 filed with the IRS—will also meet the legal requirement for disclosure, provided that it is a complete and accurate copy of what was filed with the IRS, with the exception of certain donor information on Schedule B of Form 990, which may be kept confidential. GuideStar, which gets copies of all Forms 990 from the IRS and posts them as a matter of course, redacts signatures from the documents to protect against misuse. As a technical matter, the redaction means that the GuideStar version is not a perfect copy of the return filed with the IRS. Still, as it contains all the other information someone making a legitimate request could want to see, it should be rare for a nonprofit to encounter someone wanting a return who is not satisfied with what is available on GuideStar. It is important to note, however, that there is often a significant delay in GuideStar's postings from the time of filing; therefore, someone wanting the most current filing may need to obtain it directly from the organization.

# Implications of Serving as an Information Exchange

## Defamation and Other Torts

### General rule

Any organization may be held liable for defamation or invasion of privacy, based on statements about individuals made by the organization (such as in a publication) or by persons associated with the organization (including a nonprofit's volunteers).

### Internet applications

**Potential organizational liability for the provision of listservs, chat rooms, and social media.** A nonprofit corporation may determine that its purposes are served by the provision of listservs (electronic mailing lists), chat rooms, social media, and similar technological meeting places, available to organization members or other interested persons. Messages exchanged and information made available in these forums have the potential to reach a very large audience. Consequently, there is an increased potential for claims that the content of an individual message is defamatory, invades privacy, or constitutes impermissible political activities. Messages sent through these forums by employees and others who may be seen as agents for the corporation may be attributed to the organization for purposes of these tort claims.

A corporation offering or using listservs, chat rooms, social media, and other such services may therefore wish to incorporate online disclaimers noting that the statements made in these contexts are solely those of the participants and are not endorsed or in any way attributable to the corporation.[27]

**Potential organizational liability for e-mail messages and use of social media.** Defamation, privacy, and similar concerns are also present in e-mail and social media use by an organization's employees and volunteers. The nonprofit corporation's board should therefore make sure that employees and others using the corporation's e-mail system or communicating via social media on behalf of the corporation are regularly reminded about the organization's policy of the appropriate use of e-mail and social media, and to avoid making or distributing offensive or other derogatory remarks or material by e-mail.

## Liability Protection Available by Registration as an Internet Service Provider

The Digital Millennium Copyright Act of 1998 (DMCA) permits organizations acting as "Internet service providers" or "ISPs" to avoid liability for copyright infringement when users post material on a website the organization maintains.[28] This law defines a "service provider" as "an entity offering the transmission, routing, or providing of connections for digital on-line communications, between or among points specified by a user, of material of the user's choosing, without modification to the content of the material as sent or received."[29] Operating a chat room or other interactive site may cause an organization to be treated as a service provider for purposes of this law even if it does not otherwise provide users with Internet access.

To qualify for the DMCA protections, the ISP must: (1) not receive a financial benefit directly attributable to the infringing activity, where the ISP has the right and ability to control the activity; (2) not have knowledge that the material or activity is infringing or be aware of facts or circumstances that make the infringement apparent; (3) expeditiously remove or disable access to the material if it learns of the infringement or receives a notification of infringement from a copyright holder or an agent of the owner; (4) designate an agent to receive DMCA notifications and register the agent's name and contact information with the United States Copyright Office and make this information available on its service; (5) accommodate technical measures used by copyright owners to identify or protect copyrighted works; and (6) adopt, implement, and inform subscribers and account holders of a policy and procedure for terminating a repeat infringer's subscriptions and accounts.

To invoke the liability protection available under this law, the organization must register the name of an agent with the U.S. Copyright Office, which is designated to accept complaints from those who believe their copyrights have been infringed on a website maintained by an ISP.

In addition, the Communications Decency Act of 1996, which generally imposes criminal sanctions for knowingly transmitting obscene messages or materials over the Internet, provides broad immunity for online providers, including website and forum operators, with respect to postings by third parties using their services.[30]

# Tax Consequences of Providing Internet Access to Others

Providing access to the Internet in exchange for a fee constitutes a trade or business, and unless that business is substantially related to the organization's tax-exempt purpose, the income generated will be subject to federal taxation as UBI. For example, providing Internet access for a fee substantially below cost to community centers in poor neighborhoods may be considered a charitable activity for a § 501(c)(3) organization, rather than an unrelated trade or business, if the activity is related to the organization's charitable purpose.[31] If providing Internet access is the organization's only function, it may qualify for tax-exempt status as an integral part of another exempt organization.

Thus, a corporation may serve as an ISP to members of a nonprofit university community and qualify as an integral part of the university, or perhaps as a § 501(c)(12) organization. (The latter category includes rural telephone cooperatives, electric cooperatives, and the like.)

Note: Trade associations should take care before offering Internet access to members. Trade associations violate the requirements for continuing federal income tax exemption if they provide "particular services" to members. The IRS has not yet ruled as to whether providing Internet access to individual account holders qualifies as a particular service. On the other hand, providing a listserv, chat room, or website for exchange of information among association members is unlikely to run afoul of the particular services restriction.[32]

# Protecting Electronic Records Information

If a nonprofit organization maintains, in electronic form, medical records, student records, or other records that it is legally bound to keep private, it should verify that effective systems are in place to assure that unauthorized users cannot obtain access to those records through the organization's Internet connections. Because hackers continually become more proficient at finding ways to breach computer-based security systems, the board should require appropriate management personnel to periodically confirm that adequate security measures have been taken to prevent unauthorized access to confidential information of others or of the corporation that is stored in electronic form or transmitted over the Internet.

Moreover, the organization should make sure that it keeps abreast of legal requirements relating to the electronic storage and transmission of different kinds of personal information relating to the organization's activities. For example, nonprofit health care providers must comply with the detailed federal rules issued under the Health Insurance Portability and Accountability Act (HIPAA), regarding the use and disclosure of electronic and other medical records. The Children's Online Privacy Protection Act of 1998 (COPPA) also provides special rules that apply to websites that attract children.[33] The rules implementing COPPA set out what a website operator must include in a privacy policy, when and how to seek variable consent from a parent, and what responsibilities an operator has to protect children's privacy and safety online.

## Identity Theft

Some nonprofits may be subject to the "Red Flags Rule" that requires them to implement a written identity theft prevention program to detect warning signs of identity theft in the day-to- day operations.[34] The rationale for such a program is that by identifying "red flags" in advance, the organization is better able to identify suspicious activity that might arise and takes steps to prevent its going further. A program requires that the organization (1) identify relevant patterns, practices, and specific forms of activity (called "red flags") that could give rise to possible identity theft; (2) incorporate business practices to detect red flags; (3) describe appropriate responses to red flags in order to prevent and mitigate identity theft, and (4) update the program periodically to reflect changes in risk from identity theft.

The Red Flags Rules apply to "financial institutions" and "creditors" that hold consumer accounts designed to permit multiple payments or transactions. Many nonprofits were subject to the Red Flags Rule by virtue of being deemed creditors; however, recent amendments to the definition of creditor significantly limited the types of parties covered. Under the amendments, a creditor must regularly and in the ordinary course of business, meet one of three general criteria: (1) obtain or use consumer reports in connection with a credit transaction; (2) furnish information to consumer reporting agencies in connection with a credit transaction; or (3) advance funds to or on behalf of someone, except for funds for expenses incidental to a service the creditor provides to that person.

*See the Suggested Questions and Checklist following the Endnotes below to review the issues discussed in this chapter.*

## Endnotes

1.  Approximately forty states and a relatively smaller number of cities and counties require registration of organizations that conduct charitable solicitations in that state or other jurisdiction. *See* The Unified Registration Statement, The Multi-State Filer Project, www.multistatefiling.org/#yes_states. For a copy of the Unified Registration Statement, *see* www.multistatefiling.org.
2.  *See, e.g.,* CAL. BUS. & PROF. CODE § 17510.4; CODE ANN. § 43-17-8; MINN. STAT. § 309.556.
3.  *The Charleston Principles: Guidelines on Charitable Solicitations Using the Internet* is available at www.nasconet.org.
4.  *See* I.R.C. § 170(f)(8).
5.  *See* I.R.C. § 6115.

6. *See* IRS Publication No. 1771.

7. *See* Christina Nooney, *Tax Exempt Organizations and the Internet*, 27 EXEMPT ORGANIZATION TAX REVIEW 38, 33-39 (2000).

8. *See* Cheryl Chasin, Susan Ruth, and Robert Harper, *Tax Exempt Organizations and World Wide Web Fundraising and Advertising on the Internet*, in IRS EXEMPT ORGANIZATIONS TECHNICAL INSTRUCTION PROGRAM FOR FY 2000 139 (a good discussion of individual merchant affiliate programs). *See also* Alice Anderson and Robert Wexler, *Making Use of the Internet—Issues for Tax-Exempt Organizations*, 92 JOURNAL OF TAXATION 309 (May 2000).

9. *See* IRS Publication 598.

10. *See* Michael I. Sanders, *Joint Ventures Involving Tax-Exempt Organizations* (John Wiley & Sons, Inc., 3rd ed. 2007).

11. *See* I.R.C. § 513(i); Reg. § 1.513-4.

12. *See* Chasin, Ruth, and Harper, *supra* note 8, at 137; Donna Moore and Robert Harper, *Internet Service Providers Exemption Issues Under IRC § 501(c)(3) and § 501(c)(12)*, in IRS EXEMPT ORGANIZATIONS TECHNICAL INSTRUCTION PROGRAM FOR FY 1999 64; *see also* PLR 200303062 (October 22, 2002);.

13. *See* IRS Publication 598. *See also Federal Register*, Notice of Proposed Rulemaking (REG-209601-92, March 1, 2000).

14. *See* Reg. § 1.513-4(c)(2)(iv).

15. *See* Chasin, Ruth, and Harper, *supra* note 8, at 135.

16. *See* Anderson and Wexler, *supra* note 8, for a good discussion of issues to consider when developing a linkage policy. *See generally*, SUBCOMMITTEE ON INTERACTIVE SERVICES & COMMITTEE ON THE LAW OF COMMERCE IN CYBERSPACE, ABA SECTION OF BUSINESS LAW, WEB-LINKING AGREEMENTS: CONTRACTING STRATEGIES AND MODEL PROVISIONS (American Bar Association, 1997).

17. *See* Publication 557, Ch. 3.

18. A good survey of copyright and trademark issues for nonprofits can be found in Maria Malaro, *A Legal Primer on Managing Museum Collections* (Smithsonian Institute Press, 2d ed. 1998). *See also* Lisa Runquist and Jeannie Carmedelle Frey, Eds., *Guide to Representing Religious Organizations* 227 (American Bar Association 2009) (discussing copyright issues for religious organizations).

19. *See* Anderson and Wexler, *supra* note 8; Nooney, *supra* note 7, at 37.

20. *See* Anderson and Wexler, *supra* note 8; Chasin, Ruth, and Harper, *supra* note 8, at 135-37. *See* IRS Announcement 2000-84.

21. *See Privacy Online: Fair Information Practices in the Electronic Marketplace: A Federal Trade Commission Report to Congress*, May 22, 2000, *available at* http://www.ftc.gov/privacy.

22. *See* Controlling the Assault of Non-Solicited Pornography and Marketing Act (CAN-SPAM Act), 15 U.S.C. §§ 7701-13. The Federal Trade Commission has implemented regulations under the CAN-SPAM Act under 16 C.F.R. Part 316.

23.    *See* 15 U.S.C. § 7702(17)(A).

24.    *See* 15 U.S.C. § 7704; 16 C.F.R. § 316.5.

25.    *See* I.R.C. § 6104(d)(1)-(2).

26.    *See* I.R.C. § 6104(d)(4).

27.    Thoughtful commentary can be found in Elizabeth deGrazia Blumenfeld, *Privacy Please: Will the Internet Industry Act Protect Consumer Privacy Before the Government Steps In?*, 54 Bus. Law. 349, 349–83 (1998). *See also* Robert Sprague & Corey Ciocchetti, *Preserving Identities: Protecting Personal Identifying Information Through Enhanced Privacy Policies and Laws*, 19 Alb. L.J. Sci. & Tech. 91 (2009).

28.    17 U.S.C. § 512.

29.    17 U.S.C. § 512(k)(1)(A).

30.    *See* 47 U.S.C. § 230.

31.    In a Technical Advice Memorandum, the IRS concluded that an Internet Service Provider that gave Internet access solely to low-income people and other § 501(c)(3) organizations for fees set substantially below cost qualified as a § 501(c)(3) organization. I.R.S. Tech. Adv. Mem. 200208069 (Jan. 18, 2002).

32.    *See generally* Moore and Harper, *supra* note 12, at 55-66.

33.    15 U.S.C. § 6501 et. seq. Details and current releases relating to COPPA can be found at http://business.ftc.gov/privacy-and-security.

34.    15 U.S.C. § 1681m; 12 C.F.R. § 222.90.

# Suggested Questions for Directors Regarding Supervision of Internet Activities

(1)    Does the corporation currently have, or is it considering creating, a web page, or does it engage in other activities using the Internet?

(2)    If the corporation engages in fundraising over the Internet, is it required to register under the charitable solicitation rules or foreign corporation laws of any other state, locality, or non-U.S. jurisdiction?

(3)    Does the corporation receive donations from the Internet sites or activities of other entities? Has the corporation's board approved these activities? If other entities are collecting donations on the organization's behalf, are those other entities properly authorized to serve as agents for the organization?

(4)    If the corporation has a website, does its site contain any acknowledgements or advertisements for corporate sponsors? Does

the board understand the difference? If it contains advertisements, is there a way those advertisements can be converted to acknowledgments to limit UBIT?

(5)   If the corporation is making sales over the Internet, has it investigated any responsibility it has for collecting and paying over sales tax to those states where it has a physical presence or where its customers are located?

(6)   If the corporation is making sales over the Internet, are the sales related to its exempt purpose? If not, are the sales regularly carried on? If so, how is the organization handling any UBIT liability?

(7)   Has the board evaluated whether and in what manner it may wish to engage in lobbying activities over the Internet? If it chooses to use the Internet for lobbying, has the corporation—if it is a § 501(c)(3)—made an election under IRC § 501(h)? Has it developed policies informed by IRS definitions of lobbying that will allow for strong advocacy while limiting lobbying expenditures? If it chooses to do some lobbying over the Internet, does it have an accounting system in place to gather the data necessary to allocate common costs for things like website maintenance and website hosting?

(8)   Is the board aware of the distinctions between activity that would constitute permissible public education on broad issues of public policy and democratic engagement, on the one hand, and impermissible involvement in political campaigns, on the other? If the organization intends to engage in activities that may fall into the first category, has the board developed a website policy that will help all staff and volunteers produce website content that will not cross the line and become political campaign intervention?

(9)   Has the organization reviewed the copies of its IRS returns that are available on www.guidestar.org to be sure they are accurate?

(10)  If the organization uses the Internet to collect information about people, what privacy notices or protections is the organization required to place on its site?

# Checklist: Internet Activities:  Fundraising, Selling Goods and Services, Lobbying, and Other Activities

*Note:*   For simplicity. these and other chapters describe a corporation having a chair, who pre-sides over the board of directors; a chief executive, who may be a staff person; an executive committee; a governance/nominating committee; and an audit committee. (We recognize, however, that in many smaller and other nonprofits, these committee functions may be performed by either the executive committee or the board as a whole.) We also assume a legal counsel—someone, paid or unpaid, having primary responsibility for the corporation's legal affairs. Many corporations, especially larger nonprofits, may have other committees established for specific purposes, such as establishing executive compensation; monitoring compliance with legal requirements; and overseeing investments and other financial matters.

| Subject | Review By | How Often | Comment |
|---------|-----------|-----------|---------|
| 1. Does the corporation raise money through contributions solicited or received over the Internet? | Chair, chief executive, legal counsel | At least quarterly, with annual reports to the full board | There are multiple ways of fund-raising over the Internet. Despite the relative ease of doing so from a technical and resource perspective, directors need to be aware of the legal implications of this activity. |
| 2. In what states and localities may the corporation be required to register under the charitable solicitation laws as a result of its Internet fundraising activity? | Chair, chief executive, legal counsel | At least annually | Application of the charitable solicitation laws to Internet fund-raising is not always clear, but standards can be expected to evolve rapidly. Smaller nonprofits lacking the funds to pay registration fees in multiple jurisdictions may want to take steps to limit the focus of their Internet fundraising to a few or even a single state. |

| Subject | Review By | How Often | Comment |
|---------|-----------|-----------|---------|
| 3. Do individuals or entities act as fundraisers or sources of contributions to the corporation? If so, do we understand the legal implications of this activity for the corporation and our donors? | Chair, chief executive, legal counsel | At least annually | If the corporation raises funds through websites or the assistance of other organizations, the board should ensure that management staff and legal counsel have reviewed the arrangements for compliance with laws governing charitable solicitations, charitable fundraisers, and tax-exempt contributions. |
| 4. Are there acknowledgements or advertisements of for-profit companies on the corporation's website? | Chair, chief executive, legal counsel | At least annually | The board may want to adopt a policy for sponsor acknowledgments and third-party advertising on the corporation's website. |

| Subject | Review By | How Often | Comment |
|---|---|---|---|
| 5. Does the corporation provide links to the website of for-profit companies, nonprofit advocacy organizations, or candidates for political office? Or, are we aware of any such organizations that have links to *our* website on their site? What legal issues are raised by such links? | Chief executive, chief information officer (CIO), or lead technology staff person | At least annually | If a link on a tax-exempt corporation's website is determined to constitute involvement in a political campaign or promotion of a candidate for political office, the corporation's tax-exempt status could be threatened. |
| 6. Does the organization engage in lobbying activity over the Internet? If so, does this activity meet the general "insubstantial" test, or if applicable, the standards for organizations that have made the election to have their lobby activity covered by § 501(h) of the Internal Revenue Code? | Chief executive, legal counsel, fundraising staff | At least annually for report to the full board, with frequent monitoring at the staff level | Internet lobbying activities may not be costly but directors should be aware that the IRS's position on the appropriate ways to measure these activities is still developing. |

| Subject | Review By | How Often | Comment |
|---|---|---|---|
| 7. Are the corporation's copyrights, trademarks, and service marks properly protected on the corporation's website and through e-mail activities of corporation employees? | Legal counsel, consultation with lead technology staff person or chief information officer | At least annually | |
| 8. Are copyright restrictions on works by third parties complied with before these works are posted on the corporation's website? | Legal counsel, consultation with lead technology staff person or chief information officer | At least annually, with educational reminders to staff | Staff should be educated regarding use of copyrighted works on the corporation's website. |
| 9. Does the corporation sell goods or services over the Internet? If so: | Chief executive | | |
| a. Have UBI and sales tax issues been examined? | a. Legal counsel | a. Upon inception of any such activity; at least annually thereafter | |
| b. Does this activity require registration as a foreign corporation in any states? | b. Legal counsel | b. Upon inception of any such activity; at least annually thereafter | |

| Subject | Review By | How Often | Comment |
|---|---|---|---|
| c. Are the names, credit card numbers, and other personal information of customers adequately protected from unauthorized disclosure, or hackers, and does the corporation otherwise comply with applicable privacy laws (and corporation privacy policies) regarding this information? | c. Chief executive, lead technology executive, and/ or technology consultant staff person | c. Ideally, at least quarterly | |
| 10. Does the corporation make its Form 990s available on its website or the website of a Form 990 compiler? | Chair, chief executive | At least annually | If the corporation relies on another organization to list the corporation's Form 990 on that organization's website, the corporation should periodically check the accuracy of the posted information. |

| Subject | Review By | How Often | Comment |
|---|---|---|---|
| 11. Has the corporation taken appropriate steps to limit claims by third parties resulting from: | | At least annually | Defamation claims may be made by individuals or other entities based on comments made in these electronic settings. |
| a. chat rooms, listservs, and social media either provided or used by the corporation? | a. Technology legal counsel | | |
| b. employee e-mail and social media activity? | b. Technology legal counsel | | |
| 12. If the corporation provides chat rooms or listservs, has it registered as an Internet service provider? | Chief executive, technology counsel, or consultant | When such activities begun; at least annually thereafter | |

# Chapter 7:
## Volunteers

# Chapter 7
# Volunteers

*Many nonprofit corporations find it useful or even essential to use the services of volunteers. The nonprofit director should understand not only how volunteers can be used to enhance the corporation's mission, but also the potential legal issues relating to the use of volunteers.*

*There is a prevalent use of volunteers in the nonprofit sector. In some circumstances, use of volunteers is essential to implement the corporate purpose, especially when the nonprofit corporation simply does not have the resources to perform its services without volunteers. In many cases, use of volunteers is itself demonstrative of the corporation's mission. The board should periodically evaluate what part volunteers should play in the corporation. For example, is there a role or need for volunteers in implementing a new program or service? Are there services that volunteers might provide that would enhance the corporation's fulfillment of its mission and involve more of the nonprofit's community in its activities? If so, what are the legal implications of using volunteers?*

## Risks Associated with Using Volunteers

Volunteers working on behalf of a nonprofit corporation are agents of the nonprofit corporation in the eyes of the law. That is, their acts or omissions and their care or negligence in performing their activities as volunteers are, within limits, considered to be the acts or omissions of the nonprofit corporation. *As a general rule, the nonprofit corporation will not be exonerated from liability arising from the conduct of the agent simply because the organization is a nonprofit corporation or because the agent was uncompensated or a volunteer.*

Nonprofit corporations can be and are held responsible for the actions of their volunteers and are expected, within reason, to foresee and address the risks associated with the use of volunteers. The potential risks include situations in which a volunteer is used to represent the nonprofit corporation to the public or in providing services consistent with the organization's purposes—for example, a program in which the nonprofit corporation sends volunteers into homes to provide services, uses volunteers to work in a position of trust with vulnerable individuals such as minors or the developmentally disabled, or uses volunteers to drive or to perform other potentially dangerous activities.

# Minimizing the Corporation's Liability

Because of the potential for liability involved in the use of volunteers, the nonprofit corporation should develop standards, guidelines, and procedures for the use of volunteers rather than enlisting the assistance of volunteers on a random or sporadic basis. This does not mean that there must be a large number of staff devoted to developing and administering a volunteer program. Rather, the decision to use as well as the use of volunteers should include an evaluation of the requirements for each volunteer position and written standards for selection, training, and supervision.

### *Selection of volunteers: written standards*

Nonprofit corporations should develop written standards for selecting volunteers. Depending on the nature of the volunteer position, the standards for selection may include education, experience, training requirements, consideration of the volunteer's ability to commit time to the position, and the volunteer's suitability for the particular position, such as working with children. The nonprofit corporation should then use these standards to verify a volunteer's suitability for the position. This can include requiring a written volunteer application form, personal interview, background check, driving record, reference check, and other methods to verify that the volunteer is an appropriate individual for the position. If a criminal or other background check is determined to be necessary for a volunteer position, the nonprofit corporation should obtain a signed release from the applicant authorizing the corporation to obtain the necessary information from the appropriate agencies. The board should consult with legal counsel in preparing the release form.

### *Oversight of volunteer activities: policies and procedures*

The nonprofit corporation should develop written materials for training and supervising volunteers. These materials may include written procedures, policies, or guidelines for a volunteer to use when acting on behalf of the nonprofit corporation. The corporation should provide any volunteer with clear directions and sufficient training. Developing written policies and procedures is important because a nonprofit corporation may be directly liable for its own conduct if a volunteer injures a third party due to the corporation's inadequate training or supervision of the volunteer.

### Insurance

The board should make sure that the nonprofit corporation is covered by the corporation's insurance for the activities of its volunteers. For example, if a nonprofit corporation is engaged in the distribution of goods or services involving the volunteer's use of his or her own automobile, the corporation may be liable for injuries caused by the volunteer's negligent driving of that automobile, even though the nonprofit corporation does not own the automobile or pay the driver.

The nonprofit corporation's insurance policies should be reviewed and modified, if necessary, to ensure that they cover the potential liability of the nonprofit corporation due to the conduct of a volunteer. *Such coverage is not automatic*, and may be an issue under several types of coverage, such as the corporation's general liability insurance and directors and officers insurance. Some insurance policies specifically address the unique organizational aspects and activities of nonprofit corporations, including volunteer activities. It is good practice to review all policies with legal counsel or an insurance broker experienced in working with nonprofit insurance issues, to confirm that the organization's activities and its agents are properly insured.

# Protecting the Volunteer from Individual Liability

Volunteers also may be sued individually for injuries they cause while acting in a volunteer capacity. The nonprofit corporation should consider what it should do to protect its volunteers in such situations.

# Statutes Protecting Volunteers

Most states have volunteer protection statutes limiting the liability of volunteers. Although the scope of the protection differs somewhat from state to state, most states provide at least some degree of immunity from civil liability for a volunteer if the volunteer acts within the scope of his or her duties, in good faith, and the injury is not caused by the volunteer's willful or wanton conduct.[1] There is also a federal Volunteer Protection Act, enacted in 1997, that provides some liability protection for volunteers of a nonprofit organization or governmental agency. In general, under the federal statute, volunteers will not be held liable for harm they caused if they were acting within the scope of their responsibilities, they were properly licensed or certified (if required), the harm was not caused by their willful or criminal conduct, gross negligence, or reckless conduct, and the harm was not caused by the volunteer operating a vehicle for which the operator must have a license or that must be insured.[2]

The federal statute preempts state law to the extent that it is inconsistent with the federal statute unless the state law provides additional protection from liability relating to volunteers. *The board of directors should make sure it understands the scope of available state and federal statutory protection for volunteers by consulting with legal counsel knowledgeable in the area.* To the extent that these statutes do not provide complete protection, the board should evaluate whether the corporation has adequate insurance coverage for volunteer activities. The board also should consider alerting volunteers to the potential need for personal insurance coverage for their own activities. (See further discussion in the section "*Insurance for Volunteers*" below.)

## Insurance for Volunteers

Volunteers should examine whether their individual insurance may cover any injury that they cause while acting as a volunteer. The board should make sure that, if possible, the corporation's volunteers are insured under its insurance policies, that is, the policy covers not only the corporation's liability for the acts of its volunteers, but also directly covers the volunteers. Special insurance riders or policies may be required to insure volunteers for a special occasion or fundraising event, such as a walkathon, run, or other event. In these circumstances, an insurer may require that the corporation obtain a waiver and release of liability from the volunteers for the event.

## Indemnification of Volunteers

The board should examine whether it can, or should, provide indemnification for volunteers. The nonprofit corporation acts in some states expressly permit indemnification of agents—such as volunteers (who are not directors). In these states, the board should review its articles of incorporation and bylaws to determine whether they address indemnification of volunteers. For instance, it is not unusual to find that the indemnification provisions of a nonprofit corporation's bylaws mandate that the corporation "shall" provide indemnification to the "fullest extent permitted by law." Although the scope of such required indemnification may be limited to the officers and directors, it also may specifically apply to the corporation's "agents"—a category within which most volunteers would presumably fit.

Before broadening the corporation's indemnification obligations to include volunteers, the board should assess the corporation's actual financial ability to indemnify volunteers and whether the corporation's obligation to indemnify its volunteers could be broader than its insurance coverage, potentially requiring the corporation to dip into its own assets to fulfill the indemnity obligations. In those states in which the nonprofit corporation act does not expressly address indemnification of volunteers, the nonprofit can still choose to indemnify its volunteers.[3]

# Claims by Volunteers against the Corporation

Use of volunteers may expose the nonprofit corporation to claims by the volunteer against the corporation. These can include a claim that the individual is an employee, not a volunteer, and therefore is entitled to compensation and benefits. This can also include a claim for compensation for injuries suffered while acting as a volunteer.

## Volunteer or Employee?

As discussed in *Chapter 8, Employees,* nonprofit corporations are subject to most state and federal statutes that address employer responsibilities and liabilities. Consequently, it is important for a nonprofit corporation to be sure it is appropriately categorizing individuals as employees or volunteers. An individual's status as a volunteer rather than an employee may sometimes be difficult to establish. If an individual volunteers on a consistent basis for a nonprofit organization in a position that is similar to a paid position at the organization, under certain circumstances that person may be considered, or claim to be, an employee of the nonprofit corporation and therefore entitled to compensation and other benefits.

To avoid this possibility, the nonprofit corporation should periodically review the activities of its volunteers and the benefits they receive to evaluate whether some volunteers might be considered employees rather than volunteers under the law. For example, under the Fair Labor Standards Act, an individual is prohibited from volunteering to do the same work that he or she is paid to do by the same employer; that is, a nonprofit corporation cannot ask its paid staff to "volunteer" part of their time to the organization.

Beyond this rule, the corporation should focus on such factors as whether the volunteer is doing the same work that some of the corporation's employees are being paid to do or that similar organizations often use paid staff to perform. If so, is the volunteer being paid or receiving other financial or other benefits, such as meals, shelter, stipends, insurance, medical benefits, a savings or retirement plan or credit toward the volunteer's degree? Or is the individual volunteering solely for a civic, charitable, or humanitarian reason? If the answers to these questions raise the possibility that a volunteer may be considered an employee (i.e., one who performs work for compensation), the board or chief executive should consult with legal counsel to review the volunteer's status.

## Employment Laws and the Volunteer

If volunteers are compensated for their efforts in a manner that makes them look more like employees, the nonprofit corporation may be subject to the minimum wage and overtime requirements of the Fair Labor Standards Act or a similar state law, federal or state discrimination statutes, and requirements regarding payment of employee benefits. For a discussion of issues that may arise with respect to employees of nonprofit corporations, *see Chapter 8, Employees.*

Even though equal employment opportunity laws may not apply to volunteers, the board should consider whether to adhere to the principles discussed below in the selection, supervision, and termination of its employees for its volunteers. Using a structured procedure for selecting and screening volunteers replaces a potentially arbitrary process with a fair and defensible method. Similarly, consistent application of performance and evaluation criteria for terminating volunteers will help prevent not only mistakes and hard feelings, but also potential discrimination complaints (whether or not valid).

## Obtaining a Waiver and Release of Liability

Many nonprofit corporations may use volunteers for events or in situations that present a particular risk of harm to the volunteer, such as volunteering for a race or other outdoor event. Volunteers also may be injured by other volunteers or employees of the nonprofit corporation. Unlike an employee covered by workers' compensation, the volunteer, if injured, may be able to sue the nonprofit corporation for injuries that occur while acting as a volunteer. To address these risks, the nonprofit corporation should consider whether to include the volunteer in the corporation's workers' compensation insurance, if possible, or obtain a written waiver and release of liability from the volunteers before permitting them to participate in the nonprofit corporation's activities.

One potential problem in seeking a waiver and release is practical, in that volunteers may not be willing to serve if required to sign a release. In addition, the fact that a release has been obtained does not guarantee liability protection for the organization. For example, some courts have found releases signed by parents on behalf of minors to be unenforceable.[4]

## Workers' Compensation Insurance

Workers' compensation laws vary from state to state. In some states, particular volunteers are covered by workers' compensation by statute; for example, in Colorado, volunteer firefighters for a municipal entity are automatically covered. Some workers' compensation laws may permit a nonprofit to elect to include volunteers in its existing workers' compensation insurance. One risk of including a volunteer in the workers' compensation insurance is the possibility that the volunteer would be considered an employee for other purposes. Again, this is an area in which the board should consult legal counsel in deciding how to address the organization's potential liability to its volunteers for injuries to the volunteer.

# Ownership of Materials Created by a Volunteer

To the extent that volunteers are creating written curricula, videotapes, audiotapes, printed publications, photographs, or other works for the nonprofit corporation, care should be taken to make sure that the nonprofit corporation is the owner of the work (with all rights to the work product) or that it obtains a license sufficient for its uses of the work. Therefore, *before* any works are produced, the nonprofit corporation should require any volunteer who produces work that would be protected under copyright laws to sign a statement that the work is "for hire" and owned by the nonprofit corporation or to provide a license or assignment to the organization. (See the section *"Works for Hire"* in *Chapter 8, Employees.*).

*See the Suggested Questions and Checklist following the Endnotes below to review the issues discussed in this chapter.*

# Endnotes

1.  For example, in Colorado, the statute does not provide protection for the negligent act of a volunteer involving the operation of a motor vehicle. Col. Rev. Stat. § 13-21-115.5. In Utah, the statute does not apply if the nonprofit organization fails to provide a financially secure source of recovery for individuals injured by the volunteer. Utah Code Ann. § 78B-4-102.

2.  The federal statute does not apply to conduct that constitutes a crime of violence, an act of international terrorism, a hate crime, a sexual offense, or a violation of a federal or state civil rights law; or that occurred when the defendant was under the influence of drugs or alcohol. 42 U.S.C. § 14501 *et seq.*

3.  The Model Act does not expressly address indemnification of employees, volunteers, and other agents. Still, a nonprofit corporation has the power to indemnify and advance expenses for employees, volunteers, and other agents under traditional contract and agency law principles. *See* Model Act, Introductory Comment, Subchapter E (Indemnification and Advance for Expenses), Chapter 8.

4.  *See, e.g.,* Galloway v. State of Iowa, 790 N.W.2d 252 (Iowa 2010).

# Suggested Questions for Directors Regarding Volunteers

(1)  Which of the nonprofit corporation's programs use volunteers?
(2)  How were they recruited?
(3)  What functions do they perform?
(4)  Do written guidelines, standards, or procedures exist for the nonprofit corporation's selection of volunteers?
(5)  Is there a training program in place for the nonprofit corporation's volunteer programs?
(6)  Do the corporation's insurance policies cover claims against the corporation based on acts of its volunteers?
(7)  Do the corporation's insurance policies cover the volunteers individually?
(8)  Do the corporation's insurance policies cover claims against the corporation by a volunteer?
(9)  Do the corporation's articles of incorporation, bylaws, or policies require or permit indemnification of volunteers?

        a.     If they do, should they?

        b.     If they don't, should they?

(10)  Have the corporation's volunteer positions been reviewed to evaluate whether they may be employees instead of volunteers?

(11)  Should the corporation require that its volunteers sign a waiver and release of liability for claims arising from the volunteer's activities for the corporation?

(12)  Should the corporation obtain workers' compensation insurance for its volunteers?

# Checklist: Volunteers

*Note:*    For simplicity, these and other chapter checklists describe a corporation having a chair, who presides over the board of directors; a chief executive, who may be a staff person; an executive committee; a governance/nominating committee; and an audit committee. (We recognize, however, that in many smaller and other nonprofits, these committee functions may be performed by either the executive committee or the board as a whole.) We also assume a legal counsel—someone, paid or unpaid, having primary responsibility for the corporation's legal affairs. Many corporations, especially larger nonprofits, may have other committees established for specific purposes, such as establishing executive compensation; monitoring compliance with legal requirements; and overseeing investments and other financial matters.

| Subject | Review By | How Often | Comment |
| --- | --- | --- | --- |
| 1. Does our corporation have a volunteer program? | Chief executive, full board | Annually, or at inception of new program | Volunteer programs should be formally approved by management. |

| Subject | Review By | How Often | Comment |
|---|---|---|---|
| 2. Has the program been approved by the board? Are its functions defined in the corporate resolutions or policies? | Chief executive, full board | Annually, or at inception of new program | Volunteer programs should be formally approved by management. |
| 3. Who administers the program at staff level? | Chief executive | As needed, but reviewed annually | |
| 4. Are volunteers properly screened when selected? | Chief executive, legal counsel | As needed, but reviewed annually | |
| 5. Is volunteer training adequate so that volunteers can competently perform their tasks? | Chief executive | As needed, but reviewed annually | |
| 6. Are the volunteers covered by the corporation's insurance program? | Chief executive, legal counsel | Annually | Directors should understand that the inclusion of volunteers is not automatic. |
| 7. Are volunteers subject to indemnification under the corporation's articles of incorporation, bylaws, or policies concerning indemnification? | Chief executive, legal counsel | Annually | Directors should understand that the inclusion of volunteers is not automatic. |

| Subject | Review By | How Often | Comment |
|---|---|---|---|
| 8. Do volunteers perform functions giving rise to significant risk, such as driving automobiles on the corporation's business? | Chief executive, legal counsel | Annually | It may be prudent to examine volunteer's driving record, and personal auto insurance coverage. |
| 9. Are volunteers covered by the corporation's workers' compensation insurance? Can they be? Should they be? | Chief executive, legal counsel | Annually | The corporation's insurance broker can review the available options. |
| 10. Do any volunteers receive compensation or benefits, such that they should be classified as employees rather than as volunteers (and to whom the Fair Labor Standards Acts and other laws applicable to employees would apply)? | Legal counsel | Annually, or at inception of a new program | |

# Chapter 8:
## Employees

# Chapter 8
# Employees

*Most nonprofit corporations employ staff to assist in carrying out the mission and activities of the corporation. The nonprofit director should have a basic understanding of the legal risks and obligations that go with having employees.*

*Although some nonprofit corporations may rely solely on volunteers to accomplish their missions, most nonprofit corporations employ paid staff to carry out at least some of these activities. The size of the staff can vary from a single part-time employee in a small, grassroots organization to a staff of a hundred or a thousand full-time employees. All nonprofit corporations generally must comply with federal and state employment laws. Some legal requirements may vary depending on the number of employees.*

*Nonprofit corporations often have the employment relationship with the chief executive defined by a formal contract, which should be approved by the board of directors or a committee of the board. In addition to being aware of the terms of the contract, directors should be aware of the law applicable to that employment relationship. The board of directors may also approve policies and employment terms applicable to other employees. In addition, because a significant number of the lawsuits generally brought against nonprofit directors and officers involve employment-related matters, it is important for directors to have a basic understanding of the range of legal requirements and potential liabilities that may arise in connection with employees. It is becoming more common for nonprofit corporations to obtain employment practice liability insurance. This chapter will outline some of the considerations and general legal requirements for nonprofit corporations that hire employees.*

# Executive Employment Relationships

## Chief Executives and Other Management Employees

Nonprofit corporations commonly hire a chief executive or CEO, sometimes called an executive director, who is responsible for day-to-day operations of the organization, including hiring and supervising other staff. The chief executive reports directly to the board of directors.

## Executive Employment Agreements

The board, or a committee of the board, typically will define, negotiate, and approve the chief executive's contract. Especially if the executive works directly with clients or the public, the board may want to conduct a background check before the initial hiring of an executive or approval of the contract. The executive's employment agreement should outline job responsibilities, compensation, and benefits (including any performance incentives), and contain termination provisions.

## Evaluation of Chief Executive

Performance evaluations can be a good shield against potential employment-related liability if they are done well. If they are poorly done, they can be a potent sword in the hand of a former employee. Thus, it is better to do performance evaluations correctly, or not at all.

The board should establish a process for annual performance reviews of the chief executive. This process, which may be done by a committee of the board, should be designed to give the board sufficient information to evaluate the chief executive's contribution to the organization. For instance, the evaluation process might include interviews with clients or other constituencies served by the nonprofit corporation, interviews with other staff, and review of objective measures of the organization (e.g. budget, membership numbers, etc.)

# Employment Laws Applicable to Nonprofit Corporations

Generally, nonprofit corporations are subject to the same federal and state laws as other employers. These laws include statutes regarding equal employment opportunity, wage and hour issues, employee benefits, workers' compensation, and unemployment insurance. Nonprofit corporations are also subject to common law claims such as breach of contract or negligence. Because many of these laws apply to corporations with just one employee, even the smallest nonprofit corporations should have a staff member, counsel or other adviser who is responsible for and familiar with human resources issues. Likewise, legal counsel for the nonprofit corporation should review employment policies and practices for compliance with applicable law.

## Federal Equal Employment Opportunity Laws

Several federal statutes prohibit discrimination based on a particular status. As set forth below, these statutes apply to nonprofit corporations that employ at least a specified minimum number of employees.

| Statute: | Prohibits discrimination based on: | Applies to corporations with at least: |
|---|---|---|
| Title VII of the Civil Rights Act of 1964 | Race, gender, national origin, religion[1] | 15 or more employees |
| Americans with Disabilities Act | Disability or perceived disability | 15 or more employees |
| Age Discrimination in Employment Act | Age (over 40) | 15 or more employees |
| Equal Pay Act | Discrimination with regard to compensation | No minimum number employees |
| Immigration Reform and Control Act | National origin or citizenship | 4 or more employees |

| Statute: | Prohibits discrimination based on: | Applies to corporations with at least: |
| --- | --- | --- |
| Pregnancy Discrimination Act | Pregnancy or childbirth | 15 or more employees |
| Genetic Information Nondiscrimination Act[2] | Genetic information | 15 or more employees |
| Uniformed Services Employment & Reemployment Rights Act | Veterans and members of the armed forces | No minimum number of employees |

Nonprofit corporations that are subject to these federal statutes may not discriminate in hiring, compensation, working conditions, promotion, discipline, termination, or other employment practices. Boards of nonprofits that are not subject to some of the above laws (at least given current employee numbers) may nevertheless choose to adopt policies that conform to these laws. Even if not legally required, such policies will serve to help prevent inadvertent violations when the number of employees increases, as well as discriminatory incidents that could result in public embarrassment, even if not legally actionable. In addition, the Genetic Information Nondiscrimination Act prohibits employers from even obtaining genetic information on employees and employee family members except in very limited circumstances.

## Reasonable Accommodation for Disabilities

The Americans with Disabilities Act (ADA) mandates the giving of "equal opportunity" to persons with disabilities, by requiring an employer (whether nonprofit or for-profit) to provide "reasonable accommodation" to employees with disabilities.

Reasonable accommodation under the ADA may require

(a)    making existing facilities used by employees readily accessible to and usable by individuals with disabilities; and

(b)    job restructuring, part-time or modified work schedules, reassignment to a vacant position, acquisition or modification of equipment or devices, appropriate adjustment or modifications of examinations, training materials or policies, the provision of qualified readers or interpreters, and other similar accommodations for individuals with disabilities.[3]

Nonprofit corporations that also serve as public accommodations (schools, theaters, libraries, hospitals, etc.) likely will have additional responsibilities to provide equal access and reasonable accommodations to members of the public with disabilities.

## State and Local Equal Opportunity Laws

In addition to federal law, nonprofit corporations usually are subject to state or local equal employment opportunity laws that may impose the same or additional requirements. For example, some state laws parallel the federal requirements, but apply to employers of all sizes—*regardless of the number of employees*. Other state and local statutes and ordinances may prohibit discrimination based on a status, such as sexual orientation, not covered by federal law. Still, as under federal law, state laws may provide certain exemptions for religious corporations with respect to laws prohibiting employment discrimination based on religion.

## Equal Opportunity Policies

To formalize commitment to equal employment opportunity and comply with relevant laws, nonprofit organizations should adopt a formal equal employment opportunity policy. This policy should be approved by the board of directors and comply with all relevant law. The policy should state the organization's commitment to equal employment opportunity, provide a procedure for reporting any alleged discrimination, and prohibit retaliation against anyone who makes a report or complaint. Once approved, the policy should be posted publicly and distributed to staff. The board should review the policy annually, and confirm that it conforms to current legal requirements.

## Antiharassment Policies

In addition to an equal employment opportunity policy, boards of directors of nonprofit corporations should adopt an antiharassment policy for the corporation. Under certain circumstances, employers that have such a policy may be able to assert an affirmative defense to liability based on the existence of a written policy and a victim's failure to make a complaint under it. This policy should contain a statement that harassment will not be permitted, a complaint procedure for victims or others to report harassment, and a prohibition of retaliation. The policy should be expressly applicable to both employees and volunteers.

## Family and Medical Leave

Under the federal Family and Medical Leave Act of 1993 (FMLA), nonprofit corporations with fifty or more employees are required to provide twelve weeks of unpaid leave for qualified employees upon the birth or adoption of a child, or if the employee or a family member has a serious health condition. The FMLA permits a spouse, son, daughter, parent, or next of kin to take up to twenty-six work weeks of leave to care for a member of the armed forces who is undergoing medical treatment, recuperation, or therapy or is otherwise in outpatient or disabled. The law also permits an employee to take FMLA leave for any "qualifying exigency ... arising out of the fact that the spouse, or a son, daughter or parent of the employee is on active duty or has been notified of an impending call or order to active duty." The organization must maintain the employee's position and benefits during the leave.

Some states have their own laws regarding family and medical leave that may place additional burdens on employers, including nonprofit organizations. *Nonprofit corporations that are subject to FMLA and/or state leave statutes should enact a family and medical leave policy that complies with all applicable statutes and regulations.* In addition, if the nonprofit corporation is subject to FMLA, strict notice and recordkeeping requirements apply.

## Wage and Hour Issues: Fair Labor Standards Act

Many nonprofit organizations are subject to the federal Fair Labor Standards Act (FLSA), which requires that employers pay at least the federal minimum wage and provide overtime pay (one and one-half the regular rate of pay) to nonexempt employees who work over forty hours in a single work week.

### *Does the FLSA apply?*

FLSA applies to hospitals, schools, and other organizations engaged in interstate or foreign commerce or in the production of goods for commerce, either directly or indirectly through one or more affiliates.[4]

Nonprofit organizations are *not* exempted automatically from coverage under the FLSA, even if they have no obvious commercial activities. Moreover, some kinds of organizations, such as those that operate hospitals, schools, and similar institutions, are covered by the FLSA irrespective of whether they are "engaged in interstate commerce." Other nonprofits are subject to the FLSA if they meet two tests: first, they have two or more employees engaged in commerce or in the production of goods for commerce, or employees handling, selling, or otherwise working on materials that have been moved in or produced for commerce by any person; and second, they have an annual gross volume of sales of $500,000 or more.

Whether a nonprofit corporation is "engaged in commerce" or "the production of goods for commerce" as defined by FLSA will depend on the activities of it and its affiliates. When a nonprofit engages in a commercial activity of any kind, it is considered a business purpose, which makes it subject to the FLSA, just as a for-profit commercial entity would be. Neither tax-exempt status nor charitable purposes render an otherwise commercial activity exempt from coverage. For example, fraternal orders and country clubs are considered to be operated for a business purpose, and thereby subject to the FLSA, despite their nonprofit status. On the other hand, religious and other nonprofit corporations may escape FLSA coverage if they solely engage in nonprofit activities, or only use true volunteers for their commercial activities.

With regard to the requirement that the commercial activities be "interstate," this definition has been applied broadly to a wide variety of activities, including the use of supplies produced in another state.

Because courts and the Department of Labor are likely to strain to make FLSA apply and because it is a prudent business practice to pay minimum wage and overtime to nonexempt employees, *many nonprofit organizations may find it wise to comply with FLSA, even if a plausible argument can be made that it does not apply.* A nonprofit board should make sure that the organization has received legal advice before concluding that it need not comply with the provisions of the FLSA, if it otherwise meets the coverage description set forth above.

### Exempt employees under the FLSA

Even if a nonprofit corporation is subject to the FLSA, not all of its employees are covered by the act. FLSA exemptions apply to certain executive, administrative, and professional employees who are compensated on a salary basis and whose job functions meet the tests set forth in the FLSA. Special care should be given to classifying an employee as "exempt" or "nonexempt," since a disgruntled former employee may challenge his or her classification after the fact, demanding overtime and penalties from the nonprofit corporation.

## State Wage and Hour Laws

In addition to federal law (and even if the nonprofit is not subject to FLSA), most states have wage and hour laws that apply to nonprofit organizations. These laws may impose additional burdens such as a state minimum wage, requiring overtime pay for all hours over twelve worked in a single workday, payment for unused vacation pay upon termination, compensation for on-call or sleep time (also covered by FLSA), and payment of expenses related to uniforms.

# Employee Handbooks and Personnel Policies

Nonprofit boards of directors often approve employee policies that make up employee handbooks. Commonly, employee handbooks are a collection of policies ranging from attendance, to benefits, to compensation, to workplace violence. An employee handbook that does not contain conspicuous disclaimer language may be considered a contract that alters the otherwise "at-will" nature of employment.[5] For example, language in a handbook regarding progressive discipline, termination procedures (e.g. defining "for cause"), or even broad promises of "fair treatment" may change this status. An employee who is terminated might use the handbook as the basis for a breach of contract claim, arguing that the organization is bound to use progressive discipline procedures outlined in the employee handbook. To avoid these results, consideration should be given to introductory language that states the purpose of the handbook. A prominent disclaimer that states that the handbook does not alter the "at-will" nature of employment should also be included. The board of directors should make sure that legal counsel familiar with employment-law issues reviews the handbook or policies before they are approved and distributed to staff.

## Grievance Procedures

Some nonprofit corporations have grievance procedures (often contained in the employee handbook) in which officials in the organization (such as the chief executive) or the board may hear and rule upon employee grievances with management. These grievances most typically involve adverse actions taken against an employee such as discipline, denial of promotion, or termination. Boards should decide whether or not to have such policies—since the existence of a grievance procedure or other appeal process, like a progressive discipline policy in an employee handbook, may be deemed to alter the "at-will" status of employees. If the board decides to have a grievance procedure that includes review of an employment action by the board, board members should make sure they understand their role in the grievance process and whether the board's decision is binding or merely advisory.

## Workplace Violence

As part of an employee handbook or as a separate standalone policy, it is recommended that a nonprofit corporation have an antiviolence policy that prohibits violence and weapons on the premises or any place where activities of the corporation may be conducted. Such a policy will also assist the organization to comply with Occupational Health and Safety Administration (OSHA) rules requiring a safe workplace.

## Employee Benefits

Nonprofit boards of directors often approve employee benefit plans to be offered to the organization's employees. Such plans include retirement and deferred compensation plans, welfare benefit plans (health, disability, life insurance, etc.), and various fringe benefit arrangements. Directors should make sure they are informed regarding the duties and liability exposure created by such benefit plans. Some key issues relating to employee benefit plans are discussed below.

## Reasonable Compensation

The value of employee benefit plans must be considered part of an employee's overall compensation in determining whether an employee is receiving reasonable compensation for services. If the value of a key employee's total compensation package is less than what similar organizations provide, the corporation may be in danger of losing the employee. On the other hand, an overly generous benefits package may, when combined with the employee's salary, raise private benefit/inurement concerns for tax-exempt organizations (see the discussion in the section *"Limitations on Private Benefit and Private Inurement"* in *Chapter 4, Taxation*). With respect to § 501(c)(3) and § 501(c)(4) tax-exempt organizations, this is especially important in avoiding the excise tax on excess benefit transactions that can be imposed both on recipients and responsible organization managers under the IRS's intermediate sanctions powers.

The process for determining the compensation of chief executive has become a focus for the IRS. The Form 990 requires a tax-exempt organization to state whether the process for determining compensation for the chief executive and other officers and key employees includes a review and approval by a governing body or compensation committee composed of "independent" persons, use of data as to comparable compensation for similarly qualified persons in functionally comparable positions at similarly situated organizations, and contemporaneous documentation and recordkeeping with respect to deliberations and decisions regarding the compensation arrangement. The factors are important for purposes of establishing reasonableness of compensation. (The intermediate sanction powers of the IRS, as well as these procedures for establishing reasonableness with compensation, are discussed further in the section *"Intermediate Sanctions: Excise Tax on Public Charities' Excess Benefit Transactions"* in *Chapter 4, Taxation*).

## ERISA Requirements

Most types of employee benefit plans are subject to the requirements of the Employee Retirement Income Security Act of 1974, as amended (ERISA), unless the plan is one adopted by a church or governmental plan exempt from ERISA and, in the case of a church plan, the organization has not elected to be governed by ERISA. ERISA imposes a number of reporting and disclosure requirements, creates certain minimum rights for plan participants, and imposes numerous fiduciary responsibilities. The employer organization, and under certain circumstances one or more of its employees, officers, or board members, is typically viewed as a fiduciary with respect to the plan. In addition, for certain employee benefits that are intended to receive favorable tax treatment, there are a number of technical requirements under the Code that must be satisfied, including rules intended to prevent discrimination in favor of highly compensated employees.

## Plan Documents

Most types of employee benefit plans must be maintained pursuant to written plan documents. These documents should be carefully reviewed by the human resources manager or an outside benefits expert to ensure that they reflect the actual practices for operating the employee benefit plans and that they satisfy the technical requirements of ERISA and the Code.

## Special Rules for Nonprofits

Employee benefits offered by tax-exempt organizations are subject to some special rules, particularly with respect to retirement and deferred compensation plans.

### *Tax deferral arrangements*

Unlike taxable organizations, tax-exempt organizations are somewhat more limited in the amount of tax-deferred compensation that can be offered to the organization's executives or other key employees. Although the restrictions on tax-deferred compensation arrangements were significantly loosened beginning in 2002, tax-exempt organizations are still subject to certain maximum amounts ($16,500 in 2010 and 2011, adjusted annually by the IRS based on inflation) of deferred compensation that can be provided in any year to an employee, pursuant to a nonqualified plan that is an "eligible deferred compensation plan" within the meaning of 26 U.S.C. § 457(b). The limit takes into account both employer and employee contributions.  Such limits are now in addition to—and are no longer offset against—any amounts that the employee has elected to defer under the organization's 401(k) or 403(b) plan. If a tax-exempt organization desires to provide any additional deferred compensation beyond the new § 457(b) limits, this compensation must be subject to a "substantial risk of forfeiture" as determined under 26 U.S.C. § 457(f).

Directors of tax-exempt organizations should make sure that their organization has taken advantage of recent liberalizations in the tax-deferred compensation rules. These changes may make it easier for tax-exempt organizations to attract and retain qualified executives, by lessening the difference between the kind of deferred compensation arrangements that can be offered by tax-exempt corporations compared to those provided by for-profit organizations.

### Section 403(b) and Section 401(k) plans

Tax-sheltered annuity or mutual fund custodial account arrangements described in § 403(b) may only be offered by tax-exempt organizations described in § 501(c)(3). Other types of nonprofit organizations cannot contribute to § 403(b) plans. Previously, nonprofit corporations were not permitted to maintain § 401(k) plans; however, nonprofits are now permitted to offer such plans to their employees.

# Other Laws Relating to Employees

## Background Checks

The Fair Credit Reporting Act (FCRA) requires employers who use third-party consumer reporting agencies to conduct background checks to obtain applicant authorization before conducting such checks.[6] The law also requires employers to provide prior notice to the employee before taking any adverse action against the applicant, including a decision not to hire the applicant based on the information obtained.

## Employee E-mail Monitoring

The Electronic Communications Privacy Act prohibits an employer from intercepting or monitoring employee e-mail and voicemail except when such interception occurs in the ordinary course of the employer's business or the employee consents to the monitoring.[7] In certain circumstances, nonprofit employers may be allowed to monitor employee e-mail if it is stored on the employer's computer system. To avoid ambiguity, the organization should notify employees, through employee handbooks or other means, that it may monitor e-mail in the ordinary course of business and as otherwise permitted by law.

# Identity Theft Protection

Many states require employers to limit access to documents containing an employee's personal information, including Social Security number.

# Tax Withholding and Payroll Taxes

Nonprofit corporations are also required to comply with state and federal laws regarding tax withholding and payment of payroll taxes. Directors, especially director/officers, may be personally liable for any unpaid taxes or penalties if they are found to be responsible for the unpaid taxes.[8] In comparison, directors who do not participate in day-to-day or financial operations, and who have no responsibility for the payment of payroll taxes and no knowledge of the failure to pay payroll taxes, would generally not be liable for unpaid payroll taxes and any accompanying penalty.[9]

# Workers' Compensation and Unemployment Insurance

Nonprofit corporations with employees are subject to state laws regarding workers' compensation and unemployment insurance. These laws vary from state to state, but typically, a nonprofit organization, like any other employer, is responsible for obtaining insurance for on-the-job injuries (workers' compensation) or the effects of terminating employees (unemployment). In some states, nonprofit corporations may elect to self-insure for unemployment compensation claims; in that case, the nonprofit does not make standard state unemployment tax payments, but pays its share of actual unemployment claims. Further, many states specifically exempt churches from unemployment insurance obligations. Board approval of workers' compensation insurance policies is recommended if the policies would be material to the corporation, unless the board has delegated such approval to the corporation's chief executive or other managerial personnel.

## Immigration Laws

The Immigration Reform and Control Act of 1986 (IRCA) prohibits the employment of unauthorized aliens (i.e., noncitizens who are not authorized by the Immigration and Naturalization Service to work in this country). IRCA applies to nonprofit corporations and places administrative burdens on nonprofit corporations to verify that all employees are authorized to work in the United States. IRCA also has nondiscrimination provisions that prohibit discrimination on the basis of national origin or citizenship.

## Work for Hire

To the extent that employees, volunteers, or third parties are creating curricula, videotapes, audio tapes, printed publications, photographs, or other works for the nonprofit corporation, care should be taken to make sure that the nonprofit corporation is the owner (with all rights to the work product) or that it obtains a license sufficient for its uses of the work. An employee's original works of authorship are deemed to be authored and owned by the employer if the work was prepared by the employee within the scope of his or her employment. On the other hand, work done by an independent party, or an employee working outside the scope of his or her employment, is deemed to be authored and owned by the original author unless the parties expressly agree, in a signed writing executed *prior* to the work's creation, that the work shall be considered a work made for hire.

## Confidential Information

The nonprofit corporation should also exercise care to protect its confidential and proprietary information. Employees, volunteers, and others may have access to trade secrets or confidential information such as donor or member lists, personnel information, medical records, patient or client information, or other data or materials that must be kept confidential. The nonprofit corporation should adopt a confidentiality policy and should take reasonable precautions (such as passwords, limited distribution, stamping materials "CONFIDENTIAL") to protect against unauthorized dissemination of the organization's confidential information.

# Liability to Others for Acts of Employees

## Negligent Hiring and Supervision Claims

Negligent hiring and negligent supervision are typically raised by clients or members of the public who allege they have been injured by an employee (such as a child who is allegedly sexually abused by a daycare worker) and claim that the corporation failed to properly screen the employee before hiring, or to supervise him or her once hired. To avoid such claims, and as a prudent business practice, the corporation should screen candidates for employment, especially if they work with children or other vulnerable populations. Likewise, systems should be in place to monitor and supervise employees. (Similar issues apply to volunteers who work independently with the public or vulnerable groups; see the discussion in the section *"Risks Association with Using Volunteers"* in *Chapter 7, Volunteers.*)

# Liability to Employees

## Wrongful Discharge in Violation of Public Policy

Employees may bring a wrongful discharge claim if they believe they were terminated because they refused to participate in an illegal act on behalf of the corporation or because they asserted rights under a statute, such as filing a workers' compensation claim.

## Right to Privacy: Disclosure and E-mail Review

Most states recognize a common law right of privacy of some kind. There are generally four types of privacy rights that may be asserted by employees: intrusion upon physical solitude, public disclosure of private facts, false light in the public eye, and appropriation of name or likeness. An employee could bring an action against the nonprofit corporation if the organization did an egregious act that violated the employee's right to nondisclosure of private facts, such as disclosing publicly that an employee had AIDS.

Privacy concerns are magnified with the employer's monitoring of electronic mail and Internet usage. As noted above, in *"Other Laws Relating to Employees:*

*Employee E-mail and Other Monitoring,*" employers are generally permitted to conduct such monitoring in the ordinary course of business. It is good practice, and in certain circumstances legally required, to notify employees in advance that the organization's e-mail and Internet systems are subject to monitoring at any time without further notice. Such statements often are contained in a written e-mail or Internet policy that may be a freestanding policy or part of an employee handbook.

## Lifestyle Discrimination

Many states prohibit discrimination against employees who use tobacco products outside of the workplace. Other states have broader language that prohibits discrimination for lawful activities carried on by employees outside the workplace.

# Collective Bargaining

Nonprofit corporations of a certain size or in certain industries may face issues involving unions or unionization activities. A discussion of these issues is outside the scope of this *Guidebook*.

*See the Suggested Questions and Checklist following the Endnotes below to review the issues discussed in this chapter.*

## Endnotes

1. In some cases, there may be exceptions for religious corporations to laws prohibiting discrimination on the basis of religion, where the religious organization employs individuals of a particular religion to perform work connected with the carrying out of the religious corporation's activities. *See* 42 U.S.C. § 2000e-1 (exemption to Title VII prohibition on discrimination on the basis of religion).

2. 42 U.S.C. § 2000ff.

3. 42 U.S.C. § 12111(9).

4. 29 U.S.C. § 203(s)(1).

5.   In most states, employment is presumed to be "at-will," meaning that either side may terminate the relationship at any time for any reason or no reason at all.

6.   15 U.S.C. § 1681.

7.   18 U.S.C. § 2510 (as amended by the Stored Communications Act and Patriot Act).

8.   *See* I.R.C. § 6672(a).

9.   *See* I.R.C. § 6672(e).

# Suggested Questions for Directors Regarding Employees

(1)   How many employees does the corporation have?

(2)   Which employees report directly to the board?

(3)   Are there written employment contracts with these employees?

(4)   How are performance reviews conducted for the chief executive?

(5)   Does the corporation have an equal opportunity policy?

(6)   Does the corporation have an antiharassment policy?

(7)   What kind of family and medical leave policy exists?

(8)   Does the corporation pay minimum wage and overtime pay to nonexempt employees?

(9)   Who classifies employees as exempt or nonexempt?

(10)  Does the organization have an employee handbook?

(11)  Does the employee handbook contain a disclaimer regarding employment at will?

(12)  Does the organization have a grievance procedure in which employment actions may be reviewed by the board? If so, what is the board's role?

(13)  Does the corporation comply with applicable laws regarding workers' compensation, unemployment insurance, and tax withholding?

(14)  Does the corporation comply with relevant requirements of the Immigration and Naturalization Service?

(15)  Does the corporation have "work for hire" agreements with third parties (or employees acting outside their scope of employment) who produce copyrighted works?

(16)  Does the corporation take adequate precautions to protect trade secrets and confidential information?

(17)  If employees work with children or other vulnerable people, does the corporation do adequate preemployment screening and background checks?

# Checklist: Employees

*Note:*    For simplicity. these and other chapter checklists describe a corporation having a chair, who pre-sides over the board of directors; a chief executive, who may be a staff person; an executive committee; a governance/nominating committee; a personnel committee; and an audit committee. (We recognize, however, that in many smaller and other nonprofits, these committee functions may be performed by either the executive committee or the board as a whole.) We also assume a legal counsel—someone, paid or unpaid, having primary responsibility for the corporation's legal affairs. Many corporations, especially larger nonprofits, may have other committees established for specific purposes, such as establishing executive compensation; monitoring compliance with legal requirements; and overseeing investments and other financial matters.

| Subject | Review By | How Often | Comment |
|---|---|---|---|
| 1. What employment arrangements are in place with chief executive? | Chair, chief executive, personnel committee, or full board | Annually or when chief executive or terms of employment change | Key terms of employment agreements with chief executives should be approved by the full board. |
| 2. How is the performance of the chief executive evaluated? | Chair, personnel committee | Annually | The chief executive's performance should be evaluated annually by the board. |
| 3. Does the corporation have an equal opportunity policy? | Chief executive, legal counsel, board | Annually | The board should approve an equal opportunity policy. |

| Subject | Review By | How Often | Comment |
|---|---|---|---|
| 4. Does the corporation have an antiharassment policy? | Chief executive, legal counsel, board | Upon adoption, then reviewed annually to keep updated | The board should approve an antiharassment policy. |
| 5. What kind of family and medical leave is provided to employees? | Chief executive, legal counsel | Upon adoption, then reviewed annually to keep updated | Family and medical leave policies should be in writing and comply with applicable law. |
| 6. How are employees classified as exempt/ nonexempt? | Chief executive, legal counsel | As job descriptions and positions are created | Compliance with the Fair Labor Standards Act should be monitored by legal counsel. |
| 7. Does the organization have an up-to-date employee handbook with appropriate disclaimers? | Chief executive, legal counsel, full board or personnel committee | Upon adoption, then reviewed annually to keep updated | Boards often review and approve employee handbooks since they often contain mission statements and broad policies. Special care should be taken to have appropriate disclaimers and that policies comply with applicable laws. |
| 8. Does the board "hear" appeals or employee grievances? | Chief executive, full board or committee of board per policy | As grievances are filed | Most nonprofits will not have such a process. If they do, the board should be familiar with the process and its role. |

| Subject | Review By | How Often | Comment |
|---|---|---|---|
| 9. Does the corporation have systems to comply with applicable laws regarding tax withholding, immigration, workers' compensation, and unemployment insurance? | Chief executive, legal counsel | Annually | Legal counsel and the officers of the board should make sure contracts and systems are in place to ensure compliance. |
| 10. Does the corporation own rights protecting original materials under the Copyright Act? | Chief executive, legal counsel | As works are created or commissioned | "Work for hire" agreements should be entered into with independent contractors and volunteers. |
| 11. Does the corporation protect its confidential information? | Chief executive, board | Upon adoption, then reviewed annually | A confidentiality policy should be adopted and other precautions taken to protect secrecy of confidential information. |
| 12. Does the corporation adequately screen employees before hiring? | Chief executive | As employees are hired | Thorough background and reference checks should be conducted on all employees who work with children or other vulnerable populations. |

| Subject | Review By | How Often | Comment |
|---------|-----------|-----------|---------|
| 13. Does the corporation have an organizational chart? | Chief executive | Annually | An organizational chart of management and management reporting relationships should assist the board in understanding the organization. |

# Chapter 9:
## Duties of Directors Under Special Circumstances: Change in Control, Sale of Unique Assets; and Bankruptcy

# Chapter 9

# Duties of Directors Under Special Circumstances

*This chapter discusses the duties of a director for the following special circumstances: (1) mergers, sales, or other change of control events; (2) disposition of unique assets; and (3) insolvency or bankruptcy.*

## Mergers, Sales, and Other Change of Control Events

In the course of a nonprofit corporation's existence, there may come a time when its board is faced with a traumatic decision: Will the corporation's mission be better served if the corporation merges with another entity, sells all or some of its assets, converts to for-profit status, changes its membership, or undergoes some other event that will result in change of control over the corporation's operations? The processes that a nonprofit board uses to make a change of control decision must be sufficient to satisfy the directors' fiduciary duty obligations to the corporation and its mission, as well as other applicable legal requirements.

When faced with a prospective change of control, a nonprofit corporation director should understand what actions may be required to be taken to satisfy the director's fiduciary duties to the corporation with respect to such an event. Further, the director should ask management staff or legal counsel to determine if the state attorney general or other regulatory authorities have notice rights or approval powers over the change of control decision. In addition to regulators, community interest groups may seek to change or influence the board's decision; thus, the directors will need to evaluate to what degree and in what manner the board will provide information to or seek input from these interest groups.

# Application of Duties of Care and Loyalty to Change of Control Decisions

## *In general*

As discussed in *Chapter 2, Duties and Rights of Nonprofit Corporation Directors,* directors of nonprofits are considered fiduciaries with duties of care and loyalty to the corporation. When a change of control is contemplated, the processes used by the directors to evaluate the potential change—including decisions among various alternatives—is likely to be subject to scrutiny. Persons and groups outside the board may have reason to evaluate whether the board's decision process was handled in a manner that satisfied the directors' duties.

Nonprofit directors should be aware that they may be judged in part by standards that have developed in the for-profit world, in case law challenging the propriety of board actions in change of control situations.[1] Although some issues arising in nonprofit change of control circumstances do not arise in the for-profit world (and vice versa), a number of basic guidelines drawn from the for-profit arena are equally applicable to nonprofit boards. These guidelines generally focus on what actions are necessary or sufficient to show that the directors have fulfilled their fiduciary duties of care and loyalty in connection with a change of control event.

## *Satisfying the duty of care*

**How and when the duty of care applies.** The director duty of care requires that the process by which a change of control decision is made should mirror the significance of the decision. (For further discussion of a director's duty of care, see the section *"The Duty of Care"* in *Chapter 2, Duties and Rights of Nonprofit Corporation Directors.*) Sometimes, the decision process is initiated by an external prompt—for instance, another nonprofit with a similar mission proposes a merger to maximize joint corporate resources and community support, or a nonprofit or for-profit entity approaches the corporation about purchasing some or all of the nonprofit's assets and operations. More often, the corporation's own management or board initiates an evaluation process to determine the corporation's options in light of declining revenues, an inability to garner community support for new projects, loss of a stable source of volunteers, or other factors that make it difficult to fulfill the corporation's mission. Occasionally, the need for change is not recognized until the corporation is in or near the brink of insolvency. Unless this situation was brought about precipitously by unexpected events, the late discovery of such a problem may indicate a failure by the board to properly oversee the corporation's operations. (See discussion in the section *"Insolvency or Bankruptcy"* below for other board considerations in the event of insolvency.) In most cases, however, the board is aware for some time of the factors leading up to a potential need for change.

**Duty to be informed.** The primary means for satisfying the director's duty of care in any situation is to be adequately informed before making a decision. The recommended information gathering and evaluation process that meets the board's duty of care in a change of control context has two main components: first, identifying the nature and quality of information that should be obtained to make an informed decision, and second, ensuring that independent consultants and/or committees composed of disinterested directors take the lead in evaluating aspects of change of control decisions in which some members of the board have an interest or potential interest.

**Key issues to be addressed.** While each change of control decision is unique, certain issues are typically present. Directors should make sure that they have thorough and reliable information on these and other material issues:

(1)   What are the factors requiring or motivating the board to consider a change of control of the corporation?

(2)   What is the current economic environment?

(3)   Would a change of control of the corporation be consistent with the purpose/mission of the corporation?

(4)   What are the alternatives to change of control generally?

(5)   What are the pros, cons, and alternatives for any considered form of change of control and has an independent appraisal been obtained?

(6)   Should an auction or a bidding process be used to maximize the value to be paid for the corporation's assets (if applicable), or to broaden the search for parties who may be interested in engaging in a change of control transaction with the corporation? Alternatively, will the mission of the corporation be better served by a transfer of the assets to another nonprofit organization?

(7)   What is the fair market value of the corporation's assets and activities? Will or should the corporation obtain a valuation prepared by an independent valuation specialist?

(8)   What nonmonetary criteria should be considered by the directors when making a change of control decision?

(9)   What experts and other resources are available to assist the board in analyzing the relevant issues pertaining to the change of control decision?

(10)   If the assets of the corporation are to be sold to another (nonprofit or for-profit) entity, what will happen to the proceeds?

(11)   What governmental authorities must receive notice or give their approval for a change of control transaction?

(12)   When and how will beneficiary groups and other parties be informed of a proposed change of control? Should the change of control evaluation process include a mechanism for obtaining input from any such groups?

**Board evaluation process.** The time available for the board to evaluate a proposed change of control is dictated by the circumstances at hand. In some cases, directors have some luxury of time; in other cases, financial or other circumstances require fairly quick action. In either case, however, the board should be aware that the *process* they use to make their decision—as well as the ultimate decision itself—may be subject to a high degree of scrutiny, before or after the change is completed. Once the board has identified the key issues to be addressed, it is faced with the decision of how to address them. The use of independent legal and financial advisers is highly recommended; in some cases, failure to obtain objective and expert opinions on certain key issues (such as the value of the corporation's assets or whether the terms of the proposed transactions are fair to the corporation) may be regarded as a breach of the directors' duty of care.

**Independent board committees.** For some change of control decisions, certain members of the board may have a personal interest or stake in the decision. In particular, board members who are also employees of the corporation and who may lose their positions, or gain new positions with a merged or acquiring entity, have conflicts of interest that make it difficult for them to objectively evaluate change of control decisions. Because of these conflicts, both for-profit and nonprofit corporations are well advised to appoint a committee consisting solely of independent (i.e., nonmanagement) directors to evaluate a change of control decision and make a recommendation to the board. The independent committee may engage its own independent experts (i.e., ones not regularly employed by the corporation), including attorneys, accountants, and other consultants, to assist it in evaluating the proposed transaction.

## Duty of loyalty issues

The duty of loyalty requires each nonprofit director to act in the best interests of the corporation, and to not make decisions that further the director's own interests at the corporation's expense. If a change of control decision presents a conflict of interest for one or more directors—such as a director who is also the organization president, and who may lose or keep her job depending on who acquires the corporation's assets—the entire board must take steps to make sure that this conflict of interest does not affect the board's decision as to what is in the corporation's best interest.

First, directors who have a conflict or potential conflict of interest related to a proposed change of control (or relating to one of several alternatives) must disclose the conflict, and follow the board's usual procedures for handling conflicts of interest. Second, the directors should evaluate whether the nature of any conflicts suggests that a special committee of independent directors should be used to evaluate a change of control proposal.

If "insider" directors are involved in the negotiation of change of control transactions, they need to be aware of both actual and perceived conflicts of interest. Such directors should make sure to document that decisions they make and actions they take in the course of negotiations were in the best interests of the company. In addition, these directors should assure that other directors are aware of any conflicts of interest and have taken the necessary steps (such as obtaining the advice of independent consultants) to allow the board to make decisions based on objective criteria.

## Role of State Attorney General

Nonprofit corporations contemplating a change of control may be required to give the state attorney general notice of the proposed change. In some states, the attorney general must approve the proposed change before it occurs. Such notice and approval requirements may be set forth in the state nonprofit code or other statute, and may apply to all public benefit corporations, or only to those in specific industries (for example, health care).[2] Such statutes may apply even if the proposed acquiring or successor entity is another nonprofit, or only when a for-profit corporation is proposed to assume control of the nonprofit's operations. Even in states in which no statute specifically requires a nonprofit to give notice to or obtain approval from the attorney general in connection with a change of control transaction, the attorney general may assert rights to notice or approve the transaction based on the doctrine of *cy pres*. In many states, a state attorney general is generally considered a necessary or appropriate representative of the public interest with the power to review and/or approve a transaction that may change the charitable purpose of a nonprofit, public benefit corporation. Directors of nonprofit corporations that are considering a change of control transaction should obtain the advice of counsel as to whether and how the state attorney general may become involved in the change of control decision process.

## Other Regulatory Approvals

Depending on the nature of the nonprofit organization, regulatory authorities other than the state attorney general may be required to receive notice of or approve the change of control, or some aspect of the change. As part of evaluating a change of control proposal, the board should ensure that legal counsel has identified what governmental approvals are required to implement the change, and at what stage. For instance, where only notice is required, should such notice be given a certain number of days before or after the change is to be effective? If approval is required before the change is effective, how long will the approval process take? The directors should factor in regulatory approval periods when determining the date that a change of control will occur. The board should also be informed as to whether the approval process would be routine or involve intensive review and potential requests for changes to the structure of the transaction.

## Other Interest Groups Affected by a Change of Control

A nonprofit corporation's beneficiaries, donors, funders, and employees, as well as other members of the community, may all have an interest in—or an opinion on—a nonprofit's proposed change of control transaction. From a legal perspective, these groups generally lack any legal right to receive advance notice, evaluate, or comment on a nonprofit change of control (unlike the state attorney general, who may have such rights in his or her role as the representative of the public interest and/or a charity's beneficiaries).[3] Nonetheless, beneficiaries and other groups who learn about a proposed change of control may believe they have a right to participate in, or even to challenge, a nonprofit's proposed change of control. Such groups may also animate the interests of local politicians or governmental bodies in the proposed change. As part of the board's change of control planning and evaluation process, the directors should consider the likely reaction of key constituencies to the proposed change, then decide whether any specific actions should be taken to inform these constituencies or give them opportunities to formally express their views and concerns. In some cases, professional public relations consultants may be able to assist the directors in effectively addressing community concerns. In addition, if significant funding is received from a governmental entity, approval of the change by the entity may be required (or advisable even if not required) before the transaction is completed, to ensure that the funding will continue after the change is completed.

## Summary

It is unlikely that directors of a nonprofit corporation will enter into a change of control decision lightly. Still, directors should be aware of the high level of legal and public scrutiny that may be applied both to their ultimate decision, and the process by which they arrived at the decision. In addition, directors should know that there is legal precedent (often drawn from for-profit cases) regarding what actions and procedures are and are not considered sufficient means for directors to fulfill their fiduciary duties when making a change of control decision. Change of control decisions present a challenge to nonprofit directors to exercise their decision-making authority consistently with their fiduciary duties. In addition, the directors must be able to justify and explain their decision to numerous interested constituencies.

# Disposition of Unique Assets

## Circumstances in Which Disposition Issues May Arise

Some nonprofits, particularly museums (but also a wide variety of other entities), may find that legal restraints, public perceptions, and functional necessities require the sale or other disposal of property that cannot be placed on the market in a conventional manner. Thus, an art museum may decide that a given painting lacks sufficient quality to merit a regular place in its galleries, or its original attribution to a great artist proves to be erroneous. A social service institution may find that an original settlement house, no longer practical as a center for its services, is nonetheless regarded as a symbol of the community's commitment to serve the underprivileged. A church may occupy a building that is an architectural masterpiece but the congregation that built it and supported it has moved away from the neighborhood.

There is no one-size-fits-all policy that addresses disposition of unique property, but there are examples. In the case of art museums, the problem is both eased and made more difficult because a ready market exists for works of art, even those that a museum considers unworthy of its walls. On the other hand, the possibility, real or apparent, of an officer or trustee of such a museum exploiting a deaccessioning decision to acquire, for personal use or resale, an arguably disposable object is too obvious to be disregarded.[4]

## Board Considerations in the Sale of Unique Assets

A nonprofit board finding itself with the need to dispose of unique assets should seek the aid of other organizations with expertise related to the property at issue, possibly including nonprofit organizations that have an interest in protecting the particular kind of property at issue. For example, a nonprofit organization evaluating disposition of a landmark piece of architecture could seek advice from a nonprofit entity dedicated to such functions. Similarly, in the case of vacant land, a local conservation group would likely be delighted to work with the board to help identify options that serve both the corporation's and the community's interests. Further, if the property was donated to the organization or constitutes a significant portion of the corporation's assets, the corporation should determine whether it has an obligation under state law to either notify or receive approval for the sale from the state attorney general, with respect to change of control of a major charitable asset.

Because such dispositions are by their nature unique, the best advice for board members is to proceed with care—and consider the best way to balance any competing community interests—before making a final decision.

# Insolvency and Bankruptcy

It is important that the board of directors of a nonprofit corporation facing insolvency be aware of special duties that arise with regard to the operation of a nonprofit corporation that is in the "zone of insolvency" as well as when the nonprofit is in bankruptcy. Most of the rules and issues confronting for-profit corporations in such situations also are present for nonprofit corporations. Still, there are certain unique issues relating to insolvencies and bankruptcies of nonprofit corporations, which generally reflect their unique public interest nature, mission, and corporate structure.

## The "Zone of Insolvency"

### Insolvency

The law suggests two separate standards that may be applied in determining insolvency depending on the jurisdiction involved. The "equitable insolvency test" considers a corporation to be insolvent when it is unable to pay its debts as they become due. The "balance-sheet insolvency test" considers a corporation to be insolvent when its total liabilities exceed its total assets.[5] A corporation also may be considered to have entered the zone of insolvency if it enters into a transaction that leaves the corporation with an unreasonably small capital base, making insolvency reasonably foreseeable.[6]

### Creditors' Interests

Zone-of-insolvency concepts, which have been applied to commercial ventures for years to shift some of the duties of the board and officers of corporations approaching or entering insolvency from solely protecting stockholder interests to also considering creditors' interests, have been viewed as increasingly relevant to nonprofit corporations. As a result, if a nonprofit enters the "zone of insolvency," the board may be required to consider (and refrain from actions unreasonably threatening) the interests of creditors in being paid, even if those decisions limit or conflict with absolute fulfillment of the charitable purpose of the nonprofit. In other words, as the corporation approaches and even enters the zone of insolvency, the board of directors may have an increasing duty to consider the impact of its decisions on creditors and the corporate enterprise and not to just "roll the dice" so as to unreasonably sacrifice creditor recoveries.

### What Should Boards Do Differently if the Organization Is Insolvent or Nearly Insolvent?

When in the zone of insolvency, the nonprofit board should pay particular attention to the financial impact of proposed corporate transactions and may feel compelled to refrain from funding programs even if consistent with its mission where the expenditure threatens ultimate payment to creditors. In this regard, the board may consider retaining a financial adviser to advise on whether insolvency is being approached and the appropriateness of such material expenditures. Boards of nonprofit corporations approaching or within the "zone" also may consider protections that may have been or should be undertaken to assure that donor-restricted funds are held in trust or will not be used in an inappropriate manner (e.g., used in an unrestricted manner for general operations).

In situations where a nonprofit board is faced with a zone of insolvency tension between financial interests and charitable purpose duties (e.g., where a business decision might benefit or be protective of financial or creditor interests, but not strictly adhere to the charitable mission), it may even be appropriate to consult the state attorney general before such a decision is finalized.

## Interests of Creditors vs. the Charitable Mission

Tax-exempt nonprofits may be subject to more limits than for-profits in taking actions to limit expenditures or to sell and turn assets into cash that can be used for overall operations and debt service. Nonprofits may be subject to criticism as well as public or attorney general scrutiny of transactions such as the sales of facilities and use of their proceeds, even if those transactions were designed to and would ultimately benefit the overall financial viability of the nonprofit.

State attorney general review of corporate transactions in many states generally has been limited to nonprofit to for-profit asset sales (or "conversions") or transactions involving outright self-dealing or *ultra vires* conduct. In some cases, however, the nonprofit transactions that have drawn fire from state officials have involved straightforward asset transfers to other nonprofit corporations and, in particular, transactions in which a financially strained nonprofit corporation seeks to sell or close a struggling facility, exit a community, or entirely divest itself of a portfolio of in-state holdings, with the goal of using the proceeds to fund other of its charitable facilities at different locations.[7] State attorneys general similarly have objected to specific expenditures by some financially challenged nonprofit corporations (including fees for hiring restructuring or bankruptcy professionals) and have suggested that nonprofit corporation funds can be viewed as held in a constructive or implied charitable trust and may only be expended in accordance with charitable mission objectives rather than made available for creditor recoveries or other purposes that might facilitate a restructuring.[8]

To the extent that attorneys general have advanced the argument that the assets of a nonprofit system are held pursuant to a constructive or implied charitable trust for the benefit of the community, the assets of a nonprofit organization may be viewed as less committed or available to fund the ongoing operations of the nonprofit organization or to pay creditors and, instead, as designated for the support of underperforming nonprofit assets or for furthering local community enterprises. Such a position creates potential problems and concerns for parties attempting to effect restructurings and other transactions involving entities, as well as creditors seeking recoveries from the assets of nonprofit organizations.

Directors of tax-exempt nonprofits that hold restricted gifts and are in or near the zone of insolvency should assume that no restricted funds are to be used (or "borrowed" with the intent to repay) to cover general operation expenses including restructuring costs, even if done with the intent to preserve the organization and its ability to continue to serve its charitable mission. If the organization's directors determine that, in order to survive, the organization must change its mission or purpose, it may be necessary to proceed through a *cy pres* proceeding to permit use of restricted funds for a new purpose or to change the nature of its charitable activities.

In the insolvency context, application of the "charitable trust" theory could be used to severely limit the ability of creditors, including tax-exempt bondholders, to recover against system assets that are deemed to be encumbered by trust obligations. Such assets could be deemed only available for designated charitable purposes and thereby excluded from a bankruptcy estate.

# Loan/Bond Defaults and Out-of-Court Restructurings

## *Loan/Bond Debt*

In addition to commercial lending resources that may be available, one of the significant advantages enjoyed by certain kinds of operating or revenue-producing nonprofits is the ability to secure long-term financing at lower market interest rates through the issuance of state authorized tax-exempt bonds. Still, such nonprofits are not always able to service that debt or to avoid the incurrence of other defaults on the bonds and under the bond indenture. This and other cash flow problems may force the nonprofit to attempt to restructure its bond debt or secure other accommodations from the bondholders (or in the case of insured bonds, the bond insurers) and the indenture trustee that represents the bondholders.

Negotiations with bondholders or bond insurers and their indenture trustees may include a range of options to address debt payment concerns, such as: (1) agreeing to a temporary forbearance agreement not to exercise remedies; (2) restructuring the debt in or out of bankruptcy by changing its terms including reduction of debt, reduction of interest rate, stretching of payments, extension of maturity, and waiving or eliminating covenants; or (3) exchange offers or buy-outs where new debt or cash consideration is given to reduce the debt burden or even extinguish some of the bond debt.

For organizations with tax-exempt debt, restructurings may be subject to particular tax and other rules that control tax-exempt financings, including the requirements to maintain the tax-exempt status. For example, interest payments may only be deferrable or accrued for a limited time. Certain restructuring terms may need to be approved by the state agency which authorized the bond issuance.

### Operational and Trade Debt

If the nonprofit's financial issues extend to difficulties or an inability to pay more currently owed debts—whether to suppliers, employees, or other service providers—the board may need to assure that the appropriate attention is given to, first, cash management, and then to the possibility of negotiating a stretch-out or discounting of current debt obligations. Such accommodations may even be included in a more global out-of-court restructuring or can be incorporated in a bankruptcy plan.

# Bankruptcies

Bankruptcy is a method of dealing with and ultimately discharging (forgiving) unpaid debts either through the liquidation of assets or the reorganization of the debtor's financial affairs. Bankruptcy is authorized under the Bankruptcy Code—a uniform federal law administered by bankruptcy judges who serve as units of the United States district courts.[9] Bankruptcy may be necessary or advisable if an out-of-court restructuring cannot be achieved or to bind all creditors to a restructuring of their debt negotiated with some creditors prior to bankruptcy. Bankruptcy is also used as an interim strategy to stay collection actions or foreclosure, or to allow for rejection of disadvantageous contracts or leases.

There are two types of bankruptcy applicable to private nonprofit entities— Chapter 7 and Chapter 11. Chapter 7 bankruptcy involves liquidation of the assets of the debtor administered by a trustee appointed by the court or elected by the creditors. The debtor's operations are wound down and the assets are disposed. After the assets are converted to cash, the trustee distributes the proceeds to creditors on a pro-rata basis according to priorities established by the Bankruptcy Code.

In Chapter 11 bankruptcy, the debtor's management ordinarily remains in control and possession of the assets and continues operations (as a so-called "debtor-in-possession"), although, in cases of fraud, dishonesty, incompetence, or gross mismanagement, the bankruptcy court may appoint a Chapter 11 trustee to manage the affairs of the debtor during the reorganization process.[10] The ultimate goal is for the debtor to reorganize and continue its operations pursuant to a plan approved by a majority of creditors and the court. Alternatively, the debtor-in-possession can conduct an orderly liquidation and distribute the proceeds, much as in Chapter 7.

A debtor's access to its cash is crucially and dramatically altered by a bankruptcy filing. It is common for secured lenders and bondholders to have a security interest in a debtor's cash or cash equivalents (defined by the Bankruptcy Code as "cash collateral.") A trustee or debtor-in-possession may not make use of such cash, even in the ordinary course of the debtor's business, without court approval (upon a finding that the security interest is "adequately protected") or consent by the creditor(s) whose interest is secured by the cash collateral.[11]

Reflecting the public interest mission of many nonprofits, there are at least two significant procedural differences in bankruptcy law applicable to insolvent nonprofit organizations, as compared to for-profit entities: First, nonprofit entities generally cannot be forced into involuntary bankruptcy by their creditors.[12] Second, nonprofit entities cannot be converted from a Chapter 11 reorganization to a Chapter 7 liquidation by a third-party motion.[13]

Nonetheless, creditors of a financially distressed nonprofit may have other leverage (such as threats to foreclose on collateral or cease providing needed supplies) to force the nonprofit to declare bankruptcy or take other significant action to protect creditors' interests.

## Role of State Attorney General in Bankruptcy

When a nonprofit corporation becomes a debtor under the Bankruptcy Code, the state attorney general may exercise an oversight role, in or outside the bankruptcy court. The attorney general may participate in the bankruptcy case as a party in interest and may be able to engage in enforcement action outside the bankruptcy court, if that action falls within the state's police powers, which are not stayed by the Bankruptcy Code.[14] Still, the attorney general may be subject to the bankruptcy court's jurisdiction in areas traditionally governed by bankruptcy law.[15]

# General Bankruptcy Process

## 1.    *Retention of Professionals and Appointment of Creditors' Committee*

A trustee or debtor-in-possession generally will retain restructuring counsel, consultants, and financial advisers to provide assistance in managing or liquidating its business in Chapter 7 or 11. These professionals, in addition to playing a critical role in operations and liquidating assets, may also pursue litigations and assist in formulating and implementing a debtor's reorganization plan. As a debtor-in-possession, a debtor has duties to creditors (and in the case of for-profits, stockholders) and is obligated to protect and conserve its property for the benefit of all parties in interest. The interests of unsecured creditors in a Chapter 11 will generally be represented by a creditors' committee, the members of which are appointed by the United States Trustee. Both the creditors' committee and Trustee generally will be active participants in a Chapter 11 case.

## 2.    *Creation of the Bankruptcy Estate*

Upon the filing of a bankruptcy petition, a bankruptcy estate is created by operation of law and all property of the debtor, including any legal or equitable interest of the debtor, becomes "property of the estate."[16] One of the unique issues that may arise in a case in which there are *donor-restricted funds* is whether those funds, regardless of intent, can be found to be part of the debtor's estate available for general operating expenses or to pay general creditors instead of remaining segregated and restricted for specified purposes. (The answer ultimately may turn on how well the organization has previously identified which funds provided by donors are restricted and how a court resolves the tension between charitable mission and creditor rights).

## 3.    *The Automatic Stay*

Also upon the filing of a bankruptcy petition, section 362(a) of the Bankruptcy Code operates automatically to enjoin, or "stay," all actions by creditors against both the property of the estate and the debtor, with certain limited exceptions. Prohibited actions include not only direct acts to collect on a prepetition obligation of the debtor or obtain possession of property of the estate, but any action affecting the debtor and its property, including the commencement or continuation of litigation proceedings against the debtor relating to enforcement of debt or the creation or perfection of liens on the debtor's property. The automatic stay affords the debtor a reasonable opportunity to reorganize its affairs or proceed with an orderly liquidation.

### 4.    *Operation of the Debtor's Business While in Bankruptcy*

A trustee, debtor-in-possession, or municipal debtor may continue to undertake transactions that are in the "ordinary course" of a debtor's normal, day-to-day business actions—without bankruptcy court approval. Any extraordinary policy or business decisions, however, are subject to court approval. A health care or other nonprofit business, for example, would need to obtain bankruptcy court approval to consummate any significant asset sale or to obtain secured credit, among other things.[17]

### 5.    *Assumption and Rejection of Executory Contracts and Unexpired Leases*

Section 365 of the Bankruptcy Code allows a trustee or debtor-in-possession, in its business judgment and estimation of economic sense, to either (a) assume (in conjunction with curing any defaults) and continue to be bound by an "executory contract" (generally defined as a contract under which performance remains due on both sides) or unexpired lease or (b) reject and free itself from such agreements. It is often crucial to a debtor's operational reorganization that while certain agreements need to be kept current and in place, other agreements will no longer be necessary or economically beneficial to its business and should therefore be rejected.

### 6.    *Avoiding Preferences and Fraudulent Conveyances to Increase the General Estate Available for Distribution to Creditors*

The Bankruptcy Code allows a trustee, debtor-in-possession, or municipal debtor to seek to unwind or avoid certain transactions that occurred during the months and years prior to the filing which may have unreasonably reduced the estate available to pay general creditors. In addition, a trustee or debtor-in-possession may unwind so-called "fraudulent transfers"—transactions relating to, among other things, transfers made within two years of the commencement of the bankruptcy case (or, if applicable, a longer statutory period under state law) on the grounds that the transfer was actually or constructively fraudulent. In proving a fraudulent transfer, a debtor must demonstrate, among other things, that the transfer was intended to hinder, delay, or defraud other creditors, or that the debtor did not receive reasonably equivalent value in exchange for the transfer, and was either (a) insolvent at the time of the transfer, (b) rendered insolvent as a result of the transfer, (c) left with an unreasonably small amount of capital as a result of the transfer, or (d) incurred debts beyond its ability to pay when due. In some cases, preferential payments to vendors connected to an officer or director of a financially distressed organization will be subject to challenge as a preferential transfer.

### 7.   *Reorganization Plan Issues for Nonprofit Debtors Exclusivity*

Initially, the debtor-in-possession in a Chapter 11 case has 120 days (extendable by the bankruptcy court to 180 days) from the date of the filing in which to prepare and file a "plan or reorganization" and "disclosure statement" containing information about the plan sufficient to allow creditors to vote on its acceptance or rejection.  This "exclusive period" can be extended by the bankruptcy court "for cause" to up to 18 months after the filing date.

**Plan Terms.**  In a typical Chapter 11 plan, a debtor proposes to extend maturities of outstanding debt, reduce or extinguish the amount of principal or interest payable on debts, convert debt to other debt and/or equity, or any combination of the foregoing.  It is also not uncommon for a plan to provide for the sale of certain of the debtor's assets.

**Creditor Approval.**  Each creditor whose legal or contractual rights are altered by the proposed plan is entitled to vote on the plan.  If the plan is accepted by at least one class of impaired creditors, it can be "crammed down" against the remaining nonapproving classes as long as their treatment under the plan is "fair and equitable," consistent with the "best interests of creditors test" and the other confirmation requirements.

If, during the course of a Chapter 11 case, the court determines that rehabilitation is not possible or there is no feasible plan of reorganization, the case can be converted to a Chapter 7 and the debtor's assets liquidated for the benefit of creditors.

**Special Nonprofit Plan Issues.**  To the extent the assets of a nonprofit may be single purpose or have little alternative value, they may have limited liquidation value and be particularly difficult to value.

In some cases, however, there may be an alternative value to nonprofit property that may exceed its value in the context of use for a specified charitable mission—such as an aged hospital in an urban area in which real estate values are high.  In these situations, meeting the *best interest of creditors test* (requiring receipt of no less than Chapter 7 liquidation value to a dissenting creditor) can be a particular problem in a nonprofit case, requiring a balancing of the public interest argument against strict adherence to the test.

Application of the *absolute priority rule* to nonprofits that have members as opposed to shareholders can also be complicated, although courts have generally found that the absolute priority rule allows confirmation of Chapter 11 plans for nonprofits that retain or continue the control of members even if creditors are not paid in full.[18]

## Summary

The board of a financially strained or insolvent nonprofit may need to take action to more strictly control its cash and assets.  Alternatively, the board may wish to attempt an out-of-court restructuring, including Chapter 11 reorganization. Although most of the rules and issues confronting for-profit corporations in these situations also apply to nonprofits, certain unique protections and issues arise with nonprofits, of which not-for-profit directors and officers should be advised and aware.

*See the suggested Questions and Checklist following the Endnotes below to review the issues discussed in this chapter.*

# Endnotes

1.  *See* Colin T. Moran, *Why Revlon Applies to Nonprofit Corporations,* 53 Bus. Law. 373 (1998). *See also* Revlon, Inc. v. MacAndrews & Forbes Holding, Inc., 506 A.2d 173 (Del. 1986). Under *Revlon* and other cases, courts have found that once a board has determined that a change of control of the corporation is inevitable, the board has a duty to effect the change that best maximizes the price to be received by the company's shareholders. However, the *Revlon* maximization principle does not apply in all change of control circumstances; *see* Paramount Communications, Inc. v. Time, Inc., 571 A.2d 1140 (Del. 1989). In nonprofit change of control transactions, the state attorney general or others may argue that the changing corporation should be sold to the highest bidder, thus maximizing the proceeds available to be transferred to a charitable foundation or to be used for other charitable purposes. Still, other considerations—such as whether to sell to a nonprofit or a for-profit—may also be valid factors for the board to evaluate, depending on the circumstances.

2.  *See, e.g., A Guide to Mergers and Consolidations of Not-for-Profit Corporations under Article 9 of the New York Not-for-Profit Corporation Law* (State of New York Attorney General), *available at www.ag.ny.gov.*

3.  *See* State of Tennessee, ex rel Adventist Health Care System/Sunbelt Health Care Corp. v. Nashville Memorial Hospital, Inc., 914 S.W.2d 903, 910 (Tenn. Ct. App. 1995), holding that because the state attorney general had reviewed and approved a proposed sale of a nonprofit hospital to a for-profit corporation, other parties had no standing to challenge the sale, stating that "[t]he decision of the … Attorney General in those matters in which he is the legislatively designated representative of the public interest must bind everyone who might claim to represent that interest." Still, in other states, unsuccessful bidders for the assets of a nonprofit have been allowed to file suit challenging a nonprofit board's change of control decision. *See* Leo T. Crowley, *Hospital Case: Significant Governance Questions,* 223 N.Y.L.J. 3 (February 10, 2000), discussing case before the state

Supreme Court, County of New York, involving opposition by the state attorney general to a nonprofit corporation's petition to sell its specialty hospital building, and in which two hospitals that had previously sought business combinations with the proposed selling corporation were allowed to intervene.

4.  The American Association of Museums, Code of Ethics-Collections sets forth policies with regard to deaccession. (www.aam-us.org/ museumresources/ethics/coe.cfm). Similarly, the Association of Art Museum Directors has a policy on deaccessioning. (www.aamd.org/ papers/documents/FinalDeaccessioning_Report_6_25_10.pdf).

5.  *See, e.g.*, Geyer v. Ingersoll Publications Co., 621 A.2d 784 (Del. Ch. 1992).

6.  *See* In re Healthco International, Inc., 208 B.R. 288, 302 (Bankr. D. Mass. 1997).

7.  *See* Manhattan Eye, Ear & Throat Hosp. v. Spitzer, 715 N.Y.S.2d 575 (N.Y. Sup. Ct. 1999) where the New York Attorney General successfully blocked the sale of an acute care facility on very valuable central New York City real estate, where the proceeds would have been used to fund the operations of diagnostic and treatment centers in medically underserved areas of New York City, as changing or refocusing the original charitable mission.

8.  *See* In re Nat'l. Benevolent Ass'n. of the Christian Church (Disciples of Christ), et al., Case No. 04-50948-RBK (Bankr. W.D. Tex.).

9.  The Bankruptcy Code is contained in Title 11, United States Code.

10.  11 U.S.C. § 1104(a)(1).

11.  11 U.S.C. § 363(a).

12.  11 U.S.C. § 303(a).

13.  11 U.S.C. § 1112(c).

14.  11 U.S.C. § 362(b)(4).

15.  Bankruptcy Code Section 363(d)(1) was amended in 2005 to require that any nonprofit asset sale in bankruptcy must comply with applicable nonbankruptcy law governing nonprofit assets transfers. 11 U.S.C. § 363(d)(1).

16.  11 U.S.C. § 541.

17.  11 U.S.C. §§ 363, 364.

18.  *In re* Wabash Valley Power, Inc., 72 F.3d 1305, 1320 (7th Cir. 1995); *In re* Whittaker Memorial Hospital Association, Inc., 149 B.R. 812, 816 (Bankr. E.D.Va. 1993); *In re* Corcoran Hospital District; 233 B.R. 449, 458 (Bankr. E.D.Cal. 1999).

# Suggested Questions for Directors Regarding Duties of Directors under Special Circumstances

## Mergers, Sales, or Other Change of Control Events

(1)   What information does the board need to properly evaluate a proposed change of control? What alternatives were considered? Has the fairness of the transaction from a financial standpoint been evaluated by an independent party?

(2)   What board members, officers, or other corporate insiders may be personally affected by a change in control?

(3)   What processes should the board put in place to address conflict of interest issues during the consideration of a potential change of control, as well as during any negotiation with third parties? Should a committee of independent board members be appointed to make recommendations to the board regarding a proposed change of control, or to negotiate key deal terms?

(4)   Will approval of the state attorney general or other regulators be required before a change of control may be effected?

(5)   How will community groups, employees, and constituencies of the corporation likely react to news of a change of control proposal or event? Should such concerns be addressed as part of the board's evaluation and negotiation process? Should public relations professionals be used to help communicate information about a change of control?

## Disposition of Unique Assets

(1)   Why is a unique corporate asset being considered for sale?

(2)   Could any directors, officers, or other corporate insiders personally benefit in any way from the sale?

(3)   What other organizations, such as specialized nonprofits, appraiser agencies, or other groups, could assist the corporation in maximizing the benefits of a sale, while minimizing concerns of the community or other interested groups?

(4)   Are there any organization stakeholders, such as donors, community members, or state or local officials, who may be concerned about such disposition or with whom the organization should consult or inform prior to the disposition becoming effective?

## Insolvency or Bankruptcy

(1)    Is our organization in a "zone of insolvency"? Are we able to pay our debts as they come due? Can we foresee a day in the near future when that will not be true?

(2)    What actions can our various creditors take if we default on our obligations or fail to make required debt covenants?

(3)    Is our organization eligible to file for bankruptcy?

(4)    Are there any organization stakeholders, such as donors, community members, or state or local officials, who may be concerned about such disposition or with whom the organization should consult or inform prior to the disposition becoming effective?

(5)    What are the potential benefits and disadvantages of declaring bankruptcy, as opposed to trying to work out a debt restructuring directly with one or more major creditors?

(6)    Have steps been taken to protect restricted funds from inappropriate use?

(7)    Have any payments been made that could be challenged as fraudulent transfers?

(8)    If the corporation is or becomes insolvent, do we want to reorganize and continue, or liquidate and "close up shop"?

(9)    Are there members or others affiliated with our organization who derive economic benefit from its activities who might be considered its "owners"? If yes, should they be asked to contribute to a reorganization effort? Can we legally require them to do so?

(10)   What is the fair value of our corporate assets? What would they realize in a forced liquidation?

# Checklist: Duties of Directors Under Special Circumstances

*Note:*    For simplicity, these and other chapter checklists describe a corporation having a chair, who pre-sides over the board of directors; a chief executive, who may be a staff person; an executive committee; a governance/nominating committee; and an audit committee. (We recognize, however, that in many smaller and other nonprofits, these committee functions may be performed by either the executive committee or the board as a whole.) We also assume a legal counsel—someone, paid or unpaid, having primary responsibility for the corporation's legal affairs. Many corporations, especially larger nonprofits, may have other committees established for specific purposes, such as establishing executive compensation; monitoring compliance with legal requirements; and overseeing investments and other financial matters.

| Subject | Review By | How Often | Comment |
|---|---|---|---|
| 1. Change of Control Event | | | |
| a. When and how should transaction counsel, financial advisers, and other experts needed be selected to assist the board and management in evaluating and accomplishing the transaction? | Chief executive, chief counsel, and chief financial officer, in consultation with board chair | As soon as possible after proposed transaction becomes a serious consideration | Given the significance of sales, mergers, and other change of control transactions, it is important to obtain guidance from experienced consultants and counsel |
| b. What special meetings or executive sessions of board (or designated special committee) meetings will be necessary to evaluate and discuss terms and implications of proposed transaction? | Chief executive and board chair, in consultation with chair of special transaction committee if any | At start of transaction and at major milestone marks (e.g., before signing a letter of intent; on completion of due diligence; before signing a definitive agreement, etc.) | Change of control transactions often involve a host of significant considerations that must be evaluated prior to approval by the board |

| Subject | Review By | How Often | Comment |
|---|---|---|---|
| c. Who will coordinate internal and external communication regarding a proposed or approved change of control to assure consistent messages are being delivered? | Chief executive, marketing/ communications staff, or consultants | Prior to public announcement and ongoing until transaction is completed | Change of control transactions create a significant anxiety in employees, beneficiaries, donors, and other stakeholders. It is good practice to provide board members with talking points, and to designate one board member (e.g., board chair) and/ or executive as the "point person" for communications with media and key stakeholders |
| 2.  Disposition of Unique Assets | | | |
| a. How will need for and alternatives to disposition be evaluated, approved, and documented? | Chief executive, legal counsel | Promptly after disposition is identified as a possible option to address the relevant organizational concerns | Evidence of a reasonable evaluation process to support a board decision to sell or dispose of a unique asset helps avoid potential challenges to the decision and may result in a smoother disposition process. |

| Subject | Review By | How Often | Comment |
|---|---|---|---|
| b. What legal and other requirements (including stakeholder communications) must be met before completing the asset disposition? | Chief executive, board chair, legal counsel | Prior to or immediately after board disposition decision | By definition, disposition of unique assets are uncommon events. Board members should be assured that a thorough review of legal and other considerations has been conducted prior to approval or closing of the sale |
| 3. Insolvency and Bankruptcy | | | |
| a. What process should the board follow to evaluate the options and implications for an organization that is or may soon be insolvent? | Chief executive, chief financial officer, legal counsel, followed by discussion with full board | As soon as possible after the chief financial officer identifies a possible or actual insolvency condition for the organization | Because some board duties may change for insolvent organizations, it is important for the board to engage qualified financial and legal advisers to avoid inadvertently taking actions that could later be challenged by creditors |

| Subject | Review By | How Often | Comment |
|---|---|---|---|
| b. What actions may the board need to take to assure creditors in the course of restructuring debt or other workouts needed to maintain the organization's ability to continue operations? | Chief financial officer, finance committee chair, followed by discussion with full board | After discussions with creditors and prior to board approval of debt restructure or work-out arrangement | The board should be assured that constraints imposed by lenders are feasible before approving a debt restructuring |
| c. If bankruptcy, dissolution or similar actions become necessary, what is the board's role after approval of the action? What preapproval steps should be taken to avoid director liability and to satisfy the concerns of key stakeholders? | Special bankruptcy counsel, in consultation with chief executive and board chair, followed by discussion with full board | Shortly before or in conjunction with determination to pursue Chapter 7 or Chapter 11 bankruptcy or a similar process | Bankruptcy and similar proceedings (including dissolution) involve technical legal rules, and will require the board and management to obtain special bankruptcy or other legal counsel and accounting or other financial experts. |

# Chapter 10:
## Investments and Expenditure of Endowment Funds

# Chapter 10

# Investments and Expenditure of Endowment Funds

*Many nonprofit organizations benefit from large gifts from donors that are intended to be invested with only the income expendable on an annual basis. With limited revenue resources, many nonprofits actively seek these types of gifts. Although these gifts are extremely important to the vitality of the nonprofits, in recent years—with the economic turmoil—many nonprofits have seen their endowment and other funds plummet in value. This has resulted in questions being raised as to whether the proper type of investments were made and whether the board of directors of these nonprofits properly managed their investments.*

## Gifts

Nonprofit corporations can receive various forms of financial support, including gifts from donors. These gifts can be "unrestricted," meaning they can be used in a manner deemed appropriate by the corporation, or "restricted," meaning that the gift is to be used in a manner specified by the donor. Many nonprofits receive gifts in the form of endowments under which the growth and income of the gift may be used for various purposes but the "corpus" of the gift is to remain intact.

# Potential Liability and Other Issues

Nonprofit corporations can be held liable when they improperly use funds through extravagant spending, negligent management, or outright misdirection of funds.[1] In addition, the failure to fulfill a donor's specified gift intent can result in adverse publicity, donor challenge, and state attorney general review.[2] Liability also can arise when the organization fails to invest the donated funds prudently or uses the funds in a manner that is inconsistent with the donor's intent.

# Standards for Investment of Institutional Funds

Many states have adopted a uniform law that creates a standard of conduct for managing and investing institutional funds. The original uniform law was the Uniform Management of Institutional Funds Act or UMIFA. The recent version of this law, called the Uniform Prudent Management of Institutional Funds Act or UPMIFA, addresses, among other things, the standards for the investment of institutional funds.[3] An institutional fund is a fund held by an institution but does not include program-related assets or assets held by an institution primarily to accomplish a charitable purpose of the institution but not primarily for investment.

According to the drafters of UPMIFA, both UMIFA and UPMIFA are supported by two general principles: (1) that assets of charitable organizations are to be invested prudently in diversified investments that seek growth as well as income, and (2) that appreciation of assets can prudently be spent for the purposes of any endowment fund held by a charitable institution. The drafters of UPMIFA describe UPMIFA as an update and successor to UMIFA that establishes an even sounder and more unified basis for charitable fund management than UMIFA has done.

In terms of investments, UPMIFA recognizes the application of the duty of care and duty of loyalty imposed on directors (discussed in *Chapter 2, Duties and Rights of Nonprofit Corporation Directors*) and requires investment "in good faith and with the care an ordinarily prudent person in a like position would exercise under similar circumstances." It requires prudence in incurring investment costs, authorizing "only costs that are appropriate and reasonable."

UPMIFA provides specific factors for investing in a prudent manner. When making investments, boards are required to consider the following factors:

- general economic conditions;
- possible effect of inflation or deflation;
- expected tax consequences;
- the role that each investment or course of action plays within the overall portfolio of the fund;
- expected total return from the income and appreciation of investments;
- other resources of the organization;
- the needs of the organization and the fund to make distributions and preserve capital; and
- an asset's special relationship or special value to the organization's purposes.

UPMIFA emphasizes that investment decisions must be made in relation to the overall resources of the institution and its charitable purposes. In other words, decisions on fund management and investment decisions cannot be made in isolation. UPMIFA also requires that a fund's investments be diversified unless the governing board can justify nondiversification under special circumstances. A decision for nondiversification should be reviewed at least annually.

## Investment Committee

Organizations with large endowments should have investment committees that may be delegated duties with regard to development of an investment policy, proposing amendments to the policy, oversight of the investment performance, and delegating investment authority to others, including third parties. It is extremely important that an investment committee be composed of board members with expertise of relevance to investments made by the organization. As noted below, it is permissible to delegate duties with regard to investments to others; however, an investment committee should be responsible for overseeing any such delegation and the performance of the organization's investments.

## Investment Policy

A nonprofit corporation that intends to satisfy the UPMIFA standard of care should develop an investment policy that considers the corporation's short-term, mid- term, and long-term financial needs, and its tolerance for risk. The policy as written should be reviewed regularly by the investment committee with any changes approved by the full board. Such review should occur at least annually, in light of the changing needs of the organization, economic conditions, and any other factors that may affect the corporation's tolerance of risk and need for income. It is important for the investment committee to reassess the policy from time to time with appropriate professional counsel.

Following the development of an investment policy, the investment committee should determine appropriate asset-class allocations needed to satisfy the policy objectives. Here again, the committee should consult with professional investment counsel in determining proper allocations of the corporation's investments. After determining appropriate asset-class allocations, the individual asset decisions should be made. Consistent with UPMIFA, it is important that the decisions on the assets to be acquired and maintained not be made in a vacuum. Instead, the investment committee should make each of these determinations in light of its other investments and the total portfolio's consonance with the standards of the investment policy. Particular attention should be paid to the portfolio's overall level of compensated risk.

# Delegation of Duties

It is permissible to delegate management and investment functions to external agents, such as investment managers, as long as certain requirements are met. In particular, such delegation, which generally would be done by either the board of directors or an investment committee, requires compliance with the duty of care the board acts in good faith and with the care that an ordinarily prudent person in a like position would exercise under similar circumstances with regard to selecting an agent, establishing scope and terms of delegation, and requiring periodic reviews and supervision of the agent. This means that the board, investment committee, or other board delegate thoroughly investigates the proposed external agent and the organization enters into a written agreement with regard to the scope of the external agent activities. UPMIFA provides that an agent has a duty of reasonable care in performing such delegated functions. In addition, an institution may delegate management and investment functions to its committees, officers, or employees.

In recent years, many nonprofits have come to rely substantially on the recommendations of professional money managers, and the law generally permits the board to rely on professional investment counsel's advice.[4]

# Standards for Expenditure of Endowment Funds

Various restrictions are imposed on nonprofits that maintain endowment funds. An endowment fund generally is limited to funds held by a nonprofit organization in respect to which the donor designated the fund as an endowment fund or the donor imposed limitations on spending from the fund. A fund from which spending is restricted by the nonprofit itself is not an endowment fund under UPMIFA.

Under the predecessor uniform law, UMIFA, there was a requirement that asset growth and income could be appropriated for program purposes, subject to the rule that an endowment fund could not be spent below its "historic dollar value." This resulted in a corporation not being able to spend any amounts, regardless of whether they constituted income from the fund, when the total amount of the fund was less than the amount of the original gift at the time of the gift.

UPMIFA provides more specific guidance on prudence and eliminates a floor on spending. In particular, UPMIFA states that, subject to the donor's intent as expressed in a gift instrument, an institution may spend or accumulate as much of an endowment fund as the institution determines is prudent for the uses, benefits, purposes, and duration for which the endowment fund is established." Still, if the gift instrument states a particular spending rate or formula, that rate or formula will apply and the board has no discretion in determining the spending policy with respect to the particular fund.[5] Otherwise, a prudent person standard is applied, which involves consideration of the following seven criteria to guide an institution in its expenditure decisions:

- the duration and preservation of the endowment fund;
- purposes of the organization and the fund;
- general economic conditions;
- possible effect of inflation or deflation;
- expected total return from income and appreciation of investments;
- other resources of the organization;
-  the organization's investment policy; and
- where appropriate, alternatives to spending from the endowment fund and possible effects of those alternatives on the organization.

UPMIFA includes an optional provision that a minority of states have adopted that provides that spending in excess of 7 percent of the fair market value of the fund in one year creates a presumption of imprudence in spending.[6] This does not mean that such spending is in violation of the law; however, the entity—if challenged—would need to show that the expenditure was "prudent."

It is important that board members understand the prudence standard for spending and that there are clear and accurate minutes detailing how the above-described factors were considered when making a spending decision.

In addition, to prevent problems from occurring, the organization should be involved in assisting donors in articulating any gift intent in advance or in connection with making the gift and ascertaining the donor gift intent upon receipt of the gift. Directors also should carefully consider any proposed restrictions placed on gifts to the entity. To the extent the proposed restrictions are inconsistent with the purposes or mission of the entity, the board should give serious consideration to declining the gift.

The organization also should have one or more spending policies in place that help ensure the implementation of the donor gift intent as well as monitoring the administration of the gift to make sure the donor gift intent has been implemented.

To the extent a nonprofit corporation has an investment committee responsible for the investments of the corporation and a finance committee responsible for preparing the budget, it is important that these two committees coordinate to ensure that there is a common understanding with regard to issues of common concern, such as liquidity of assets for purposes of program operations.

# Out-of-Date or Impractical Restrictions on Gifts

A restriction on a gift can, after time, become outdated or impractical. This would be the situation where a gift made to a nonprofit college in the form of a scholarship fund was limited by its terms to scholarships of $50 a year. Such a restriction is impractical today. In the past, the nonprofit has had to go to the donor to seek a modification to the restriction if the donor was still living. If not living, the organization often had to seek court relief through a proceeding called *cy pres.*

UPMIFA recognizes and protects donor intent broadly by providing a comprehensive treatment of the modification of restrictions on charitable funds. Among other things, UPMIFA provides that a court may release or modify a restriction where the restriction is, among other things, impracticable or wasteful, or the purpose is unlawful, impracticable, impossible to achieve, or wasteful. For small funds with a value of less than $50,000 and where more than twenty years has elapsed since their establishment, the institution may institute a release or modification without court approval.

# Accounting Treatment of Institutional Funds

For nonprofit organizations that have a donor-restricted endowment fund or board-designated endowment fund, there are special accounting rules for the treatment of these funds. In particular, the Financial Accounting Standards Board (FASB) issued FASB-No. FAS 117-1 with the dual objective of providing guidance on net asset classification of donor-restricted endowment funds for nonprofits subject to UPMIFA and providing increased disclosures about an organization's endowment funds, whether or not the organization is subject to UPMIFA.

Under this accounting rule, the assets in these endowment funds are to be classified as "temporarily restricted," "permanently restricted," or "unrestricted." A temporarily restricted asset relates to an asset that is subject to donor-imposed restriction that permits the organization to use up or expend the donated assets as specified and is satisfied either by passage of time or by actions of the organization. A permanently restricted asset is created when the donor requires that the asset be maintained permanently. That amount must be kept permanently in accordance with explicit donor restrictions, or if no restrictions are specified, the organization's governing board determines the amount that must be retained permanently consistent with relevant law. An unrestricted asset is an asset that has no restrictions by the donors. Under the accounting guidelines, investment income (including appreciation) is to be treated as temporarily restricted until appropriated for expenditure. This creates a time restriction that must first be satisfied in addition to any purpose restriction.[7]

# Donor-Advised Funds

The type of possible funds that can be maintained by a nonprofit corporation are outside the scope of this book. Still, a brief description of one type of fund that has received significant attention from both nonprofits and regulators is provided.

Donor-advised funds have become a popular means for managing charitable donations on behalf of an organization, family, or individual. Often, a donor-advised fund is maintained by a sponsoring public charity, such as a community foundation. Donors are able to receive the maximum tax deduction available, while avoiding excise taxes and other restrictions imposed on private foundations. Donors contribute tax-deductible assets to the accounts, and may periodically advise the sponsoring charity on how it should invest the assets. Donors also are able to recommend grants from their accounts to charitable organizations of their choice. The sponsoring charity can accept donations of almost any asset including cash, stock, and real estate.

In recent years, there has been legislation to regulate donor-advised funds. This legislation has resulted in, among other things, the imposition of excise taxes for distributions that do not meet a charitable purpose or for certain distributions where the expenditure responsibility is not exercised.[8] The IRS has established procedures for processing applications of organizations that are applying for exemption and are planning to maintain donor-advised funds. Among other things, the IRS will determine whether the organization is in a position to ensure that  accomplishing the charitable purposes through the distribution can occur.[9]

*See the Suggested Questions and Checklist following the Endnotes below to review the issues discussed in this chapter.*

# Endnotes

1.  *See* Lisa A. Runquist and Jeannie Carmedelle Frey, Eds., *Guide to Representing Religious Organizations* (American Bar Association 2009), at 96.

2.  *See* discussion on donors in *Chapter 1, The Nonprofit Corporation and its Directors, What They Do, How They Do It, and For Whom.*

3.  Uniform Prudent Management of Institutional Funds Act (http:\\www.uniformlaws.org).

4.  *See* Cynthia R. Rowland, *UPMIFA, Three Years Later:  What's a Prudent Director To Do?,* ABA BUSINESS LAW TODAY, Volume 18 No. 6 (July/August 2009).

5.  *See* Rowland, *UPMIFA, Three Years Later, supra* note 4.

6.  *See, e.g.,* New York Prudent Management of Institutional Funds Act, NPLL § 551, et al.

7.  *See, e.g.,* Kelly Thornton, *FSP No. FAS 117-1, Endowments of Not-for-Profit Organizations:  Net Asset Classifications of Funds Subject to Unenacted Version of the Uniform Prudent Management of Institutional Funds Act, and Enhanced Disclosures for all Endowment Funds* (ABA Section of Taxation September 12, 2008).

8.  *See* Pension Protection Act of 2006, Pub. L. No. 109-208; IRS Notice 2006-109 (Interim Guidance Regarding Supporting Organizations and Donor Advised Funds).

9.  *See* Runquist & Frey, *Guide to Representing Religious Organizations, supra* note 1, at 101-102.

# Suggested Questions for Directors Regarding Investments and Expenditure of Endowment Funds

(1)    Does the corporation receive gifts in the form of endowments?

(2)    Does the corporation have a gift policy?

(3)    Does the corporation have an investment policy?

(4)    What has been the experience (in terms of rate of return) of the corporation's investments? How does such experience compare to other similar entities?

(5)    Does the corporation utilize the services of an external party with regard to its investments? If so, has the term of the agreement with the agent been recently reviewed? Also, what is the experience (in terms of rate of return) with the external agent?

(6)    Does the corporation have a spending policy?

# Checklist: Investments and Expenditure of Endowment Funds

*Note:*    For simplicity, these and other chapter checklists describe a corporation having a chair, who presides over the board of directors; a chief executive, who may be a staff person; an executive committee; a governance/nominating committee; and an audit committee. (We recognize, however, that in many smaller and other nonprofits, these committee functions may be performed by either the executive committee or the board as a whole.) We also assume a legal counsel—someone, paid or unpaid, having primary responsibility for the corporation's legal affairs. Many corporations, especially larger nonprofits, may have other committees established for specific purposes, such as establishing executive compensation; monitoring compliance with legal requirements; and overseeing investments and other financial matters.

| Subject | Review By | How Often | Comment |
|---|---|---|---|
| 1. Does the corporation actively seek to obtain gifts from donors that may be subject to donor restrictions? | Chair, chief executive | At least annually | |
| 2. If the corporation seeks gifts in the form of endowments, does the corporation have in place a gift policy? | Chair, chief executive, legal counsel | At least annually | A gift policy can be important in assisting the organization in making sure that, among other things, any restrictions placed on a gift to the organization are manageable by the organization. |
| 3. Does the corporation have any endowment funds? | Chair, chief executive | At least annually | |
| 4. What type of endowment funds does the corporation have? Donor-created or board-created? What are the restrictions? | Chair, chief executive, legal counsel | At least annually | |
| 5. Does the corporation have an investment policy? | Chair, chief executive, legal counsel, investment committee | At least annually | An investment policy should comply with the terms of UPMIFA. |

| Subject | Review By | How Often | Comment |
|---|---|---|---|
| 6. Does the corporation utilize the services of an investment manager or other third party with regard to the management of its investments pursuant to the terms of a written agreement? | Chair, chief executive, legal counsel, investment committee | At least annually | Any delegation of investment management duties should be pursuant to a written agreement between the corporation and third party. |
| 7. Does the corporation review the performance of the investment portfolio and the performance of the investment manager? | Chair, chief executive, investment committee | At least quarterly | |
| 8. Does the corporation comply with applicable requirements relating to the spending of any donor-restricted or board-restricted funds? | Chief executive, legal counsel | At least annually for report to the full board, with frequent monitoring at the staff level | |

# Chapter 11:
## Director Liability Risks and Protections

# Chapter 11
# Director Liability Risks and Protections

*The failure (or alleged failure) of directors of nonprofit corporations to fulfill their duties may expose them to liability to third parties, or to the corporation. Directors should therefore be aware of protections that may be available against such liability.*

*In recent years, litigation against directors of many varieties of nonprofits has increased in frequency.[1] The demise of the charitable immunity exemption that was previously available to many kinds of nonprofit corporations has increased the frequency of suits against directors and officers of public benefit and religious corporations.[2] (Mutual benefit corporations and their directors have never enjoyed the protection of the charitable exemption.) Regardless of the size of the nonprofit or its activities, all directors need to understand the actions that may be taken to protect them against liability claims related to their service on a nonprofit corporation's board.*

*A nonprofit corporation director should understand what the corporation's basic documents provide as to indemnification and insurance, and know if there are any statutory exemptions or other legal provisions that may limit the director's liability.*

## The Director's Exposure to Liability

A director's possible liability in litigation does not arise simply because the corporation may be liable for a matter. It arises because the director is charged with some breach of duty or other harm done to the corporation or to a specific party. A director should understand that the corporation itself may be the party asserting a claim.

A director's liability does not automatically arise from corporate liability. For directors to be endangered by litigation, they must hold a duty to, or have directly harmed, some party entitled—or allegedly entitled—to sue the director. Suits against directors are typically brought in one of three ways:

(1)  An outside party may attempt to sue a member of the board directly, in a suit alleging some injury done *by* the corporation, but claiming the director to be a principal or implied coconspirator in connection with the injury.

(2)  An aggrieved party may assert some right of the corporation against the director, suing to remedy claimed harm done to the corporation; lawsuits of this type are referred to as "derivative actions."[3] In effect, someone is suing the director on behalf of the corporation, generally because of the director's breach of the duty of care or the duty of loyalty. (See the discussion of director duties in *Chapter 2, Duties and Rights of Nonprofit Corporation Directors.*)

(3)  The director may be held *personally* liable under various federal and state laws dealing with issues such as environmental claims, tax delinquencies (for example, failure to pay sales taxes, payroll taxes, or make proper withholding), antitrust claims, or employment claims.[4]

Although a director's exposure to potential liability claims may vary according to the size of the entity, the nature and degree of exposure will be determined more by the type of nonprofit corporation than by its size. Generally, liability exposure is based on allegations of negligence or failure to oversee.

# Avoiding Liability Risks

Some litigation risk may be avoided. As discussed in *Chapter 9, Duties of Directors under Special Circumstances: Change of Control; Sale of Unique Assets; and Bankruptcy,* the board should identify areas in which the corporation is vulnerable to litigation or potential legal liability, and then make sure that appropriate procedures and reporting mechanisms are put in place to avoid or minimize these risks. In some cases, the directors may wish to employ advisers and consultants to aid in decisions that are of a kind likely to be scrutinized by regulators or others. Use of outside advisers may help the board demonstrate that it satisfied its duty of care when it made a particular decision.

Similarly, in situations in which duty of loyalty issues are present, the use of an outside opinion, even to verify what seems obvious, may be prudent, and offer legal protections not otherwise available. For example, under the IRS's excess benefit rules, transactions with insiders that are approved by the board or a disinterested committee may be afforded a presumption of reasonableness if the transaction is ever challenged as involving an excess benefit (see discussion of excess benefits liability in *Chapter 4, Taxation.*)

# Director Indemnification

The director should seek a program of corporate indemnification to the maximum extent permitted by applicable corporation law. Such a program of indemnification should be sought even if the corporation's liquid net worth may make the protection limited in value.

Although the value of indemnification depends on both the legal and financial ability of the corporation to pay, the legal right of the director to be indemnified in connection with a lawsuit or other proceeding depends on the type of loss the director has incurred. In some instances, the corporation is required to indemnify a director, while in other cases the corporation is permitted to indemnify, if the board chooses to do so. A corporation also may advance certain litigation expenses to the director in certain circumstances.

## Discretionary Indemnification

Initially, it should be noted that even if the board of directors wants to indemnify another director, such an indemnification must be consistent with state law and the corporation's articles and bylaws. Mere goodwill of the board is not sufficient to authorize indemnification.

Most, if not all, states provide for indemnification rights of nonprofit officers and directors by statute.[5] The Model Act gives the corporation discretion to indemnify the director if the director has acted in good faith and with the reasonable belief, in the case of conduct in an official capacity, that his or her actions were in the best interests of the corporation, and, in all other cases, that the individual's conduct was at least not opposed to the best interests of the corporation.[6] Indemnification may include sums due under a settlement agreement. Indemnification for proceedings by the corporation against the director (whether direct or derivative) is generally limited under the Model Act to the reasonable expenses the director incurred in connection with the proceeding.[7] Indemnification may be made mandatory in most situations by appropriate provisions in the corporation's articles of incorporation or bylaws.[8]

## Mandatory Indemnification

Under the Model Act as well as most state laws, directors have the *right* to indemnification from the corporation under certain circumstances.[9] Although individual state statutes may differ from the Model Act, the issues treated by the Model Act are ones that the director must face in any event. Under the Model Act, a corporation is required to indemnify a director for reasonable expenses if the director is "wholly successful" in his or her defense of any proceeding of which the director is a party as a result of being a director of the corporation.[10]

Note, however, that such mandatory indemnification is contingent on a director's being deemed wholly successful in defense of the matter for which indemnification is sought. Such success seems clear when there is a verdict or final ruling in the director's favor (including dismissal with prejudice) in a lawsuit, arbitration, or other legal proceeding. Still, depending on the facts and the applicable state, a settlement of a proceeding may or may not trigger a director's mandatory indemnification rights under the Model Act.[11]

The director should endeavor to have corporate indemnification to the fullest extent permitted by applicable law. This means that the corporate obligation should be set forth in the articles of incorporation or bylaws, in language as broad as the applicable statute permits. A director also may wish to have a separate contract with the corporation providing for indemnification.

Despite the indemnification protections that might exist, directors must recognize that the corporation's uninsured obligation to indemnify may be of little value, if the corporation's net worth is insufficient to cover the directors' expenses or their exposure.

## Advancement of Expenses

A director should know what specific measures the corporation has adopted to provide for advancement of legal expenses. A director will want the corporation to have taken actions that will maximize the corporation's ability to advance expenses of directors who are made parties to proceedings because of their director status. In some states, the ability to advance expenses is provided for under state law.[12] In other states, advancement of expenses may be permitted (or required) only if set forth in a corporation's articles or bylaws.[13]

The director should not underestimate the importance of a procedure permitting the corporation to advance expenses, since having a right of indemnification does not mean that the director can require the corporation to immediately assume the costs of litigation or other proceeding while the matter is being pursued. Rather, indemnification rights are generally triggered only at the end of a litigation or similar proceeding, and result in reimbursement for expenses already incurred. The right of indemnification is therefore of limited help to the director without an advance for expenses. Thus, directors should know whether the corporate documents require the corporation to advance expenses to the maximum extent permitted by the state's indemnification laws.

The Model Act sets forth conditions upon which such advances may be made. Most states have similar conditions, although certain specifics may vary. Under the Model Act, a nonprofit corporation may advance expenses to a director if:

(1)    the director furnishes a written affirmation of the director's good faith belief that the standard of conduct permitting indemnification has been met or that the proceeding involves conduct for which liability has been eliminated by the Model Act liability shield for directors of charitable nonprofit corporations or under a provision of the articles of incorporation as authorized by the Model Act; and

(2)    the director furnishes a written undertaking to repay any sums advanced if it is ultimately determined that the director did not meet the applicable standard.[14]

The undertaking must be an unlimited general obligation of the director, but need not be secured and may be accepted without reference to the director's financial ability to make repayment. In addition, authorizations under the Model Act must be made by a disinterested body or their members, if any.[15] Still, not all state laws require such determination before advances may be made.[16]

## Third-Party Indemnification

In addition, indemnification for directors may be sought from any third party who may agree to indemnify the corporation on a related matter. For instance, the owners of a group of assets sold to the corporation may agree to indemnify the corporation—and, if specified, its officers and directors—against any liability relating to periods prior to the corporation's purchase. Directors should ascertain whether such third-party indemnification runs directly to the directors, or runs only to the corporation. Directors should further ascertain at what point this protection becomes available.

## Attorney General Notice

In some states, indemnification of a director of a public benefit corporation may not occur until at least twenty days after the corporation has given written notice of the proposed indemnification to the state attorney general.[17]

# Protecting Directors through Insurance

A nonprofit corporation should obtain insurance to protect its directors and officers. A directors and officers (D&O) insurance policy *may*, subject to the applicable corporation act, provide coverage that is broader than any indemnification permitted or required by the Model Act or by relevant state law. Under the Model Act, a corporation can protect a director by insurance, even if the insurance coverage extends protection to situations in which the corporation is otherwise prohibited by applicable law from providing indemnification.[18] In addition, some state statutes prohibit indemnification against settlements and judgments in derivative actions (i.e., lawsuits asserting the corporation's rights against the director) if a director is found liable, unless the court determines that special circumstances entitle the director to indemnity despite that judgment.[19] Still, most nonprofit corporation statutes *permit* the corporation to procure insurance for the director for such events, even though the corporation could not directly indemnify from its own funds.

## Directors and Officers (D&O) Insurance

Directors should expect the corporation to provide D&O insurance (or properly funded self-insurance) protecting them from liability. If no D&O insurance is provided, directors should examine the risks of serving without it.

Even if a nonprofit corporation has expansive indemnification provisions in its articles of incorporation or bylaws, these assurances must be considered in light of the financial strength of the corporation offering them. To the extent that qualified board members may be deterred from participating because of inadequate financial reserves to pay such claims, D&O insurance may be the most viable method of providing both the perception and reality of adequate protection for both current and prospective board members. On the other hand, nonprofit corporations with good financial resources may determine that it is more cost-effective to self-insure against director and officer litigation expenses by maintaining a self-insured fund. Such a fund gives the corporation more control over the cost of director and officer protection. It also allows the corporation to more closely tailor protection to the needs of the corporation, its officers, and directors. Nonprofit corporations should not ask directors to serve without insurance coverage if adequate insurance is available to the corporation at reasonable cost.[20]

## D&O Policy Coverage Review to Determine Who and What is Covered

At least annually, the corporation's management or staff should review what individuals and entities are covered by its D&O policy. Where a corporation has (or has recently acquired) affiliates or subsidiaries, the extension of the insurance coverage to these entities should be verified. If the policy provides coverage to directors and officers specified by name, rather than position, the policy may need to be updated whenever new officers or directors are selected. The D&O policy also should be examined to determine if it covers the activities of nondirector members of committees, or other persons (such as volunteers) who may be subject to liability due to their activities on the corporation's behalf.

## Impact of Dual Roles of a Director on D&O Coverage

Many typical D&O policies do not cover the activities of directors or officers when they are acting in other capacities. For example, when a board member who is an attorney is acting in the capacity of counsel, whether paid or volunteer, his or her conduct is probably not included in the corporation's D&O protection. Such dual roles can give rise to difficult questions concerning coverage. For example, legal malpractice insurers may specifically exclude claims that arise if the attorney was acting as an officer or director of an organization. The D&O policy may have a similar provision excluding work performed as a lawyer unless the attorney is specifically named in the policy. Thus, there may be a gray area in which neither coverage applies, especially if the attorney or his or her law firm is also legal counsel to the corporation.[21] Similar problems can arise in other dual roles. These problems may be addressed by obtaining special riders or endorsements on policies; however, the need for clarification should be recognized by those individuals wearing multiple corporate hats.

## The Nature of "Claims-Made" Policies

Most D&O policies are written on a "claims-made" basis; thus, a director should understand the limits of this type of coverage.

The claims-made type of policy contrasts with an "occurrence" policy. Occurrence policies cover all claims arising out of incidents occurring during the policy period, regardless of whether the insurance policy is still in effect at the time the claim is made. Most insurance policies with which a director will be individually familiar—e.g., automobile liability, fire, and extended coverage—are occurrence policies. Thus, it is important to understand the nature and limits of claims-made coverage.

Policy coverage on a claims-made basis means that a claim is covered by insurance only if the policy is in effect at the time that the claim is made, regardless of when the event causing the claim occurred. For instance, suppose that a corporation had coverage for the past ten years, but because of a changeover in clerical staff, the policy lapsed for a month before being renewed. The corporation would not be covered for any claim made during the one month of noncoverage, even though the claim related to corporate action during the prior period in which the corporation's policy had been in effect. Furthermore, some D&O policies will limit the coverage of prior events to those arising in a specified number of years prior to the inception of the policy with that particular carrier. As can be seen, claims-made coverage may offer a very limited protection. Directors should further understand that if the corporation discontinues a D&O policy after they cease to be a directors, they may be uninsured even as to acts occurring during their term of office, if the claim is made after the policy is discontinued and no "tail" policy is obtained.

In addition to the requirement that the D&O policy be in effect as of the date a claim is made, D&O policies have other requirements that must be adhered to in order to ensure that coverage is available. For instance, D&O policies typically require the corporation to advise the insurer promptly of facts that could trigger claims, and delicate issues arise as to what constitutes adequate notice of a claim. When making a D&O claim, the corporation should make sure that the form of notice conforms to the policy requirements.

## Policy Coverage

D&O policies are typically divided into two parts. The first part covers reimbursement of individual directors and officers for losses for which they are not indemnified by the corporation. The second part provides reimbursement to the corporation for amounts that it has paid, or is required to expend, in indemnifying its directors and officers. In other words, it provides the funds that enable the corporation to discharge its obligation to indemnify.[22]

The type of coverage, retentions, exclusions, and other aspects of the policies are sufficiently complex as to require study by the corporation's insurance committee, an insurance consultant, and possibly by legal counsel experienced in this area. The corporation also should review the issues whenever insurance carriers are changed.

## Types of Coverage

When a director reviews a D&O policy, it is important to understand whether the policy covers the directors and officers (A-side coverage), the organization's obligation to indemnify its directors and officers (B-side coverage), or the entity for its own liability (C-side coverage).[23] A-side coverage can require a director who is entitled to indemnification to look first to the nonprofit rather than the insured for protection against loss. B-side coverage covers the institution regarding reimbursement for amounts advanced to satisfy indemnification claims that the directors and officers may make against the institution or entity under corporate law or organizing documents of the institution.[24] C-side coverage provides insurance for an entity itself for its own wrongful acts and to avoid an allocation of benefits between the entity and the officers and directors.[25]

## Losses Covered

The D&O policy should be analyzed to determine whether the duty to defend and the cost of defense are covered. The corporation should provide the director with a memorandum on this subject as well as the losses covered or not covered. For example, usually, there is no duty to provide attorneys to defend a lawsuit; nor do typical D&O policies provide for the payment of legal expenses, except after a final determination of liability under the policy.[26] Thus, technically, a D&O policy is an *indemnity* policy, as distinguished from a *liability* policy.

Under an indemnity policy, such as the typical D&O policy, the insurer is not required to make any payments until the insured has suffered an actual loss (as defined in the policy). In comparison, a liability policy, such as the typical automobile insurance policy, requires the insurer to make certain payments even though the insured has not yet incurred a loss or paid any out-of-pocket money.[27] It is because of the nature of a D&O policy that the advances for expenses mentioned above are so crucial for the director's protection.

A director will also want to know:

- the limits of coverage of the D&O policy (i.e., the highest amount of money the insurer will pay for each loss);

- the retention level imposed on the insureds, more commonly known as the deductible (i.e., how much of the loss must be borne by the director before the insurer will begin to provide payment for the loss); and

- the amount of coinsurance, if any (i.e., the percentage that the insured continues to be responsible for paying, even when deductibles have been satisfied and the insurance is providing coverage for a loss).

## Policy Exclusions

Virtually all D&O policies have substantial exclusions that must be fully understood.

In addition to the scope of coverage, directors should understand their D&O policy's exclusions. The excluded risks are not just limited to the exclusions section but occur throughout the policy. For example, the term "loss" may be defined to exclude fines or penalties imposed by law for matters uninsurable under applicable law, such as punitive damages. Other definitions and terms also set forth exclusions.[28]

The standard exclusions often involve some types of risks that could produce sizable claims against directors and officers. Often excluded are the following liabilities: losses covered by other insurance; sickness or death resulting from pollution; ERISA claims; fair employment claims; libel or slander actions; and liabilities arising from intentional conduct, including fraud, dishonesty, and criminal conduct. Most policies also will not cover fines, penalties, or punitive damages.

Just because an area of risk is excluded from a standard D&O policy, however, does not mean that coverage for such risk cannot be obtained. Many exclusions may be deleted by negotiation and payment of a separate premium. A few specialized exposures (such as ERISA claims) may be covered by specific policies. While a request for additional coverage may constitute the "red-flagging" of a problem, the disclosure of potential claims is required in the application in any event. Thus, it is in the interests of the corporation and its officers and directors to identify whether the corporation's activities result in a significant risk of liability for a type of claim excluded by its D&O policy. The corporation can then determine whether the exclusion can be eliminated, or if coverage for such claims can be obtained by other means.

## The Application

All applications for D&O insurance should be carefully prepared and reviewed for accuracy.

The application for D&O insurance and the statements made in it are part of the insurance contract and may be relied on by the insurer when an issue is raised as to the policy's coverage. Because of the peculiar importance of D&O insurance, all directors should be sure that not only the policy itself, but also the application for it, have been reviewed with particular care since a misstatement in the application (even if the director is unaware of it) may result in a denial of coverage.

# Statutory Protections for Directors

Many state statutes limit the liability of directors of certain kinds of nonprofit corporations.

## Eliminating Liability to Third Parties

As a partial response to the increased exposure of directors, and the possible unavailability of insurance, the Model Act and many states' nonprofit corporation statutes limit a director's liability except in special situations such as those involving gross negligence, recklessness, or willful misconduct.[29] An example of such a provision is § 8.31(d) of the Model Act, which provides that a director of a charitable corporation shall not be liable to the corporation or its members for money damages for any action taken, or any failure to take any action, as a director, except liability for (1) the amount of a financial benefit received by the director to which the director is not entitled; (2) an intentional infliction of harm; (3) an unlawful distribution; or (4) an intentional violation of criminal law.

In some states, these liability-elimination provisions apply only to directors of public benefit corporations or corporations exempt from taxation under § 501(c) of the Internal Revenue Code,[30] or to directors who serve without compensation.[31] In addition, under some state statutes, such liability-elimination only applies if the corporation has satisfied certain requirements, such as including a liability-elimination provision in its articles of incorporation or obtaining a certain level of insurance coverage.[32] Directors should make sure that the corporation has taken all actions needed to make this protection available.

# Eliminating Liability for Monetary Damages to the Corporation or Its Members

Some states provide protection to directors from claims by the corporation or its members through the business judgment rule statutes. The rule provides that board members acting in good faith and the reasonable belief that their actions are in the best interests of the organization are protected from liability for erroneous judgments. *See* discussion in *Chapter 2, Duties and Rights of Nonprofit Corporation Directors*.

Other states also allow nonprofit corporations to eliminate or limit the personal liability of a director to the corporation or its members for monetary damages resulting from the breach of the director's duty of care owed the corporation or its members.[33] Some state statutes will require such liability-elimination to be set forth in the corporation's articles of incorporation. In addition, as noted above, such statutes generally do not permit elimination of liability for intentional infliction of harm on the corporation or its members, intentional violation of criminal law, any transaction in which the director derived an improper personal economic benefit, loans to the director by the corporation, or unlawful distributions approved by the director.

# Limitations of Liability Protection Statutes

The director should be aware of several fundamental weaknesses in statutes purporting to eliminate the liability of directors. First, many plaintiffs will predictably assert in the initial complaint that the act or omission involved falls within the exception to the applicable statute, i.e., that the director *was* grossly negligent or willful, or that the matter involved breach of the director's duty of loyalty. Therefore, the director may still have to defend himself or herself in a court proceeding. Hence, once again, the need for advances of expenses (see discussion in the section *"Advancement of Expenses"* above). Second, whether or not these state statutes protect against director liability for claims arising under federal law is unclear. (Although the federal Volunteer Protection Act of 1997 may provide a similar level of protection, at least to uncompensated directors, it is subject to the same fundamental weaknesses identified here.[34]) Third, immunity from liability is not automatic under these statutes; directors must *prove* that they met the due care, good faith, and other statutory requirements for elimination of liability. Therefore, even directors who are eligible to rely on these liability-elimination statutes should still request the corporation to maximize director indemnification rights available under state law and supplement these statutory protections with a D&O policy if possible.[35]

## Protection against Certain Kinds of Claims

Other statutes limit the liability of corporations, or of volunteers other than directors, for certain types of claims. For instance, in New Jersey, nonprofit corporations are not liable for negligently causing injury to a beneficiary of the corporation.[36] To the extent these statutes effectively block claims to which the corporation (and potentially its directors and officers) are subject, they provide an added level of protection against litigation risks.

# Conflicting Interests: The Director and Legal Counsel

In general, the board of directors is the highest authority of the corporation, and, in matters concerning the entire board, the corporation and the board are roughly identical in their legal exposure. But in some instances, the members of the board and the corporation may have conflicting interests. If the corporation and members of the board are both defendants in a proceeding, the corporation may wish (or be forced for its own protection) to assert cross claims against all or some of its directors. Further, individual directors may, through their own acts or omissions, find that they have different potential liability compared to other members of the board.

With respect to the role of legal counsel in claims made both against the corporation and some or all of the directors, the director should recognize the following:

(1) The legal positions of the board of directors and that of the corporation are not *necessarily* identical; in some situations the board or a portion of the board needs to seek counsel of its own, since the corporate general counsel may be obligated to pursue or assert claims against the directors in order to avoid liability of the corporation.

(2) An individual director may need independent counsel if the director finds that his or her situation differs markedly from that of other members of the board.

# Summary

Directors and prospective directors will benefit from a thorough understanding of the protections against liability afforded them under state law, the corporation's articles of incorporation and bylaws, and the corporation's D&O policy or self-insurance fund. Directors may wish to require that senior management, board officers, or a committee conduct an annual review of the scope and limitations of these protections and evaluate whether it is feasible to take any actions to enhance them. The persons who conduct this review should report their conclusions to the full board.

*See the Suggested Questions and Checklist following the Endnotes below to review the issues discussed in this chapter.*

# Endnotes

1.  Individuals working in the nonprofit sector have faced an increased risk in personal liability. Since the 1980s, there has been a marked increase in the number of suits filed against individuals acting for nonprofit organizations. *See Developments in the Law—Nonprofit Corporations*, 105 HARV. L. REV. 1578 (1992); *see also* Directors and Officers Liability Survey: 2010 Summary of Results (Towers Watson); Stephen M. Foxman, *Directors and Officers Liability Insurance for Nonprofits*, 18 ABA BUS. L. TODAY 35 (July/August 2009).

2.  In the past, many states held that charities were immune from lawsuits arising from injuries caused by employees or agents. This immunity has virtually disappeared through legislation and judicial decision. *See* President and Directors of Georgetown College v. Hughes, 130 F.2d 810 (D.C. Cir. 1942). *See also* Sanner v. Trustees of Sheppard and Enoch Pratt Hospital, 278 F. Supp. 138 (D. Md. 1968), *aff'd*, 398 F.2d 226 (4th Cir. 1968).

3.  Derivative suits may be brought in some states by a corporation's members. *See, e.g.*, S.C. CODE ANN. § 33-31-304. In many states, the attorney general may bring a derivative suit against a director. *See, e.g.*, S.C. CODE ANN. § 33-31-304(b); PRINCIPLES OF THE LAW OF NONPROFIT ORGANIZATIONS, (Tentative Draft No. 3, 2011).

4.  *See* W. VA. CODE § 11-15-17 (tax delinquencies); CONN. GEN. STAT. § 42-110b (antitrust liability).

5.  Although a number of nonprofit indemnification statutes generally follow the indemnification provision of the Model Act or the Revised Model Nonprofit Corporation Act, a significant number have less

standard provisions. *See, e.g.,* John F. Olson, Josiah O. Hatch, III, & Ty R. Sagalow, DIRECTOR AND OFFICER LIABILITY: INDEMNIFICATION AND INSURANCE, § 11.03[2] (West Group 2008 update).

6.  *See* Model Act § 8.51(a).
7.  *See* Model Act § 8.51(d).
8.  For example, Model Act § 2.02(b)(8) permits a nonprofit corporation to include in its articles of incorporation a provision authorizing permissible or mandatory indemnification of a director. Such Section specifically excepts liability arising out of improper financial benefit received by a director, an intentional infliction of harm on the corporation or the members, an unlawful distribution, or an intentional violation of criminal law. *See also* IOWA CODE § 504.202(2)(e).
9.  *See* Model Act § 8.52.
10. Model Act § 8.50(8) defines "proceeding" broadly, to include a threatened, pending, or completed proceeding. Some state statutes may have different and more limited definitions. *See* GA. CODE ANN. § 14-3-140(26); N.C. GEN. STAT. § 55A-8-52; ARK. STAT. ANN. § 4-33-850(7).
11. See Olson et al., DIRECTOR AND OFFICER LIABILITY, *supra* n. 5, at § 5.03[4][a]. Settlement amounts paid in connection with derivative suits may not be considered liabilities payable under the indemnification provision of the Model Act. *See* Comment 5, § 8.50.
12. *See, e.g.,* COLO. REV. STAT. § 7-129-104.
13. *See, e.g.,* N.J. STAT. ANN. § 15A:3-4.
14. Model Act § 8.53.
15. Model Act § 8.53(c).
16. *See, e.g.,* ARIZ. REV. STAT. § 10-3853.
17. *See, e.g.,* ARK. STAT. ANN. § 4-33-855.
18. Model Act § 8.57.
19. *See e.g.,* MISS. CODE ANN. § 79-11-281.
20. In the past, some homeowners' policies contained coverage for specific nonprofit civic activities of the insured. These provisions have largely been eliminated. Moreover, although some corporate general liability and individual personal liability policies will cover an individual's service as a director, this coverage is rarely complete.
21. *See* Willard L. Boyd III, *Lawyers' Service on Nonprofit Boards: Managing the Risks of an Important Community Activity,* 18 ABA BUS. L. TODAY 35, 39 (November/December 2008).
22. *See* Jack B. Siegel, A DESKTOP GUIDE FOR NONPROFIT DIRECTORS, OFFICERS, AND ADVISORS: AVOIDING TROUBLE WHILE DOING GOOD, 614-617 (John Wiley & Sons 2006), Michael R. Davisson, Martin J. O'Leary, Eric C. Scheiner, Edward G. Smerdon, and Joseph

M. Smick, *Directors & Officers Liability Insurance Deskbook*, 30-31 (American Bar Association 2011).

23. *See* Siegel, A DESKTOP GUIDE FOR NONPROFIT DIRECTORS, OFFICERS, AND ADVISORS, *supra note 22, at* 614.

24. *See* Foxman, *Directors and Officers Liability Insurance for Nonprofits, supra* n. 2.

25. *See* Foxman, *Directors and Officers Liability Insurance for Nonprofits, supra* n. 2.

26. *See* Zaborac v. American Casualty Co., 663 F. Supp. 330 (C.D. Ill. 1987). *But see* Okada v. MGIC Indemnity Corp. 823 F.2d 276 (9th Cir. 1986), which held to the contrary. There is considerable dispute among courts as to when legal fees would be payable. Some courts require legal fees to be paid as they are billed and payable. *See, e.g.,* Pepsico, Inc. v. Continental Casualty Corp., 640 F. Supp. 656 (S.D. N.Y. 1986).

27. In addition, an insured can be liable for legal defense costs as well as for damages on the claim itself when they exceed policy limits. A large deductible can subject a corporate insured to paying a significant portion of the initial defense costs. *See* Siegel, A DESKTOP GUIDE FOR NONPROFIT DIRECTORS, OFFICERS, AND ADVISORS, *supra* n. 22, at 610-611. Thus, many nonprofit corporations may be underinsured.

28. Siegel, A DESKTOP GUIDE FOR NONPROFIT DIRECTORS, OFFICERS, AND ADVISORS, *supra* n. 22, at 609-610.

29. *See* IND. CODE ANN. § 23-1-35-1; IOWA CODE § 504.901; TENN. CODE ANN. § 48-58-601; CAL. CORP. CODE §§ 5239 and 5047.5.

30. *See* CAL. CORP. CODE § 5239.

31. *See* 805 ILL. COMP. STAT. 105/108.70(a) of the Illinois General Not For Profit Corporation Act of 1986, as amended (in addition, the elimination of liability provision only applies to directors and officers of tax-exempt corporations).

32. *See State Liability Laws for Charitable Organizations and Volunteers* (Nonprofit Risk Management Center http://www.nonprofitrisk.org/library/state-liability.shtml). This publication provides an excellent summary of state laws and leading court cases limiting or eliminating the liability of nonprofit corporations, directors, and volunteers.

33. *See* Model Act, Section 2.02(c). *See also* TENN. CODE ANN. § 48-52-102.

34. *See* Volunteer Protection Act of 1997, 42 U.S.C. §§ 14501-14505; *see also* Lisa A. Runquist and Judy F. Zybach, *Volunteer Protection Act of 1997: An Imperfect Solution* (available at www.runquist.com).

35. For a discussion of state laws providing for limited liability of nonprofit organizations' directors and officers, *see* Olson et. al., DIRECTOR AND OFFICER LIABILITY, *supra* n. 5, at § 11.03. For a critical view of one state's statute, *see* Louis S. Harrison & Eric L. Marhoun, *Protection*

for *Unpaid Directors and Officers of Illinois Not-For-Profits: Fact or Fiction?*, 79 Ill. Bar J. 172 (April 1991), and a critique of the latter article, 79 Ill. Bar J. 267 (June 1991).

36.    *See* N.J. Stat. Ann. §§ 2A:53A-7 and 2A: 53A-8 (immunity for claim made by the hospital's intended beneficiaries for damages in excess of $250,000); *referenced in State Liability Laws for Charitable Organizations and Volunteers, supra* n. 32, at 8, 72-76.

# Suggested Questions for Directors Regarding Director Liability

(1)    What exposure do I and others have to claims or litigation that may be brought? Who could potentially assert such claims and for what reasons?

(2)    Have the directors of the corporation, past or present, been subject to litigation or threats of it? Why, and with what result?

(3)    Do I know of a similar corporation in which the directors have been sued?

(4)    What provisions do the corporation's articles and bylaws have with regard to the director's risk, indemnification, and insurance?

(5)    Of those provisions, which ones are mandatory ones upon which I can insist, and that require some approval or ratification? By whom? According to what standard?

(6)    Do the mandatory provisions include the advance of expenses?

(7)    Do I know what our corporation's D&O policy provides? What is not covered by it?

(8)    What is the earliest date for which a matter would be covered even if a claim comes within the policy period?

(9)    Who has read or examined the corporation's D&O policy, and how recently?

(10)   Have I been provided with a memorandum describing our D&O coverage, available indemnification, and statutory protections available?

(11)   Have I been informed as to the interrelationship of the corporation's D&O coverage and other policies insuring me, such as professional malpractice or umbrella liability policies? Are there gaps in my protection?

(12)   If I cease to be a director, for how long a period, if any, will the corporation's D&O policy cover me?

(13) If I have D&O coverage supplied in connection with another corporation, does it cover me as a director of this nonprofit corporation?

(14) Do applicable statutes limit my liability or exonerate me? Has the corporation taken all steps necessary to make those limitations or exonerations effective?

# Checklist: Director Liability

*Note:*    For simplicity, these and other chapter checklists describe a corporation having a chair, who pre-sides over the board of directors; a chief executive, who may be a staff person; an executive committee; a governance/nominating committee; and an audit committee. (We recognize, however, that in many smaller and other nonprofits, these committee functions may be performed by either the executive committee or the board as a whole.) We also assume a legal counsel—someone, paid or unpaid, having primary responsibility for the corporation's legal affairs. Many corporations, especially larger nonprofits, may have other committees established for specific purposes, such as establishing executive compensation; monitoring compliance with legal requirements; and overseeing investments and other financial matters.

| Subject | Review By | How Often | Comment |
|---|---|---|---|
| 1. Do we have D&O insurance? What events does it cover? | Legal counsel, chief executive or board chair; prospective board members; risk manager/ risk management committee (if any) | Perform evaluation and update all directors, at least annually | Review and evaluation of the adequacy of D&O coverage may also be merited at each change in corporate activities or structure, as well as at each change of insurer or alteration in policy coverage. |

| Subject | Review By | How Often | Comment |
|---|---|---|---|
| a. What event dates are covered by D&O insurance? | Legal counsel, chief executive or board chair; risk manager/ risk management committee (if any) | At least annually | This is not just an analysis of dates of policy itself, but an analysis of how far it covers prior events. |
| b. Is the policy providing coverage on a "claims made" basis? | Legal counsel, chief executive or board chair; risk manager/ risk management committee (if any) | At least annually | The board should understand what event constitutes a claim, and the nature of a claims-made policy. A memorandum to the directors should cover this issue. |
| c. What events are not covered? Are special riders or policies available to cover specific excluded risks? | Legal counsel, chief executive or board chair; risk manager/ risk management committee (if any) | At least annually | The board should understand what event constitutes an insurable event, and what events are not covered. A memorandum to the directors should cover this issue. |
| d. What are the deductibles? What coinsurance is required? | Legal counsel, chief executive or board chair; risk manager/ risk management committee (if any) | At least annually | A memorandum to the directors should cover this issue. |

| Subject | Review By | How Often | Comment |
|---|---|---|---|
| 3. Does our D&O policy exclude coverage when an otherwise insured person is covered by another liability policy— e.g., an attorney's malpractice policy? | Legal counsel, chief executive or board chair; risk manager/ risk management committee (if any) | At least annually | Directors having dual coverage should inform audit committee and counsel. |
| 4. Have we reviewed how possible gaps in coverage can be plugged? | Legal counsel, chief executive or board chair; risk manager/ risk management committee (if any) | At least annually | Larger corporations may use professional risk consultants in this task. |

# Chapter 12:
## The Legal Environment of the Nonprofit Corporation

# Chapter 12
# The Legal Environment of the Nonprofit Corporation

*Directors need to understand the corporation's legal environment in order to ensure the corporation acts within the bounds of the law and maximizes its performance for its constituency of service.*

## The Board's Responsibility

### Understanding the Corporation's Legal Environment

To fully understand the scope of their duties, directors should have a clear picture of the corporation's legal environment, that is, the substantive law governing all the things the corporation is organized to do. *The directors must understand that this environment of laws and regulations surrounds the corporation at all times,* regardless of whether the corporation employs a lawyer, whether or not it is involved in a lawsuit, or whether some license or permit is required for the corporation's operations. Parts of this same legal landscape surround each of us individually; for the most part, we adjust to it unconsciously, without any need for professional help or guidance. The corporate director, however, must be more conscious of the corporation's legal environment, since it affects what the corporation can or cannot do.

For an analogy, think of driving a car. It is sitting in the garage; someone enters it to drive it. The law defines who that driver may be, on what side of the street the driver will drive, when the car must stop, when and where it cannot turn, and how fast it may go. The law imposes conditions of insurance, and requires pollution-free status. In some states, the law governs how many people may be in the car, or whether or not the driver must be wearing a seat belt, and other matters.

And yet, of course, no one of us gives any of this a moment's thought. Driving a car is such a normal part of our lives that we take for granted the commands of the law in doing so. If we were to drive a car from here to Mexico City, we might have different thoughts. We might find it necessary to inquire somewhere of the Mexican requirements for a permit to drive, how fast we may drive, and what we should if we had an accident. And then, if we went further and decided we wanted to take a passenger for hire to Mexico, we might see some complex legal problems emerge.

# Role of Legal Counsel

Helping the corporation to navigate safely through its legal environment is a responsibility primarily of counsel for the corporation—whether a volunteer or paid—but that responsibility is most effectively assigned when the board of directors understands how the corporation faces the legal landscape surrounding it. On the one hand, we do not counsel the board of directors to try to resolve legal problems themselves on a do-it-yourself basis, but on the other hand, we counsel against the other extreme: assuming that the problem is entirely one to be assigned to counsel, and if counsel is not available, it is a problem that somehow ceases to exist. Counsel (whether internal or external, paid or volunteer) is a means to be used. It is the job of the board to use such means appropriately and effectively.

# What We Mean by Law

In determining a corporation's legal environment, a director should first understand what the "law" is. This question is answered in three parts:

## Predictable Acts by Authorities

The law is a question of how people holding power over the corporation—legislators, regulators, officials of various kinds, judges, and the like—will behave in certain situations. A distinguished jurist once said that the object of the study of law is prediction, "the prediction of the incidence of the public force through the instrumentality of the courts,"[1] and we adopt basically this view. A large part of the corporation's legal environment is the predictable behavior of power: power held by legislatures, by the administrators, by the judges, etc.

## Private Acts (Contracts) That Bind the Corporation

Corporations through their own voluntary actions are frequently making law: by contracts, agreements, leases, etc. These private actions, which are part of the daily business of the corporation, create a set of legal restraints that are as effective within their limited sphere as any statute or regulation. Yet no business could survive if every contract or every purchase of goods, required the services of a lawyer. The prudent board attempting to control its legal environment will expect management to separate those contracts that require the assistance of outside counsel from those that can be handled by the corporation's staff (including any in-house attorneys) as part of its day-to-day business.

## Litigation

The determination of law applicable to the corporation must include an understanding of the impact of litigation involving the corporation either as a plaintiff or a defendant. This *Guidebook* does not elaborate on this particular aspect of legal activity because in most situations if the corporation is entering the courtroom voluntarily, or forced into it involuntarily, the corporation must employ counsel.

# Analysis of the Corporation's Legal Environment

## Identifying Potential Areas of Legal Exposure

To understand the corporation's legal environment, directors should make the following inquiries:

(a)    Does the corporation's activity require that it have relatively long-term contracts or agreements with other entities or persons?

(b)    Are any activities of the corporation similar to those of other corporations that have faced litigation in connection with such activities—whether brought by a government entity or by some private entity or individual?

(c)    Do any of the corporation's activities require the concurrent expenditure of money or provision of effort by another party—such as a joint venture partner?

(d)    Do any of the corporation's activities require a license or permit? Is there a government body that can require reports or make inspections?

From a list such as that set forth above, the directors can note those issues where the expectations of the corporation (or the party contracting with the corporation) may not be met and where a failure to meet expectations would seriously impact the corporation. These are the areas in which the board should probably consult counsel. The board's recognition of the corporation's potential legal exposures will help the directors determine what actions may be taken in advance to minimize the likelihood that the corporation would suffer any damage in connection with any particular relationship or activity.

## Annual Review

A general review of the corporation's legal environment should be conducted once a year. This review serves in part to promote consciousness-raising, to help make the board aware of its potential problems and legal vulnerabilities, even though no immediate solution may be needed. *This* Guidebook *does not assume that the answer to all of the demands of the corporation's legal environment is, automatically, the employment of a lawyer.* Still, once the board has performed a review of its legal vulnerabilities and needs, it will be in a better position to determine when counsel is and is not appropriate.

# The Corporation's Contractual Environment

### *When to involve outside counsel in the contracting process*

The section *"Private Acts (Contracts) That Bind the Corporation"* above refers to the private law-making function of the corporation, that is, the drafting and execution of contracts and agreements. The board should establish, or request management staff to propose guidelines regarding when outside counsel should be retained, in connection with a contractual matter, such as the following:

- The moneys to be committed by the corporation, or to the corporation, are a significant fraction of its budget.
- The contract involves more than two parties.
- The proposed contract involves the employment of a key person.
- The agreement is material to the corporation's activities.
- The performance to be promised (by either party) requires clear definition to avoid potential misunderstandings (such as for certain consulting or management services).
- The terms of the contract extend beyond one year.
- The activity touches on controversial issues such as fair employment, public health disputes, etc.
- The activity exposes the corporation to substantial risks, even if indemnification and insurance are available.

### *Use of in-house attorneys*

Nonprofit organizations of sufficient size and resources may hire one or more in-house attorneys to draft and review contracts or provide other legal services. In some cases, the executive officer or other senior manager may be an attorney or otherwise capable of reviewing basic contracts without engaging outside counsel. To the extent such individual is not licensed to practice in the jurisdiction where the nonprofit is located, such review should not be treated as a formal legal review.

Board members may volunteer to review contracts; however, this practice raises a variety of legal and role-definition issues and should be done cautiously if at all. See *"Special Issues of the Board Member as Counsel"* below.

# The Litigation Environment

Litigation differs from other aspects of the legal landscape in its potential expense, the necessity of the use of legal counsel, and its unpredictable outcome.

### Insurance and indemnification to limit litigation risk

The possibility that the corporation may be exposed to litigation is a risk of loss against which the board should shield the organization by insurance or indemnification if it is feasible.

Any exposure to litigation generally means an exposure to costs of significant size. Litigation requires the use of paid counsel, with substantial uncertainty as to cost. Even if a lawsuit against the corporation is frivolous, and the corporation may be awarded its attorneys' fees by a court or its costs are covered by insurance, by the time all expenses, including diversions of staff time and lost opportunities have been totaled up, the corporation will still have been adversely affected. If the corporation finds that other corporations having similar activities have been exposed to litigation, directors should examine why this has been so, and what differences, if any, exist between their corporation and the other corporations.

If litigation on behalf of the corporation seems essential to protect the corporation or to fulfill its purpose, it must be budgeted as best can be done. Still, in a lawsuit of anything more than routine nature, such budgeting is extremely difficult; this is an occasion on which the board may benefit from receiving counsel *regarding* counsel, from attorney board members or trusted attorney volunteers. A board contemplating engaging an attorney for a litigation matter should recognize the following:

- No lawyer can totally control, and hence no lawyer can guarantee, the time that a lawsuit may consume. Tactics of the opponent, unforeseen developments, and congestion in the courts all add to the unmanageable character of litigation.
- Although some lawyers may undertake to handle a lawsuit for a fixed maximum fee, in doing so the lawyer may be either including a substantial contingency allowance in that quotation, or counting on readjusting the fee in some manner if the litigation proceeds in an unexpected fashion.
- No corporation should enter the courtroom on its own behalf on the assumption that it can withdraw at will; it may be subject to a counterclaim that holds it in the courthouse, or to substantial penalties imposed by the court.

# The Corporation's Political/Legal Environment

## Restrictions on Involvement in Political Arena

Nonprofit corporations that are tax-exempt under § 501(c)(3) of the Internal Revenue Code (Code) are prohibited from using the organization's resources on behalf of a candidate in a political campaign. (See the discussion in the section "*The Absolute Prohibition on Political Campaign Activities*" in *Chapter 4, Taxation*") Such tax-exempt corporations may, however, engage in lobbying in connection with an issue of concern to the organization, provided that such lobbying activities are limited to an "insubstantial" amount (generally 5 percent of its total activities, or other amount if the corporation elects to rely on the safe harbor under Code § 501(h)) (See the discussion in the section "*Limitations on Lobbying*" in *Chapter 4, Taxation*.) Nonprofits that engage in lobbying also must comply with federal, state, and local lobbying regulations, such as the federal Lobbying Disclosure Act and the Honest Leadership and Open Government Act of 2007.[2] Despite these restrictions and limitations on a tax-exempt corporation's involvement in the political arena, directors of § 501(c)(3) corporations and other nonprofits should still be aware of the legal/political environment in which their organization operates.

## How Nonprofits Are Affected by the Legal/Political Environment

As discussed earlier in this chapter, all nonprofits are affected by laws and regulations relating to one or more of the organization's activities. In some cases, nonprofits look to governmental sources for grants or other revenues. In all cases, the activities of nonprofits—including hiring employees and providing services to the public—are subject to various legal requirements and restrictions.

Changes in the political environment relating to a nonprofit corporation's activities can have a significant effect on the nonprofit's ability to fulfill its mission, or even to survive. For example, an arts organization that sees its public funding diminish, or another organization suddenly faced with burdensome governmental record-keeping requirements, may need to reassess a significant portion of its operations. Similarly, any changes in the Code that affect the deductibility of certain kinds of gifts—whether artwork, appreciated stock, or other assets—may have substantial consequences for nonprofit organizations. For this reason, it is important that directors have a clear understanding of the regulatory environment under which the nonprofit operates, including its public funding sources.

## Keeping the Board and Others Aware of the Impact of Proposed Legal Changes

Since many nonprofits operate on slim profit margins, directors of nonprofit corporations should stay informed regarding what impact proposed legislative and regulatory changes could have on the organization. Nonprofit boards may request that their staff or outside advisers periodically review pending legislative activity relating to the nonprofit's operations, as well as identify opportunities for the organization to receive assistance from governmental bodies in connection with the organization's mission.

Some organizations may wish to adopt a lobbying plan, to ensure that their voices are appropriately heard on issues of importance to the organization or its beneficiaries. On significant topical issues, the organization may effectively pool its resources with similar nonprofits or other groups with like concerns. Even without adopting a formal lobbying plan, a nonprofit may benefit from surveying its board members and any significant donors, to identify those with connections to legislators who are active in areas of interest to the organization, or who may otherwise be willing to listen to the organization's concerns. Nonprofits should be aware that although they must at all times adhere to the legal restrictions on lobbying activity, lobbying may occasionally, or even frequently, be an important means by which they assure their continued ability to fulfill their mission.

# Choice of Counsel

## Differences among Kinds of Nonprofit Corporations

The situation of certain nonprofit corporations should be distinguished from others with regard to employment of counsel. Large nonprofits will, and should, solve their needs for legal services much as a business corporation would: by the employment of professionals, either as salaried attorneys or as outside counsel. The considerations that lead to their choice of counsel remain very much those that would guide the director of a business corporation.

In comparison, the directors of small nonprofit corporations frequently have special problems and opportunities in the choice of counsel. First of all, some nonprofit corporations may have lawyers serving as directors. Such persons clearly offer certain benefits to the corporation, but also present certain problems, discussed below. Moreover, many such corporations have given little attention to planning or managing their legal exposures and often let them reach crisis proportions before taking action.

## Budgeting for Predictable and Recurrent Legal Needs

### *Legal budget considerations*

The first step of the board in this area is budgetary: Given the corporation's legal environment and needs, how much of its funds should the corporation set aside for predictable and recurrent needs for counsel? This estimate should be a part of an appropriate reserve for emergencies or other unbudgeted items.

Wise boards will choose to ignore available uncompensated legal services of volunteers or board members when preparing the corporation's legal budget. Such a source of services, discussed later in this chapter, may on occasion be both available and appropriate; however, the corporation should not *budget* on the assumption that legal problems of serious dimensions can be so handled. If a volunteer lawyer is available and appropriate, the saving of money should be treated as an unexpected financial benefit, not as a budgetary offset.

### *When needs exceed capacity*

If a realistic legal services budget—again, for only the predictable and recurrent legal needs—is apparently beyond the means of the corporation, it should examine, just as it would with any other excess of expected expenses over receipts, whether its resources are too small for its functional survival. The board should recognize that the risks it is unwilling to lessen or minimize here will always go somewhere: They will be borne in the disappointment of donors who see a program jeopardized or encumbered, of staff who see organizational goals unable to be achieved, or of beneficiaries who are not served. As with every other item of expense, the board must prudently provide for it, just as it must budget the corporation's income.

### *Making decisions within the legal budget*

Given a budgetary floor, the chief executive or other appropriate officer should recommend to the board whether to:

- hire (if funds permit) one or more full-time or part-time in-house attorneys;
- budget in anticipation of retaining counsel on a regular basis, as a predictably necessary part of corporate existence; or
- plan to retain counsel to deal with particular problems as needed.

The above distinctions are inevitably one of degree: Is the predictable frequency of problems such that the services of a designated lawyer or firm that deals with all of them would be more efficient? Or is the frequency so slight or the diversity of events so great that a separate choice should be made for each case?

If a single lawyer or firm handles the bulk of the corporation's work, there are significant economies in the time necessary to initiate each engagement. If the predictable volume of work indicates continuing exposure to problems, a general retainer may be advisable.

# Selecting Counsel

In selecting counsel, the corporation should enter into a professional engagement, regardless of whether counsel is compensated or volunteer. Certain generalizations can be offered about the choice of counsel, regardless of whether the lawyer is paid or unpaid.

## *Professional engagements*

The relationship between the corporation and the lawyer serving as counsel (whether for a fee or on a volunteer basis) must be a professional engagement. It should be entered into formally, with the lawyer and the corporation each specifying (preferably in writing) what they expect the engagement to entail.

## *Identifying the kind of legal counsel required*

Lawyers are not one-size-fits-all products, each one of whom is capable of doing everything or being the best person available. The services needed for the particular corporation may be unique and somewhat specialized. A large professional or trade association, for example, needs regular antitrust counsel—lawyers with some experience in this area, whose work keeps them abreast of recent developments in the field that may affect the corporation. In comparison, this specialized expertise would be of little use to the board of an art museum.

On the other hand, there are a large variety of professional skills needed by a nonprofit corporation that vary little between the largest trade association and the smallest community enterprise. All these corporations need competent tax advice; all of them, from time to time, will need skill in drafting employment contracts, reviewing leases, reviewing bank loan documents, and the like. In analyzing needs, the corporation should separate its routine, legal "housekeeping" needs from its specialized needs.

With that said—and other things being equal—it is desirable to get most legal services from a single-source supplier. This will probably save money, and it enables a lawyer to have an overview of the total activities of the corporation; as a peripheral or fringe benefit of that corporation, he or she may offer an insight into some overlooked aspect of the corporation's activities. The corporation may decide that some legal housekeeping can be done by volunteer lawyers and other problems referred to paid counsel.

### "Peacemaker" functions of counsel

There is another role that paid counsel in the proper circumstances can perform, and which may be of enormous importance. We refer to a function of an internal "peacemaker" within the corporation. Often this means simply that the lawyer conveys and certifies unwelcome truths, where other concessions to that reality may be fraught with political tensions within the board. It may be also that the lawyer, as an informed outsider, can suggest alternatives in the midst of a polarized controversy, or provide objectivity regarding certain controversial issues.

## Understanding the Corporation's Rights and Obligations vis-à-vis Its Legal Counsel

### Significance of client–lawyer relationship

The law regards the relationship of a lawyer and a client in a unique and peculiar way, *and does so regardless of whether the lawyer is paid or unpaid*. Still, the mere fact that a person who serves on a board of directors is a lawyer does not make the corporation that lawyer's client. If a client relationship does exist, certain consequences follow for both the lawyer and the corporation.

### Authority of lawyer to bind client

The corporation must recognize that, in general, a lawyer who can describe a corporation as a client has the apparent authority to bind that client to certain kinds of commitments in certain situations. This is particularly true in the courtroom. The limits of the lawyer's apparent authority are, to some degree, discernible from common sense. Nonetheless, it is always important in engaging an attorney (again, whether volunteer or paid) to define the scope of that engagement so that any generally implied authority of an attorney can be limited to specific actions. Wherever feasible, the employment of an attorney should be defined and documented in a written letter of engagement. Such contracts of engagement are, in many states, required by the rules governing the profession. Such document can further clarify the business aspects of the arrangements such as fees, payments, advancing cash expenditures, and so on.

### *Standards of loyalty*

When the lawyer is engaged, the client is entitled to expect certain minimum standards of loyalty. To some degree, these parallel the obligations a corporation may expect from anyone acting on its behalf, e.g., a real estate broker or an executive search firm. One expects such agents to keep confidences and not to use the information obtained from the organization for the agent's advantage outside the scope of the engagement.

### *Confidentiality for certain client-lawyer communications*

The relationship with a lawyer differs, however, in that the client can confide in the lawyer as to matters related to the professional engagement and the communications to the lawyer generally may not be disclosed by the lawyer (without a serious breach of his or her obligations). A court might not require the lawyer to make that disclosure, even under a subpoena. Under the attorney-client privilege, consultations with lawyers concerning complicated and frequently delicate matters are given protections that are not available in consultations with, for example, an accountant or personnel consultant.

In dealing with controversial or sensitive matters, the protection against disclosure arising under the attorney-client privilege, this distinction may be of great importance to the corporation. In certain circumstances, however, such confidentiality protection can be lost, such as when the client (through an officer, employee, or other agent) discloses the sensitive information to a third party in addition to the lawyer. Therefore, the board should caution its members and representatives of the corporation against disclosure of such matters to persons other than the corporation's counsel. This includes ex officio or honorary directors who are not actual directors with a vote, but simply advisory.

### *Potential lawyer conflicts of interest*

A cost of client confidentiality is imposed on the corporation's lawyer. The receipt of confidences from the client, whose interests may be opposed to that of another party, may prevent the lawyer from accepting certain engagements with such other parties, unless the client agrees to waive the conflict.

## Use of Volunteer Lawyers

Volunteer lawyers, whether or not members of the board, may present certain opportunities to the corporation, but they should be used with caution, and with a clear understanding of their role.

Public benefit and religious corporations frequently have lawyers as board members; they also may have outside volunteer lawyers willing to serve the organization. The availability of such resources should not be overlooked, but should be approached with caution.

It should be realized that the lawyer-volunteer could expose him or herself to a substantial risk in undertaking a legal engagement of any significant depth. The following issues need to be considered:

- The fact that the lawyer is unpaid is immaterial in terms of professional malpractice liability of the individual involved and in terms of what the corporation is entitled to expect.[3]
- Lawyers acting in an area outside their regular experience and expertise may expose themselves to heightened risks of professional liability.

## Responsibility for Monitoring the Corporation's Tax Environment

If a corporation seeks to solve most of its legal problems through the use of board members or other volunteers, at least one such volunteer should undertake to maintain regular familiarity with the tax laws affecting the corporation. A public benefit corporation should know, for example, the limits of its activities imposed by § 501(c)(3) of the Code and the distinctions between influencing legislation, where some flexibility is permitted, and engaging in political campaigns, which is absolutely prohibited. The administration of such an inquiry is time-consuming, and in fact is rarely made. Because of a director's familiarity with the ongoing activities of the corporation, this is a valuable service that may be provided by a qualified lawyer-director alone or in periodic contact with specialized tax counsel.

## Special Issues of the Board Member As Counsel

It is hardly uncommon for a lawyer who is a member of a nonprofit corporation's board to serve also as counsel for the corporation. Still, when a director serves as counsel for the corporation, there are special issues that both the corporation and the lawyer need to carefully consider. The practice of generally representing the corporation is frequently criticized for the following reasons:

- The lawyer's independence and objectivity in advising the corporation may be at least somewhat impaired.
- A confusion of roles may affect the lawyer's ability to assert, on behalf of the corporation, its right to confidential treatment of certain communications.
- Various types of conflicts can arise, such as when a lawyer is asked to pursue an objective that the lawyer, as a board member, opposed, when the

board is taking action with regard to the law firm representing the corporation (such as voting to retain the firm) and when the lawyer is asked to opine on board actions in which the lawyer, as a board member, participated.[4]

- The lawyer's ability to negotiate on behalf of the corporation, as a professional facing another professional, is sometimes impaired by the ambiguity of roles.

A further problem arises with a board member acting as lawyer for the corporation. Effective representation of any entity—whether a hospital, school, or dance troupe—requires the full and informed confidence of the persons controlling that entity. In other words, a lawyer serving on a nonprofit board should know if his or her designation as counsel had the active consent of all the fellow directors. Some board members who would prefer using outside counsel may be uncomfortable challenging a fellow director who offers his or her legal services. A board member serving as counsel may be put in a difficult position if called upon to give advice regarding a matter that touches on some controversial policy or field of activity about which the board is divided. In addition, when an attorney board member also acts as corporation counsel, it may be difficult to distinguish which "hat" the director is wearing at any given time. What would otherwise be considered protectable attorney-client communication may become subject to discovery if characterized as discussion among board members.

Frequently, outside counsel handling a problem area is able to bring to the board an objectivity concerning a decision to be made, since the lawyer stands aside from the substantive controversy involved. This is, to a certain degree, a traditional function of lawyers serving organizations and it is a role that may be difficult for an inside lawyer to perform.

At the same time, it may be unrealistic to suggest that a small public benefit entity should avoid the use of volunteer legal services and always seek outside paid counsel. In fact, nonprofits often will look to their lawyer board members for assistance on certain legal matters, such as preparation of articles of incorporation, bylaws, tax returns, or employment agreements. By providing this assistance, the lawyer board member can be viewed as having established an attorney-client relationship and becoming the lawyer for the organization.

As noted above, a lawyer sitting on the nonprofit corporation's board should proceed with caution when agreeing to provide legal services to the corporation. A lawyer board member who agrees to act as counsel should consider and discuss with the other board members the extent of the representation and the potential hazards of serving in such dual roles. The lawyer board member also should make clear to the board when he or she is acting as a board member or as the attorney for the organization.[5]

## Who Is the Client?

Lawyers representing nonprofit corporations owes their professional obligations to the corporation and not to the board as a whole, or to any individual director or officer.

In controversies involving corporate actions, a claimant may assert that both the corporation and one or more directors are accountable, or the corporation may wish to assert that certain directors bear the real responsibility for the controversial events. A director should understand *that in such circumstances the corporation's lawyer does not and cannot represent both the corporation and the affected directors.* Among other things, this means that the corporation's lawyer cannot receive confidences from a director that are kept from the corporation.[6]

When a situation arises that involves an actual or potential dichotomy of interest between the corporate entity and one or more directors, the affected directors should seek independent legal counsel, and the corporation's lawyer should so advise the directors.[7]

*See the Suggested Questions and Checklist following the Endnotes below to review the issues discussed in this chapter.*

## Endnotes

1. Oliver W. Holmes, *The Path of the Law*, 10 HARV. L. REV. 557 (1896).

2. 2 U.S.C. § 1610. For a good summary of the requirements of the Lobbying Disclosure Act, see R. Boisture, *What Charities Need to Know to Comply with the Lobbying Disclosure Act of 1995*, the Independent Sector website, *available at* http://www.independent sector.org; Assoc. of Corp. Counsel, *Lobbying: What Does It Mean for 501(c)(3) Organizations?* (June 15, 2009), *available at* http://www. acc.com/legalresources/quickcounsel/lwdimf501c3o.cfm.; Jeffrey S. Tenenbaum, *Myths about Lobbying, Political Activity, and Tax-Exempt Status* (June 5, 2007), *available at* http://www.venable.com/ myths-about-lobbying-political-activity-and-tax-exempt-status-06-02-2010/.

3. The Model Rules of Professional Conduct, promulgated by the American Bar Association, are the basis of the professional regulation of lawyers in the vast majority of states. Rule 1.1 of the Model Rules states that "[a] lawyer shall provide competent representation to a client. Competent representation requires the legal knowledge,

skill, thoroughness and preparation *reasonably necessary for the representation.*" (emphasis supplied)

4.   *See* American Bar Association *Model Rules of Professional Conduct*, Rule 1.13, Comment 35; ABA Formal Ethics Opinion 98-410.

5.   *See, e.g.*, Willard L. Boyd III, *Lawyers' Service on Nonprofit Boards: Managing the Risks of an Important Community Activity*, 18 ABA BUS. L. TODAY 35 (November/December 2008).

6.   American Bar Association *Model Rules of Professional Conduct*, Rule 1.13 states, in part:

   A lawyer employed or retained by an organization represents the organization ... In dealing with an organization's directors ... a lawyer shall explain the identity of the client when the lawyer knows or reasonably should know that the organization's interests are adverse to those of the [directors] with whom the lawyer is dealing.

7.   *See* Michael W. Peregrin and James R. Schwartz, *When Does the Board Need its Own Counsel?* TRUSTEE at 23 (April 2001).

# Suggested Questions for Directors Regarding the Corporation's Legal Environment and Selection of Counsel

## Legal Environment

(1)   Do we depend on the help of another group, individual, or entity to carry out a major part of our corporate purpose or mission? Does such a party need us in a similar way?

(2)   If we are in a position of dependency as described above, are the relationships clearly defined? How?

(3)   Is the other party involved expending money in reliance on our activity with them? Are we devoting funds to the activity?

(4)   Does the size of the undertaking or its contemplated duration suggest that the relationship be defined by a formal agreement? Do we have one?

(5)   Do any such undertakings seem to be failing to achieve their purposes? Will we, or our partner in the undertaking, lose substantial funds in the event of failure?

(6)   Have we ever been sued? Why? With what result?

(7)  Do I know of a corporation similar to ours that was sued? Why? With what result?

(8)  Is there any government agency (other than the IRS) that controls or regulates our activities? What limits does this agency place on us?

(9)  Do we engage in public controversies during which we make statements attacking or criticizing some other person or entity?

(10)  Do we regularly review the corporation's legal exposures?

(11)  Do we review the public funding sources of the nonprofit and monitor developments in these sources?

## Selection of Counsel

(1)  Do we include legal fees as part of our regular budget? If we do, how is the amount determined?

(2)  Do other corporations with activities similar to ours find it necessary to retain counsel? Why? Or, if they do not, why not?

(3)  Is there a lawyer, paid or unpaid, whom we generally look to for legal advice?

(4)  Have we analyzed that individual's particular skills in relation to our problems?

(5)  What legal skills do we need that are unique, specialized, or unusual?

(6)  Is our corporation presently a plaintiff or defendant in litigation? Why? What are the prospects of a termination?

(7)  If a volunteer lawyer is presently acting as legal counsel, do I feel she or he is qualified to serve our needs?

(8)  [If I am a lawyer:] Am I asked to provide legal advice to the board of directors? Do the board and I understand when my discussion of a problem is or is not a legal opinion that is protected by the attorney-client privilege?

(9)  [If I am a lawyer:] Have I considered the potential conflicts of interest that may arise from my dual role and discussed them with the board? How will they be handled when they occur?

(10)  [If I am a lawyer:] If I am asked to serve as counsel to the corporation for some matter, am I protected under my professional malpractice policy?

(11)  [If I am a lawyer:] If I am asked to provide legal advice to the corporation, has the extent of my representation been clearly defined?

# Checklist: The Legal Environment of the Nonprofit Corporation

*Note:*    For simplicity, these and other chapter checklists describe a corporation having a chair, who presides over the board of directors; a chief executive, who may be a staff person; an executive committee; a governance/nominating committee; and an audit committee. (We recognize, however, that in many smaller and other nonprofits, these committee functions may be performed by either the executive committee or the board as a whole.) We also assume a legal counsel—someone, paid or unpaid, having primary responsibility for the corporation's legal affairs. Many corporations, especially larger nonprofits, may have other committees established for specific purposes, such as establishing executive compensation; monitoring compliance with legal requirements; and overseeing investments and other financial matters.

| Subject | Review By | How Often | Comment |
|---|---|---|---|
| 1. The Corporation's Legal Environment | | | |
| a. Do we know in what areas our organization may be vulnerable to legal liability? | Chair, chief executive | Annually | |
| b. How does the board monitor the corporation's compliance with applicable laws? | Chair, chief executive | Annually | |
| c. What actions should the corporation take to minimize known legal risks? | Chair, chief executive | Annually | |

| Subject | Review By | How Often | Comment |
|---|---|---|---|
| 2. The Selection of Counsel | | | |
| a. Do we need regular counsel? | Chair, chief executive | Annually | An analysis of how the board solves recognized legal problems should be made. |
| b. Can we use volunteer legal counsel? | Chair, chief executive | Annually | Review must examine fitness of particular volunteer counsel's ability to meet corporation's specific needs. |

—

# Chapter 13:
## Director Orientation and Revitalization

# Chapter 13
# Director Orientation
# and Revitalization

*The corporation should institute formal actions and procedures to assure that all directors have received (and continue to receive) key documents regarding the corporation. New directors should be given specific orientation as to the corporation's history, structure, and activities, and be encouraged to share their unique perspectives with the other directors. Board members should periodically be given the opportunity to engage in strategic planning, self-evaluation, and other analysis that show how well both the corporation and the board are fulfilling their missions.*

## New Director Orientation and Materials

### Orientation

The corporation's board and management should organize specific events or meetings to welcome the new director. They also should make sure the director is provided with sufficient information to become an effective member of the board without a prolonged breaking-in period.

Effective use of new board members requires that they learn as much as possible about the organization, its mission, history, and hopes, as quickly as possible. Leaving the new arrivals to find this knowledge on their own, over a series of meetings, is a slow and inefficient process, and one in which the promise of many a board member can be lost to a corporation.

Set forth below is an outline of the type of reading material the corporation should provide to  new board members, in the form of directors' manuals. Such information should be supplemented by site tours and specific meetings with senior staff and officers (outside of board meeting reporting sessions). Meetings of this type are very effective for new board members and may be scheduled prior to a new member's first meeting. Still, it may also be useful to schedule some meetings *after* the new member has attended a few meetings and become acquainted with the range of corporate matters within the board's purview.

## Directors' Manuals or Websites

A threshold obligation of a director is to know and understand the purpose, function, and goals of the nonprofit corporation the director is serving. An invaluable tool in acclimating new directors of nonprofit corporations—as well as assisting all directors in satisfying their duties—is a manual or manuals containing important documents relating to the governance and operation of the corporation and other information that will keep the director apprised of the current state of the corporation. These may be simple loose-leaf binders, with a table of contents and a tab for each item. Use of such a binder makes updating the manual easy.  As an alternative, many nonprofits have established governance sites on their websites or on another secure Internet location, in which board and committee information is maintained. This alternative allows for updates without the need to print new documents.

Increasingly, board meeting information is provided to directors of nonprofit corporations by e-mail and posted for reference at a board website, so that directors can have easy access to meeting materials and choose how much of the materials they would like to print.

The board may wish to have two board manuals, or categories of information: one containing material that a director should have ready access to at every board meeting, and a larger set of documents and information available for reference as needed. If a two-manual/category system is chosen, then the first board manual or set would include the items listed below:

### *Basic board reference material (first manual or information reference set)*

The basic board reference material (first manual or information reference set) should contain, at a minimum, copies of the following documents:

(1)   Calendar of dates and events compiled for the year, listing board, committee, and other significant meetings, activities (such as major fundraising events) and deadlines, which can be updated periodically;

(2)    The corporation's articles of incorporation or charter, and any amendments;

(3)    The current bylaws of the corporation;

(4)    The corporate mission statement, vision statement, and any strategic plan;

(5)    Board policies;

(6)    Copies of all committee charters;

(7)    Corporate organization chart, showing any affiliated organizations, and any departments and divisions of the corporation;

(8)    Listing of names, addresses, and phone numbers of the corporation's directors and officers;

(9)    List of the corporation's committees, including the name of each committee chair and all committee members; and

(10)   List of key executive and administrative staff members of the corporation, including positions, addresses, and phone numbers.

### Additional board reference material (second manual or information set)

The following material is recommended to be made available for a director's reference as needed:

(1)    Prior minutes of board and committee meetings (these can be retained in a manual or website for one to two years, and then disposed of or filed elsewhere);

(2)    Financial statements of the corporation for the prior fiscal year and the operating and capital budgets for the current year;

(3)    Biographical data on directors and key staff;

(4)    Summary of D&O insurance, bylaw indemnification provisions, and statutory limitations on director liability;

(5)    Current news releases by or about the corporation;

(6)    Annual reports on the results of the organization's activities for the past two or three years;

(7)    Conflict of interest and other policies of the board or to which the board is subject;

(8)    Current long-range or strategic plan; and

(9)    The last two most recent Form 990s filed by the corporation.

As noted above, in lieu of hard-copy manuals, this information may be made available to board members via a secure governance site maintained on the nonprofit corporation's website or other secure Internet location.

# New Director Review of Information

Another aspect of new director orientation (or evaluation of an invitation to become a director) requires the new or prospective director to review material on the corporation's operations and resources, as well as the operations of the board. At a minimum, the new or prospective director should review carefully the material recommended above for inclusion in the director's manuals, as well as the following materials:

### *Past board and committee minutes*

The new director should review the minutes of the meetings of the board and its main committees for the last three years or so. Such a review is an excellent way to become knowledgeable regarding the recent history of the corporation, the issues faced by the board, and the board's methods for addressing these issues.

### *Past financial statements and reports*

A new or prospective director should review the financial statements of the corporation for at least the last few years, noting particularly if there are any restrictions that have been placed on gifts to the corporation. For tax-exempt corporations, the director should review the corporation's annual informational returns filed with the IRS on Form 990. For corporations that acquired tax-exempt status fairly recently, a review of the corporation's Form 1023 (Application for Recognition of Exemption) also may be useful. If the corporation has issued tax-exempt bonds, the official statement related to any bond financing that is still outstanding should be reviewed; the first appendix ("Appendix A") to the official statement can provide a useful overview of the corporation and its management.

### *Current directors and management personnel*

Ideally, before new directors join the board, they should have met the chief executive and other principal officers. The new board members also should have met the board chair and at least a few other board members—including both senior and junior members, so that the new members will not feel surrounded by strangers at their first meeting.

### *Compliance with law and internal control*

As noted throughout this *Guidebook*, the use of assets of a nonprofit corporation is subject to certain limitations. For example, corporate assets must be used for the purpose for which they are given (generally, as stated in the corporation's articles of incorporation and bylaws). The assets of tax-exempt corporations cannot be used to inure to the benefit of private individuals. (For a more in-depth discussion of limitations on tax-exempt corporations, see *Chapter 4, Taxation.*)

Prospective directors should become familiar with the role of the corporation's accountants and legal advisers in regard to matters of internal control and legal compliance. They should learn the corporation's policies and procedures regarding conflict of interest. If the corporation does not have a public accountant or regular corporate counsel, the individual should determine what steps the corporation has taken to make sure it is in compliance with any applicable limitations. In addition, some nonprofit corporations are subject to being accredited or licensed by outside agencies. Review of accrediting or survey reports, if available, can be most helpful in determining problem areas needing attention. (For additional suggestions for becoming familiar with the corporation's legal environment, see *Chapter 12, The Legal Environment of the Nonprofit Corporation.*)

### Corporation's outlook

The new or prospective board member may find it helpful to have an in-depth discussion with the chief executive and board chair about the corporation's current plans, current prospects, critical issues being or expected to be confronted, and long-range objectives.

### Board culture

Although new members are generally expected to fit in to the existing board structure and culture, they also may be able to offer new perspectives and suggestions that will help the board operate more effectively. Nonetheless, prospective board members may need to think twice before agreeing to serve on a board that operates in a fashion they believe ineffective.

# Board Revitalization: Retreats, Strategic Planning, and Self-Evaluation

## Board Retreats

Many of the most successful nonprofit organizations have periodic board (or board/management) retreats. Retreats are used to give the board members an opportunity to conduct an assessment of the corporation and renew their individual commitment to helping the corporation satisfy its mission. A retreat may take the form of an extended board meeting, or may have a different format. The agenda may focus on larger issues of mission and the future, or on particular problems facing the corporation. Retreats often include sessions designed to build relationships among board members, and thereby facilitate open discussions both then and at future board meetings. Often retreats are scheduled at locations away from the corporation's offices, where board members will be able to focus on the work at hand as well as have the opportunity to socialize and build personal rapport. Such retreats are ineffective unless all, or a very high proportion, of the board can attend. Therefore, retreats should be scheduled far in advance, and annually if possible—or at least on a regular schedule, such as every two or three years.[1]

## Reviewing the Board Decision-Making Process

All directors should be aware of board discussion and decision-making style. If a director believes the current style or culture is not conducive to effective decision-making, the director should discuss the issue with the board chair or other directors, preferably apart from the boardroom. For example, are all board members given the opportunity to participate in discussions? Is adequate time allotted for questions? Do a few board members—or the board chair—tend to dominate discussions? Does the board chair give his or her opinion before other board members have had a chance to speak? Has the corporation had difficulty retaining chief executives? If so, could board function or board members' style be a source of the difficulty? The review of the board decision process and consideration of these questions should be conducted by the governance/nominating committee.[2]

## Evaluating Whether the Board Needs to Be Restructured

Over the course of time, the board of a nonprofit corporation may require structural adjustments to enable the corporation to continue to meet its mission. For instance, the size of the board may need to be adjusted upward or downward. The resources of a large board may be more effectively channeled by using multiple committees that act in smaller groups and report back to the board. In some cases, fresh faces may be needed to help the board move away from entrenched attitudes and assumptions, and to meet changing realities affecting the corporation and its mission. Again, this subject would be appropriate for the governance/nominating committee to review.[3]

### *Periodic review of board structure*

The board should periodically provide for a process whereby the need for board structural changes can be assessed. This process may occur every three to five years at board retreats, be initiated by the board chair or chief executive, be handled by the governance/nominating committee, or consist of a report by outside advisers (in some areas, consultants or scholars in the area of nonprofit management may be available to conduct a review on a no-fee or low-cost basis). Because these reviews can be sensitive—particularly if members of the existing board feel threatened, or vulnerable to criticism for past decisions—it is recommended that such a structural review be institutionalized so that it occurs automatically every few years.

### *Self-evaluations of individual board members*

Nonprofit corporations may benefit from board members engaging in annual or other periodic evaluations of each member's performance individually as well as the board's performance as a whole. These evaluations, or assessments, can be accomplished through the use of forms developed internally or adapted from samples developed by others, including other nonprofits, local trade associations, or writers in the area of nonprofit governance. (See discussion of information resources for nonprofit corporations in the section *"Other Sources of Information, Inspiration, and Guidance"* below, and selected titles and websites in *Appendix B*.)

Individual board members may be evaluated by the board chair and the corporation's chief executive, a governance/nominating committee, or a committee of a small number of board members or former board members. (Board members on the committee should be evaluated by a similar group.) After such evaluations, the board or committee chair should discuss the results of the evaluation with each board member. These discussion should serve as an opportunity both to acknowledge the individual director's contributions as well as to suggest ways in which the director's effectiveness could be improved.

### *Evaluations of the board*

All board members should also complete periodic evaluations of the effectiveness of the board and the resources provided to it. Such an evaluation should include questions regarding each individual director's views on the strengths and weaknesses of the board and its committees, and provide an opportunity for directors to make suggestions for ways to improve board effectiveness. The evaluation should cover all aspects of board and committee functions, including new board member orientation, selection of future board candidates, adequacy of information provided before board meetings, conduct of board and committee meetings, effectiveness of board retreats, and opinions on future board needs. The governance/nominating committee should review the evaluations and make any recommendations to the board it believes will make the board more effective.

### Board Term Limits

One mechanism used by nonprofit corporations to ensure they have engaged board members as well as an overall effective board involves the use of term limits. Often a nonprofit corporation will include a requirement in its bylaws that limits the number of terms an individual may serve as a director, thereby requiring the individual to be off the board for at least one year before coming back on the board.

# Information-Gathering for Strategic Planning and Mission Measurement

Whether in the form of retreats or otherwise, many of the most successful nonprofit corporations require the board and staff members to engage in regular (often annual) strategic planning sessions. In order to make the most of these brainstorming and self-evaluation opportunities, the board should ask itself and its staff what information is available to determine whether the corporation has been successful in meeting its mission. For instance, are members/donors/visitors/users surveyed regarding their experiences, perceptions, and needs? Is such data available from or on comparable organizations? What other information is available quantifying the experience of the individuals who are the intended beneficiaries of the nonprofit corporation? What information *could* become available if the corporation sought to obtain it? Could volunteers be used to help gather this information? Have grant-makers required the corporation to compile information that could also be useful to review within the organization?

In general, nonprofit organizations, both big and small, tend to be much less sophisticated in terms of the information they routinely gather about their markets (both actual and potential) and market perceptions, when compared to for-profit organizations. Partly, this is a reflection of the unique nature of nonprofit corporations. A nonprofit corporation generally cannot measure success or failure of its mission in simple monetary terms. Often, the primary mission of the nonprofit cannot be measured in amounts of X and Y calculated by an accounting firm. But this does not mean that nonprofits should not seek to count what can be counted, rather than relying on intuition or traditional assumptions. Through the use of the Internet, computer programs, interns, and volunteers, even small nonprofits with limited resources can access a wide range of information. Such data can confirm correlations between factors that an organization assumes to be relevant, or reveal correlations between factors that are not intuitively obvious.

Without obtaining and analyzing available information on how well the organization is achieving its mission (and where improvement may be needed), it is very difficult for the board of a nonprofit organization to properly evaluate whether it is using its resources to their maximum potential. The organization runs the risk of becoming fixed in outdated perceptions—"this is the way things have always been"—without any mechanism to test the accuracy of these perceptions.

Although most nonprofits will not have the luxury of a full-time research department, nonprofit board members should regularly ask what information could and should be obtained in order to assist the board in evaluating whether the organization has been successful in meeting its mission. Such information can also provide board members with the tools they need to recognize when it is time to redefine the corporation's mission or make other changes to reflect new realities.

## Quantifying Success for a Nonprofit Corporation

Quantification of the success or failure of a corporation is a considerably more challenging exercise in the nonprofit world compared to the for-profit business environment. While the board of directors of a for-profit must consider a large number of nonnumerical phenomena related to the operation of the corporation—legalities, risks of lawsuits, employee morale, quirks of consumer preferences, etc.—at the end of the day one factor reigns supreme: the bottom line. In the long run, no conceivable success in personnel management, marketing skills, or product development, will excuse the failure of a for-profit corporation to produce a profit, or at least break even. In the nonprofit world, in comparison, it is possible to achieve an outstanding success in some mission and yet become financially insolvent.

Thus, the key challenge for any nonprofit board is both to fulfill the corporate mission and to see to it that the nonprofit survives to maximize the public benefits resulting from fulfilling its mission. A further burden on the nonprofit management is to achieve those goals with maximum efficiency. The process of assuring efficient survival will require the consideration of various numbers, including many things other than revenue dollars—such as the number of persons entering an art museum during a given month, or the increase in symphony orchestra memberships by certain minority groups and young professionals.

The subtleties of the "quantification challenge" in evaluating the success of a nonprofit corporation may be illustrated as follows: It is clear that the board of directors of an art museum must know what dollars are needed to keep the doors open and where that money can be found; it should also be able to know how many people come to the museum and when, who gives money and when, and how much a "needed" art work will cost. All these matters are capable of being reduced to numbers. But, as an institution seeking to change a visitor's behavior and perceptions, what else does it and can it know and measure? How can it compare, numerically, one painting versus another or a visitor's different experiences after viewing those paintings—or a specific collection?

No ready answers rise to the surface, but let us examine what could be determined and counted. Probably one can learn, at relatively small cost:

- how many people come to the museum;
- on what days;
- at what hours;
- how many of those are dues-paying members;
- how many attend a given exhibit;
- how many buy books describing the exhibit;
- how many of the above are adults, children, men or women; and
- how many live within certain zip-code areas.

In addition, for each of those questions, the organization can determine the correlation (or the lack thereof) of one classification with another. For example, do more women come on Tuesday morning than at any other time or any other day? The answers may be insignificant or mysterious, but they may, as one tracks them down, lead to other, more significant questions. All of the above data can be obtained without asking for any specific personal identification of those whose behavior is being measured, and none of it involves hidden cameras or other invasions of privacy.

But the board of a nonprofit institution, such as our hypothetical art museum, should not stop there. If it can cross the barrier that inhibits personal identification, it will want to know:

- how many of our sample live in which suburb or city area;
- how old are they;
- what is their race or ethnic identification; and
- did they come with others, and if so, who.

These last described questions can be asked on a voluntary basis (with the increased margin of error, as many of the subjects will refuse the information, or worse, give deliberately misleading answers).

At this point our illustrative board has obtained a mass of information that can be assembled at relatively low cost—and some of it is already assembled by most museums. But at some point, it may want to go further. It will want to know:

- how would a visitor (of one of the classifications listed above) describe the motivations that brought him or her to the institution;
- were those aims satisfied;
- what other museums (of art or other purpose) does the visitor patronize; and
- what particular object or painting drew the visitor's most prolonged attention.

Once the nonprofit staff has compiled all the above answers and presented them to our board in numerical form, the board may be able to trace the correlations between trait X and trait Y, and ask if those correlations suggest management changes in the museum's programs. But such information may also lead to further questions, such as, "What is the correlation we wish to obtain? Why are we here?" Are we fulfilling our mission as effectively as possible? These are the kinds of ultimate questions that will continue to challenge the board of directors of a nonprofit corporation throughout its existence. In exercising the rights and duties described in this *Guidebook*, successive generations of a single nonprofit board will undoubtedly find different answers to these questions.

# Other Sources of Information, Inspiration, and Guidance

Although this *Guidebook* has attempted to provide directors of nonprofit corporations with an overview of nonprofit corporation board service, there are a host of topics that we have not had space to address in depth or even at all. Board members seeking additional information on topics discussed in this *Guidebook*, or topics not addressed here, may take advantage of other resources available to nonprofit corporations in their community or available through the Internet.

For example, the Panel on the Nonprofit Sector, which was convened by Independent Sector (www.independentsector.org), has developed various reports and a guidebook for charities and foundations. *The Principles for Good Governance and Ethical Practice: A Guide for Charities and Foundations* sets forth 33 principles of sound practice that should be considered by every charitable organization as a guide for strengthening its effectiveness and accountability. In addition, BoardSource is a national organization dedicated to advancing the public good by building exceptional nonprofit boards and inspiring service. It maintains a website (www.BoardSource.org) with information on various board governance topics. In addition, BoardSource has published numerous publications on the topic.

Similarly, the nonprofit Donor's Forum (www.donorsforum.org), an association of grant-makers, presents educational programs and maintains an extensive library of materials on nonprofit governance, financing, and operational issues. Many other communities have similar nonprofit resource organizations. College and public libraries, as well as commercial bookstores, are other resources for such materials. At *Appendix B* is a nonexhaustive sampling of publications and websites that may be of interest to nonprofit corporation directors and their advisers.

*See the Suggested Questions and Checklist following the Endnotes below to review the issues discussed in this chapter.*

## Endnotes

1.  *See* Sandra R. Hughes, To Go Forward, Retreat! (BoardSource EBook Series 1999).

2.  *See* ABA Coordinating Committee on Nonprofit Governance, Guide to Nonprofit Corporate Governance in the Wake of Sarbanes-Oxley 34-35 (ABA 2005).

3.  *See* Guide to Nonprofit Corporate Governance in the Wake of Sarbanes-Oxley, *supra* n. 2, at 34-35.

# Suggested Questions for Directors Regarding Director Orientation and Revitalization

(1)  Do we have a board manual containing the corporation's basic documents?

(2)  What documents does it contain?

(3)  How do I keep it up to date?

(4)  Are the materials maintained on a board governance website? Do I frequently access the website?

(5)  What files do I keep concerning my service as a director?

(6)  Does the board have an orientation program for new directors? Does the board leadership encourage new members to participate in meetings? Are the board leadership and the more experienced board members receptive to statements from (new or continuing) members questioning aspects of board culture or procedures?

(7)  Do I know of practices of other corporations concerning director orientation and training that our corporation could adopt?

(8)  Does the board have meetings or retreats reviewing the corporation's overall policies, mission, or specific problems?

(9)  Does the board have a strategic-planning process? How have past strategic plans been evaluated and updated?

(10)  Does the board ask its directors to engage in annual or other periodic self-evaluations or evaluations of the board as a whole?

(11)  How does the board evaluate whether the corporation is fulfilling its mission? Is there information available from or about similar

corporations or grant-making agencies that could help us measure the corporation's effectiveness in meeting its mission?

# Checklist: Director Orientation and Revitalization

*Note:* For simplicity, these and other chapter checklists describe a corporation having a chair, who pre-sides over the board of directors; a chief executive, who may be a staff person; an executive committee; a governance/nominating committee; and an audit committee. (We recognize, however, that in many smaller and other nonprofits, these committee functions may be performed by either the executive committee or the board as a whole.) We also assume a legal counsel—someone, paid or unpaid, having primary responsibility for the corporation's legal affairs. Many corporations, especially larger nonprofits, may have other committees established for specific purposes, such as establishing executive compensation; monitoring compliance with legal requirements; and overseeing investments and other financial matters.

| Subject | Review By | How Often | Comment |
|---|---|---|---|
| 1. Director's manual | Chair, chief executive | At least annually, and in preparation for each meeting at which directors are elected | A specific committee to undertake this task is recommended. |
| 2. Orientation | Chair, chief executive, governance/ nominating committee | At least annually, and in preparation for each meeting at which directors are elected | A successful orientation meeting will take extensive time in planning and arranging for both board and staff participation. |

| Subject | Review By | How Often | Comment |
|---|---|---|---|
| 3. Board retreats | Chair, chief executive | Annually or at least every other year | The board may wish the retreats to be planned by staff, with input from the chief executive and a committee of junior and senior board members. |
| 4. Self-evaluations and assessments | Chair, chief executive, governance/ nominating committee | Annually or at least every other year | Results of individual director evaluations should be discussed with that director; results of overall board assessments should be presented to and reviewed by the entire board. |
| 5. Strategic planning | Chair, chief executive | Annually | Some nonprofit corporations of sufficient size have strategic planning committees that meet periodically through the year to assess the implementation of the corporation's current strategic plan, and report to the board on areas of shortcomings and recommendation for changes to future plans. |

# Appendices

# Appendix A

## Tax-Exempt Organization Reference Chart

**Organization Reference Chart from *Tax-Exempt Status for Your Organization*, Internal Revenue Service Publication 557 (Rev. October 2011)**

| Section of 1986 Code | Description of organization | General nature of activities |
|---|---|---|
| 501(c)(1) | Corporations Organized Under Act of Congress (including Federal Credit Unions) | Instrumentalities of the United States |
| 501(c)(2) | Title Holding Corporation for Exempt Corporation | Holding title to property of an exempt organization |

| Section of 1986 Code | Description of organization | General nature of activities |
|---|---|---|
| 501(c)(3) | Religious, Educational, Charitable, Scientific, Literary, Testing for Public Safety, to Foster National or International Amateur Sports Competition, or Prevention of Cruelty to Children or Animals Organizations | Activities of nature implied by description of class of organization |
| 501(c)(4) | Civic Leagues, Social Welfare Organizations, and Local Associations of Employees | Promotion of community welfare; charitable, educational, or recreational |
| 501(c)(5) | Labor, Agricultural, and Horticultural Organizations | Educational or instructive, the purpose being to improve conditions of work, and to improve products and efficiency |
| 501(c)(6) | Business Leagues, Chambers of Commerce, Real Estate Boards, Etc. | Improvement of business conditions of one or more lines of business |
| 501(c)(7) | Social and Recreational Clubs | Pleasure, recreation, social activities |
| 501(c)(8) | Fraternal Beneficiary Societies and Associations | Lodge providing for payment of life, sickness, accident, or other benefits to members |
| 501(c)(9) | Voluntary Employees' Beneficiary Associations | Providing for payment of life, sickness, accident, or other benefits to members |

| Section of 1986 Code | Description of organization | General nature of activities |
|---|---|---|
| 501(c)(10) | Domestic Fraternal Societies and Associations | Lodge devoting its net earnings to charitable, fraternal, and other specified purposes. No life, sickness, or accident benefits to members |
| 501(c)(11) | Teachers' Retirement Fund Associations | Teachers' association for payment of retirement benefits |
| 501(c)(12) | Benevolent Life Insurance Associations, Mutual Ditch or Irrigation Companies, Mutual or Cooperative Telephone Companies, Etc. | Activities of a mutually beneficial nature similar to those implied by the description of class or organization |
| 501(c)(13) | Cemetery Companies | Burials and incidental activities |
| 501(c)(14) | State-Chartered Credit Unions, Mutual Reserve Funds | Loans to members |
| 501(c)(15) | Mutual Insurance Companies or Associations | Providing insurance to members substantially at cost |
| 501(c)(16) | Cooperative Organizations to Finance Crop Operations | Financing crop operations in conjunction with activities of a marketing or purchasing Association |
| 501(c)(17) | Supplemental Unemployment Benefit Trusts | Provides for payment of supplemental unemployment compensation benefits |
| 501(c)(18) | Employee-Funded Pension Trust (created before June 25, 1959) | Payment of benefits under a pension plan funded by employees |

| Section of 1986 Code | Description of organization | General nature of activities |
|---|---|---|
| 501(c)(19) | Post or Organization of Past or Present Members of the Armed Forces | Activities implied by nature of organization |
| 501(c)(21) | Black Lung Benefit Trusts | Funded by coal mine operators to satisfy their liability for disability or death due to black lung diseases |
| 501(c)(22) | Withdrawal Liability Payment Fund | To provide funds to meet the liability of employers withdrawing from a multiemployer pension fund |
| 501(c)(23) | Veterans Organization (created before 1880) | To provide insurance and other benefits to veterans |
| 501(c)(25) | Title-Holding Corporations or Trusts with Multiple Parents | Holding title and paying over income from property to 35 or fewer parents or beneficiaries |
| 501(c)(26) | State-sponsored Organization Providing Health Coverage for High-Risk Individuals | Provides health care coverage for high-risk individuals |
| 501(c)(27) | State-Sponsored Workers' Compensation Reinsurance Organization | Reimburses members for losses under workers' compensation acts |
| 501(c)(28) | National Railroad Retirement Investment Trust | Manages and invests railroad retirement assets |
| 501(c)(29) | Consumer Operated and Oriented Plans (CO-OPs) | Consumer-governed, member-run health insurers |

| Section of 1986 Code | Description of organization | General nature of activities |
|---|---|---|
| 501(d) | Religious and Apostolic Associations | Regular business activities. Communal religious community |
| 501(e) | Cooperative Hospital Service Organizations | Performs cooperative services for hospitals |
| 501(f) | Cooperative Service Organizations of Operating Educational Organizations | Performs collective investment services for educational organizations |
| 501(k) | Child Care Organization | Provides care for children |
| 501(n) | Charitable Risk Pools | Pools certain insurance risks of § 501(c)(3) organizations |
| 501(q) | Credit Counseling Organization | Credit Counseling services |
| 521(a) | Farmers' Cooperative Associations | Cooperative marketing and purchasing for agricultural producers |
| 527 | Political Organizations | A party, committee, fund, association, etc., that directly or indirectly accepts contributions or makes expenditures for political campaigns |

# Appendix B

---

## Suggested Publications, Periodicals, and Websites

The general literature on nonprofit boards and corporations is becoming extensive and this Appendix does not purport to cover all titles, particularly in view of the uneven quality of some of the material currently offered on the market. The following, however, merit perhaps more extensive attention:

## Publications

THE MODEL NONPROFIT CORPORATION ACT, THIRD EDITION (American Bar Association, 2009); William H. Clark, Jr., editor, contains both the Model Act provisions and official commentary.

NONPROFIT GOVERNANCE AND MANAGEMENT (American Bar Association 3rd ed. 2011) is a practical guide for executive staff and boards of directors of nonprofit organizations. The book provides an overview of the basics on nonprofit governance as well as board structure and operations. It also provides 27 samples of important governance forms and guidelines.

For a basic understanding of nonprofits and the issues facing nonprofits, *see* Lisa A. Runquist, THE ABCS OF NONPROFITS (American Bar Association, 2005). The book describes how nonprofit corporations are formed, options for organizational structure, matters relating to the operation of the corporation, and basic tax issues for nonprofits.

THE GUIDE TO REPRESENTING RELIGIOUS ORGANIZATIONS (American Bar Association, 2009) addresses critical issues and risk factors of concern for religious organizations ranging from formation and governance, to taxes, fundraising, employment issues, and property rights. It outlines the general requirements of applicable law and highlights areas in which religious organizations receive special consideration under the law.

THE GUIDE TO NONPROFIT CORPORATE GOVERNANCE IN THE WAKE OF SARBANES-OXLEY (American Bar Association, 2005) provides a basic overview of the provisions of the leading Sarbanes-Oxley reforms that might be relevant to nonprofit organizations and describes governance structures, processes and procedures that have been recognized as "good governance practices."

Jim Collins's monograph on GOOD TO GREAT AND THE SOCIAL SECTORS: WHY BUSINESS THINKING IS NOT THE ANSWER (Jim Collins, 2005) applies and reconceives Collins's core lessons in his well-known book GOOD TO GREAT : WHY SOME COMPANIES MAKE THE LEAP...AND OTHERS DON'T (Harper Collins Publishers Inc., 2001), examining how the Hedgehog Concepts of good-to-great companies work in nonprofit, mission-oriented organizations.

Bruce R. Hopkins has written several excellent treatises on tax-exempt organizations, including THE LAW OF TAX-EXEMPT ORGANIZATIONS (John Wiley & Sons, Inc. 10th ed. 2011) (with annual updates).

Michael I. Sanders, JOINT VENTURES INVOLVING TAX-EXEMPT ORGANIZATIONS (John Wiley & Sons, Inc. 3rd ed. 2007) (with annual updates) provides an excellent treatise on legal issues on joint ventures involving nonprofits.

Jack B. Siegel, A DESKTOP GUIDE FOR NONPROFIT DIRECTORS, OFFICERS, AND ADVISORS: AVOIDING TROUBLE WHILE DOING GOOD (John Wiley & Sons, Inc., 2006) provides a detailed analysis of legal issues relevant to board members.

The American Law Institute is working on a project, THE PRINCIPLES OF LAW OF NONPROFIT ORGANIZATIONS, to draft legal principles for the nonprofit sector, including principles relating to governance and the duties of governing boards and individual fiduciaries. Drafts of The Principles are available from the ALI at http://www.ali.org.

# Periodicals

Periodicals focusing on the nonprofit sector include the following:

*The Chronicle of Philanthropy*, a newspaper focusing on the nonprofit world (*see* website at http://philanthropy.com). The *Chronicle* publishes annually its *Non-Profit Handbook*, with lists of books, periodicals, software, Internet sites, and other resources, organized by subject matter (such as "Advocacy," "Boards," and "Fundraising").

*Don Kramer's Nonprofit Issues* is a national newsletter reporting on tax and other legal developments affecting nonprofit organizations and available at www.nonprofitissues.com.

The *Philanthropy News Network* provides a daily online news service for nonprofit organizations, at http://www.pnnonline.org.

*Bruce Hopkins' The NonProfit Counsel*, published by John Wiley & Sons, a monthly newsletter that provides analysis of current developments in tax and related law for nonprofit organizations and their professional advisers.

*The Nonprofit Times*, a business publication directed to nonprofit management, with 12 monthly editions plus bimonthly special editions on direct marketing and financial management, and an annual nonprofit salary survey (for information and selected articles, *see* http://www.nptimes.com).

## Useful websites and organizations

A reader interested in pursuing further material in this area may consult the following organizations and their websites:

The IRS website, www.irs.gov, has a section focused on charities and nonprofits that contains extensive information on compliance with tax-exempt requirements.

The GuideStar website,www.guidestar.org, is produced by Philanthropic Research, Inc., and contains a database of information from the Form 990s of over 700,000 U.S. nonprofit organizations.

Many states' secretary of state websites and attorney general websites contain useful information for nonprofit organizations. Examples include the California Attorney General Charity Portal http://caag.state.ca.us/charities, the Illinois Attorney General Charity Portal http://www.ag.state.il.us/charities/reg_reports.html, and Iowa Secretary of State website http://www.sos.state.ia.us/business/nonprofits/index.html.

BoardSource, www.boardsource.org, which has an extended bibliography on topics relevant to nonprofit boards.

Charity Navigator, www.charitynavigator.org/ provides comparison information on thousands of charitable organizations and other information, including executive compensation studies.

The National Conference of Commissioners on Uniform State Laws (NCCUSL) maintains a website of uniform laws, which includes the Uniform Prudent Management of Institutional Funds Act, The Revised Uniform Unincorporated Nonprofit Association Act, and the Model Protection of Charitable Assets Act, at www.uniformlaws.org.

The National Council of Nonprofit Associations, www.councilofnonprofits.org, is a network of state and regional associations of nonprofit organizations, developed to provide nonprofits with services, peer support, and a mechanism for collective advocacy. Various states have nonprofit associations and resource organizations that maintain websites with resource information specific to the state. Examples include the Minnesota Nonprofit Council, www.minnesotanonprofits.org, the Larned A. Waterman Iowa Nonprofit Resource

Center, http://inrc.continuetolearn.uiowa.edu, and the New York Council on Nonprofits, www.nycon.org. The National Council on Nonprofits maintains a directory of state nonprofit associations.

The Nonprofit Organizations Committee of the Business Law Section of the American Bar Association maintains a website, http://apps.americanbar.org/dch/committee.cfm?com=CL580000, that contains various materials, including the text of the Model Nonprofit Corporation Act, Third Edition, and links to nonprofit articles.

The American Society of Corporate Secretaries and Governance Professionals, 521 Fifth Avenue, New York, NY 10175, (212) 681-2000, www.ascs.org, publishes a number of materials, mostly intended for the business corporation, but some of which are also relevant or specifically directed to nonprofit corporations. *See,* for example, "Governance for Nonprofits—A Summary of Organizational Principles and Resources for Directors of Nonprofit Organizations" available on the society's website or in pamphlet form.

The Public Counsel Law Center includes sample Form 990 policies and analysis at www.publiccounsel.org/useful_materials?id=0025.

The website for Idealist (formerly called the Internet Nonprofit Center) provides suggested book titles, practical guides, essays, and other resource information about nonprofit organizations, as well as Nonprofit FAQ, an "online encyclopedia of information" designed for use by nonprofit organizations. *See* www.idealist.org.

The National Center for Charitable Statistics (NCCS) is a repository of data on the nonprofit sector in the United States. The NCCS' activities include the development of uniform standards for reporting on the activities of charitable organizations. *See* NCCS at www.NCCS@ui.urban.org.

The Charity Channel website, www.charitychannel.com, provides a wide range of discussion forums on nonprofit topics, from "Accountability" to "Volunteer Issues."

The Nonprofit Genie website, www.compasspoint.org/askgeni/index.php, is maintained by CompassPoint Nonprofit Services, and contains links to an online newsletter for nonprofit board members (the *Board Café*) and facts on nonprofits and other publications of interest to nonprofit boards, officers, and volunteers.

The *Blue Avocado* website, www.blueavocado.org, is maintained by The Alliance of Nonprofits for Insurance, Risk Retention Group, Nonprofit Insurance Alliance of California, and Compasspoint Nonprofit Services, and contains links to a newsletter and practical advice on the operation of nonprofit organizations.

The Independent Sector provides information on and promotes the range of nonprofit organizations that comprise America's independent sector. *See* www.independentsector.org. In 2004, the Independent Sector convened the Panel on the Nonprofit Sector. This resulted in several publications, including the PRINCIPLES FOR GOOD GOVERNANCE AND ETHICAL PRACTICE: A GUIDE FOR CHARITIES AND FOUNDATIONS (2007), which contains 33 practices designed to support board members and staff leaders of every charitable organization as they work to improve their own operations. This publication, as well as other related publications of the Panel on the Nonprofit Sector, are available on the Independent Sector website.

# Index